ANCESTRAL
SLAVIC MAGIC

"Natasha Helvin's *Ancestral Slavic Magic* reminds us that our Pagan roots are as present as they are past and that they hold the key to our future. Through her sharing of Slavic Pagan lore, Helvin teaches the importance of observing cycles, spending regular time in nature, tending to our dead, and, most of all, engaging with our ancestors. The resonant teaching Helvin offers throughout this book is that true magic takes effort, and that effort must be consistent."

S. KELLEY HARRELL, AUTHOR OF
FROM ELDER TO ANCESTOR AND
RUNIC BOOK OF DAYS

"As we enter a new era critical for the survival of humanity, it becomes imperative to heed the wisdom of our ancestors' spirits. Natasha Helvin beautifully describes the essence of this new era, offering insights from the Pagan perspective of the Slavic and Rus people of Ukraine and Southwest Russia. Additionally, she explores the traditions of the Vodouists in Haiti."

NICHOLAS E. BRINK, PH.D., AUTHOR OF
THE POWER OF ECSTATIC TRANCE, BALDR'S MAGIC, AND
BEOWULF'S ECSTATIC TRANCE MAGIC

ANCESTRAL
SLAVIC MAGIC

Transcend Family Patterns and Empower Ancestral Connections

NATASHA HELVIN

Destiny Books
Rochester, Vermont

Destiny Books
One Park Street
Rochester, Vermont 05767
www.DestinyBooks.com

Text stock is SFI certified

Destiny Books is a division of Inner Traditions International

Cataloging-in-Publication Data for this title is available from the Library of Congress

ISBN 978-1-64411-957-0 (print)
ISBN 978-1-64411-958-7 (ebook)

Printed and bound in the United States by Lake Book Manufacturing, LLC
The text stock is SFI certified. The Sustainable Forestry Initiative® program promotes sustainable forest management.

10 9 8 7 6 5 4 3 2 1

Text design by Virginia Scott Bowman and layout by Debbie Glogover
This book was typeset in Garamond Premier Pro with Editor, Gill Sans MT Pro, and Pentz used as display typefaces

To send correspondence to the author of this book, mail a first-class letter to the author c/o Inner Traditions • Bear & Company, One Park Street, Rochester, VT 05767, and we will forward the communication, or contact the author directly at **natashahelvin.com**.

Contents

Your Ancestors and Your Destiny

Dear Reader,

The primary purpose of this book is to show you how you can become more assertive, both physically and spiritually. The most important power you possess doesn't need to be acquired—you already have it; you need to recognize it and learn how to use it. Everyone has this power; it's their birthright. It is the strength accumulated over the centuries of your clan's existence, the strength of life itself. It flows in your veins. To own it, you need to maintain a connection with your nature and understand how energy works between people, both in your clan and your family. How life comes into this world, how it develops, how it finds a mate and gives birth to its progeny, how it encounters death, and what can remain after life has ended is all influenced by the accumulation of your clan's strength.

Usually, to make the right choices, you need to understand who you are and where you came from. I'm convinced that, in many ways, this understanding comes from the knowledge of your ancestors and the history of your family. The strength that passed from one generation to the next for centuries to become embedded in your body and mind, like a map, all come together into specific patterns that affect your life; you need to learn how to read this map. If you learn how to read this map and see changes in these patterns, you will learn to change your destiny.

In the first part of this book, I will explain the meaning of the ancestors in Slavic Paganism and the magical tradition, as well as how important ancestors are to the Russian people and Slavs in general. I will talk about how our ancestors continue to influence our lives and answer the most important question: Is it possible to change our destiny? I convey that the ability to learn from the mistakes of previous generations is the basis of spiritual evolution and a person's life transformation. Your ancestors influence you directly; however, to change your life, you must first understand it. The influence of the ancestors and the help they can give us is almost impossible to receive without knowledge and understanding of who they were. If you respect your ancestors and learn who they were, you will learn about yourself. You will be able to direct your destiny in any direction you desire.

In line with the above, in the first part of the book I describe the nature of Slavic Paganism and its relation to the Christian tradition (the so-called dual faith), in addition to describing the Pagan mythological image of the Slavic world, including the symbolic nature of the calendar and its relation to our ancestors.

In the second part of this book, I describe the Slavic burial traditions and beliefs that have been passed down by generations. Although many of the customs have almost disappeared, they are still practiced today by a very small population in Southern and Western Russia. I will give a brief explanation of how rural witches use burial rites to perform their crafts. I will examine the material of the traditional Slavic culture associated with archaic ideas about death, the dead and their posthumous existence, the soul and the afterlife, funeral and memorial rituals, folklore, and beliefs of rural Russia as well as those found in Haiti. Part of the book is devoted to a discussion on the Christian Orthodox tradition and the church as a source of occult power, and the power of the enchanted word (prayers and spells). I propose the concept of a burial ceremony as a nonverbal message with its laws of construction and distinctive poetics.

In addition to practicing my ancestral Slavic traditions, I am also a priestess in Haitian Vodou, another important influence on my life and research. Throughout the book I will point out the connection and similarities between Haitian Vodou and the Slavic tradition of healing (folk magic), including honoring one's ancestors as a foundation for life, the existence of supernatural forces, life after death, funeral traditions, and much more. I will describe the Haitian syncretism and Catholic influence on African-based tradition and Christian influence on Slavic Paganism and how it blends with folk magic and customs. Many other religions and cultures throughout the world have beliefs that are related to veneration of the ancestors and magic; in some cases, I will briefly discuss these as well.

This information is intended as a tribute to our ancestors' culture. It is an effective tool and a source of information on primitive doctrine and dogma. Upon reading, please keep in mind the following: In everything that concerns the invisible realm, Slavic material communicates only a wide range of opinions and hypotheses. The "official" canonical picture of the invisible has never been established by tradition.

I anticipate some of you will love this book—and some will hate it. Like everything in life, it is all about balance. Without it, nothing can exist in this world.

In this book, I express my own point of view and personal reasoning, which are sometimes difficult to prove, and I do not strive to do so. However, I am confident in them on one basis or another; for example, they are informed by comparative research or some of my personal experiences. Where I have drawn on other written sources, I mention this in the text, and I have placed those references in the bibliography. The insights and knowledge I share are not for approval but reflection and, maybe, discussion. After all, only through this approach can we move forward instead of simply rewriting what has been written many times before.

A lot of the information presented in this book was passed down to me by my family in the form of ancestral knowledge. This is the most important, and only, source I have trusted since the early days of my life. Perhaps the approach I have taken to share my insights may not appeal to everyone because it is not based on proven research or primary literature sources that have survived the passage of time. However, such a discourse would simply serve to rewrite existing material and understanding, which is not my objective. I am seeking to add to current knowledge, not replicate it.

As a mindful practitioner of my family tradition and of Haitian Vodou, I strive to practice full awareness of everything I think, say, and do. I'm consciously able to mold and shape how my practice will develop. I want to point out that our spiritual realization's profundity steadily grows by infusing our actions with gentleness and awareness. Eventually, we become skilled at facing even the most challenging problems that arise in the present moment. We begin to see that every issue is a challenge, and every challenge is an experience—nothing more.

PART 1

Ancestors and the Magical Tradition

1
The Beginning

During my childhood, I had a distinct recurring dream that forever haunts my memory. The dream would consistently commence in the same manner—a vision of myself stood in a darkened room next to a window. The room is dark, dismal, and filled with a continual drizzle. The only source of meager light comes from outside the room, a limited shaft of sunlight that falls across the floor. In the distance, I can hear a vivid whistle of a strong wind that is weirdly juxtaposed against the sound of someone softly playing the piano. As the wind blows, wet leaves cascade into the room via the open window, dancing through the air in time with the piano keystrokes like a rush of souls seeking sanctuary from the inclement weather.

The shaft of sunlight casts shadows from the tree branches outside the window, forming curious patterns on my skin and clothing. Then, without warning, a foreboding cloud covers the sun, and the room descends into darkness. A new sound fills the room, that of torrential rain beating against the glass panes. But the distinct echo of the howling wind remains as menacing as before.

The leaves that once danced along the floor sweep into a tidal wave that finds sanctuary in the folds of my dress. The intense, blackened sky continues to loom farther into the room, leaving a host of trembling trees in its wake. Branches scour the walls, edging forward, looking for shelter like the ghosts of children lost in the depths of a mysterious dark forest during the storm. It feels like I am forever trapped in this endless night. It felt like eternity. The trees outside take the form of a hunched-over old hag. Her long bony fingers reach out and tap an endless rhythm on my window. I can sense that the house surrounding me is beginning to fall apart. My mind urges me to run away and seek shelter from the torrential rain. I am standing there at the window, shaken by the freezing rain. I feel like the darkness is trying to swallow me up . . .

Suddenly, everything falls silent . . . the sound of the storm and the accompanying piano chords are replaced by a distant call of circling ravens. I smell the damp scent of the earth after heavy rain and feel moist grass beneath my feet. I find myself meandering along a twisting lane through the dark forest. Behind me, I can see the lonely silhouette of the house I previously thought was inescapable. As a child, I loved to run free along this same path. My loose flowing hair gently brushes my back as the wind ruffles it into tousles of curls. I feel compelled to continue to venture deeper and deeper into the forest by some mysterious force. Before long, I am completely consumed by the darkness. Now and again, the moon's dim light successfully pierces through the gaps in the dense branches to offer me a glimpse of the way ahead. I am being called forward by the shadowy cries of women who once drowned in the lake that lies ahead. They urge me to join them, destined to be their sister. I sense that my fate awaits. The murky waters of the lake will soon consume me as I join my new family.

I dreamed the same dream for several years repeatedly, and I always wake up in a cold sweat at the same moment I felt water on my skin in my dream. I dreamed it over and over again until I accepted my calling in this world—my destination. Spirits come to me. I see and hear them and, as their messenger, I transfer those messages to people. These spirits are your ancestors. And they need only one thing that only the living can give them—remembrance.

People study nature and gods, natural sciences, and history; they comprehend the past and strive to see the future. We know this world as the flow of information processes and energy connections. We learn to foresee patterns and uncertainties and manipulate the energy around us. But we forget about our ancestors. Remembrance is the tribute we all must pay to those who brought us into this life—a commemoration of those who passed on our personalities, talents, actions, and destiny. I want to remind people of what they often forget—that people have the strength to solve anything, even the most terrible and seemingly unsolvable problems. Your strength, magic, and wisdom are in your blood, passed down through many generations—the gift you received from your ancestors, your family, and your clan. When we finally understand that life is a long learning process and it all comes to "the beginning," everything we encounter becomes small and simple. Honoring your ancestors and carrying and preserving your lineage is the most effective form of mysticism, spirituality, and magic practice.

Although an awareness of the practitioner within will gradually develop as you continue to practice, there are certain things you can do to help yourself grow. Practicing with the full knowledge and understanding that enlightenment is a real possibility within this lifetime adds an entirely new dimension and meaning to your practice. It provides you with tremendous spiritual and magical energy. You simply need to know how to find these powers and draw them out. You can only draw real strength from within yourself. Recognize and appreciate the incredible ability you already have. Recognition, acceptance, and clarity expand your mind, and the problems that cross your path no longer seem intractable.

In this book, I have paid great attention to the little things that we often miss in the hustle and bustle of everyday life. I reveal the secrets of a happy and healthy life based on the example our ancestors set for us by fulfilling natural and ancestral laws. These laws are laid down in folk traditions and customs, rituals, and amulets. The symbolism of each of them is filled with sacred meaning that makes our lives easier and fills us with the family's power.

In the contemporary world, people are cut off from their "roots" in the literal and figurative sense of the word, which causes irreparable damage to their health, personal relationships, material well-being, and social status. Many folk traditions have been improperly forgotten. Ancestral magic is the most powerful; ancestral protection is the most robust. If you have your clan standing behind you, you will be well protected and successful. Ancestral tradition is one of the oldest forms of magic; it places an emphasis on communicating with your ancestors and receiving help from them. Initially, ancestral tradition involved people worshipping their departed relatives as real gods. They sought protection from their dead relatives and turned to them for advice.

Real success in the field of magic, or manipulation of the energies as I prefer to say, can only be achieved by those who know how to think, work hard to improve, find a creative approach to everything, listen to their inner voice, read between the lines, and finally, set a goal and strive to achieve it. Put simply: you can forget about magic wands and spells working on the first try.

The harsh truth is that in magic, as with anything else, you first need to acquire at least a basic knowledge and develop your ability to work with subtle energies. Many people understand magic as the art of fulfilling their desires, but this is far from the truth. The secret of magic is not to subdue circumstances and people, but to resonate with the world and oneself. Then, instead of overcoming, let's say, illnesses and obstacles, you can avoid them, and the things you desire will present themselves to you without much effort on your part.

Magic is knowledge of the fundamental laws by which the universe operates—an understanding of how your inner world is connected with the external world, and the power of thoughts, words, and deeds. It's the ability to take responsibility for your life. Finally, it is the wisdom to live how you want. Magic is the unique view of the world and of yourself that manifests itself in all your actions. It's not an occupation but a way of life.

Among the Slavs, as with many other people throughout the world, it was customary to install a small symbolical shrine in a particular part of the house or yard. In Benin, Africa, and Haiti, practitioners construct a memorial shrine to honor (and work with) their ancestors.

Man is not purely a biological being. People do not rely on instincts alone. Culture is incredibly important for humanity—it is the main system by which we pass on our experiences to our descendants. This relationship exists at the level of universal human culture and at the individual and family level. And the culture of reverence for ancestors is what connects all people. After all, whatever faith you profess, you are someone's descendant and, if you're lucky, someone's ancestor.

When you know about your ancestors, you can hold memorial rites. Symbolic meetings are intended to pay tribute to the ancestors and strengthen the family. Introducing children to their ancestors will help to preserve lineage and help teach your children and grandchildren what can take them a lifetime to learn, if at all. Memorial ceremonies can either be family events that are closed to strangers or public affairs celebrated as festivals. Ancestral tradition itself is based on the idea that what you have is not only because of you. Many generations of your ancestors lived and accumulated power so you could possess it in your life today. You can express your respect for your ancestors by helping people around you and those who will come after you.

In Rus, the tradition of honoring dead ancestors has always been of great importance. For example, in ancient times, there was a rite in the villages that involved deliberately spilling some of the drinks on the table—this was symbolic of pouring a separate glass for the deceased as we do today. And on Maslenitsa, a hot pancake was put aside on the window for the dead. (We'll discuss holidays in detail in chapter 6.)

In my family, and that of many Russians, we had what is called a "red corner" in which wooden figurines of bearded "grandfathers" (ancestors)

Fig. 1.1. The red corner after implementation of Christianity

and pictures were displayed on a shelf that represented the symbolical clan's ancestor altar. After the implementation of Christianity, wooden figurines were replaced with Christian saint icons. The analogous concept in Western Christianity is the home altar. This tradition of installing a "house church" continues to this day in Eastern Christianity. The home is considered to be a microcosm of the church.

Symbolically, the husband and wife are the clergy of this church, and the children are the laity. In Pagan homes, particular rituals may be performed in the red corner when people who possessed sacred knowledge—sorcerers, witches—die in the local village, since long torments accompany their deaths.

2
Pagan Christianity

Paganism is the oldest and most natural tradition in the world, and I am fully convinced that it is eternal. Paganism preceded Christianity and will survive it in the hearts of Slavs. There are three main concepts in Paganism: (1) the connection of generations and bond with their land, (2) the full immersion in nature and its eternal cycles, and (3) the ongoing "search," both in the realm of the spirit and in seeking out spontaneous experiences with no predetermined outcome. In contrast to monotheism, Paganism binds people of the same community with the physical world in which they live—and does not follow a codified set of rules set between an individual and an almighty god. See "An Interview with Guillaume Faye," *Antaios* XVI (Spring Equinox 2001) for more on this topic.

In Europe, Paganism, which was the ancient religion of the region, is present in various spheres: in the form of "folklore" (without the dismissive connotation of fairy tales), traditionalism, and ethnic pantheism without belief in personified gods. Paganism also represents a massive departure from Catholicism and Orthodoxy, in ways that I will discuss in later chapters. Just some aspects of Paganism that have experienced a resurgence in more recent times include the celebration of the end of the seasonal cycles and the solstices. Celebrations that were originally Pagan but had been co-opted by the church have recently started to take on their Pagan character once again; for example, at Christmas, we see it becoming more common to use a tree (instead of a manger) to represent the winter solstice.

THE BAPTISM OF RUS

The story of Slavic Pagan Christianity begins with Prince Vladimir. Vladimir Sviatoslavich (also called Vladimir the Great) was Prince of Novgorod, Grand Prince of Kyiv, and the ruler of Kievan Rus' (modern-day Russia, Belarus, and Ukraine) from 980 to 1015. In 988, he decided to change his faith and that of his country and people. Born and living as Pagan, he initially responded to all appeals to accept Christianity with a persistent refusal, explaining that his supporters would ridicule him. Eventually, after learning about different religions, he became a sincere believer in the Christian faith, and Christianization arose. It didn't happen overnight; it was a process that stretched out over two centuries. But eventually "the light" of the Christian faith shone down on Kievan Rus' and its people. On Vladimir's orders, Kyiv underwent a baptism, followed by all the people of Rus.

Rather than being for personal enlightenment alone, the baptism of Rus was undoubtedly a step forward in the development of a feudal government. It brought Kievan Rus' closer to the rest of Europe, strengthened its cultural ties to Byzantium, and maintained it as a political entity in itself. The Pagan religion that arose during the era of the tribal system was not class-based. It did not require one person to show subservience to another. Therefore, the Pagan religion was inconsistent with the developing feudal class system of the ancient Slavic government. In pre-Christian times, Slavs did not belong to one nationality or tribe; they were members of many different tribes, each of which had its own language, culture, territory, and traditional system. While all these tribes were relatively similar, they were also heterogeneous. It was apparent to any Slavic man that the gods were related only to him, his tribe, and the people born from the people of his tribe. On foreign territory, you were obliged to worship the gods of another land, or at least those natural phenomena and objects that represented the gods of that land. Each region worshipped the respective gods differently, even if they were referred to using the same names. In addition to the common and main gods of the tribe, there were always local gods.

Prince Vladimir first attempted to adapt the old, Pagan religion he practiced earlier in his reign to the new system of government. To accomplish this, he wanted to combine the gods that the different Slavic tribes worshipped and establish a unified pantheon for all of Rus. The Slavic Pagan tradition for most of its history didn't represent a harmonious system, but was composed of regional religious beliefs, groups, and individual sects. The most famous is the cult of Perun (one of the highest gods of the pantheon, God of the Sky), which in the ninth through tenth centuries was the main competitor of Christianity in Russia. Prince Vladimir tried to create a nationwide organized religion around this cult to consolidate his own political and ideological power; but it failed, which subsequently led to the Christianization of Rus.

The Christian religion, which sanctified the exploitation and oppression of others in the name of God and could turn a slave by compulsion into a slave by conviction, was the religion most in line with the interests of the feudal military elite of the ancient Slavic state. Prince Vladimir undoubtedly took the close economic ties between Kievan Rus' and the West into account when he carried out these religious reforms in his state. Furthermore, Christianity of the Byzantine type offered another indisputable advantage from the point of view of those in power in Kievan Rus'. The Byzantine Church claimed less control over the secular government of a state than other religions or types of Christianity. This was in sharp contrast to the Western Catholic Church, which demanded political power. In this way, it was not the "true light" of the Orthodox faith, but primarily political and economic reasons that led to the Baptism of Rus and the decision to make Christianity its official religion.

Notably, the mentality of people has undergone a significant shift since Prince Vladimir's era. There are very few similarities between people of the pre-baptism era and the present generation. For centuries, the church taught people to read and write using biblical texts, instilling into a person's consciousness from infancy no resistance to evil, but only "patience" and "obedience"—that is, to be passive and suffer. The result is the current mentality. We, as a generation, have progressively deteriorated into a decrepit state characterized by banality, stupidity, debauchery, dependence, drunkenness, and cowardice. This can be primarily attributed to the fact that people no longer raise their children in accordance with ancestral traditions.

The meaning of the term *religion* comes from Latin and refers to a conscientious attitude toward someone or something; in modern times it is also defined as "a system of beliefs held to with ardor and faith" (Merriam-Webster, "religion"). There was no religion per se among the ancient Slavs; there was a faith based on knowledge and experience. For example, the belief that the sun would rise in the morning is based on the observation that it has done so many times before. Therefore, the problem of faith is a problem in the reliability of information about the source of faith and the possibilities of its objectivity or falsity. The conscience of our ancestors was based on universal moral and ethical values and an objective reflection on reality, which gave true faith in the reflected reality and the sequence of phenomena and events. In contrast, Judaism (and later Christianity) are based on actions and experiences caused by so-called supernatural interventions from the monotheistic God of the ancient Israelites; I have often wondered how relevant this religion is for Russians and Slavs in general. If the religion of our ancestors was based on a dialectical-materialistic reflection on reality, then monotheism was a subjective-idealistic view, which, in my opinion, leaves it open to lies, manipulation, and perversion. I ask, Why have we allowed this perspective to overcome the truth our ancestors passed down to us?

A poignant example of this is the creation of public property, which Christian liberals refer to as "no man's property," a view that is based on the assumption of a form of a coup by privatizing and claiming rights to the property of others, thereby dooming the workers to poverty, debauchery, and extinction. Ironically, Christian liberals accuse us, Pagans, of this wrongdoing and of renouncing God and fighting against him.

I want to note that the essence of Paganism lies in polytheism and entails a surprising absence of worship. Paganism involves revering gods as opposed to worshipping them. Worship, such as falling on your knees and banging your forehead on the floor with screams of "God forgive me for I have sinned," is a glorified form of self-humiliation, whereas reverence involves deep-rooted mutual respect.

In essence, in comparison to the Christian mentality, the Pagan mentality corresponds with the attitude ancient Pagans had toward their gods: One cannot seek consolation from the gods. The gods only respect pride and strength, not pleading. A person can become happy and healthy only thanks to the power of her spirit and will. Pagans do not prostrate themselves before their gods; they challenge them or thank them and try to earn their favor. Christianity has developed the theology of castration, declaring us all inferior and guilty by virtue of our birth. While Pagans seduce their gods or argue with them, the monotheist pleads with God and humiliates himself before him.

For Pagans, there is an element of flexibility in choosing the mode of worshipping gods. For example, when a couple is intimate, they both show sufficient respect to the God (or Gods) of Love. When a man meets the enemy who arrives bearing arms to drive him out, he honors the God of War, and so on. Creators of a new Christian religion in Rus brazenly appropriated biblical motives about the creation of the world and the main holidays of the Slavs, replacing them with new meanings.

Paganism became a serious obstacle to the spread of bloody Christianity, mainly since it affected all levels of society, especially the poor. At the same time, the followers of Christ came from a higher class of society due to particular circumstances.

The adoption of Christianity as a state religion in Rus did not mean a complete and rapid change in the way of thinking and way of life. Cities became the centers of the new religion. Dioceses were established, churches were built, public services in Pagan sanctuaries were forcibly replaced with divine services in Christian churches. Yet, there were no changes in people's worldview; there was no rejection of the beliefs of great-grandfathers. Dual faith resulted from a simple concession of the people to the new government and "true faith." The Slavs wanted to save their lives, so they put on the mask of a "Christian" while remaining faithful to their ancestors, the gods. Christian saints personified the Pagan gods: for example, Perun as Elijah the Prophet; and Veles (god of earth, waters, livestock, and the underworld) as Vlasiy, the patron saint of cattle. The belief in house and forest spirits, the elemental power of water and air, and so on, also persevered.

The official religion ousted Paganism into the realm of folk culture: the observance of Christian rituals (church services, fasts, etc.) was combined with the communal observance of agrarian cults, participation in feasts and merrymaking, with which medieval clergy. The church did incorporate the main Pagan holidays into the Christian celebrations to subordinate communal cults to its influence. Dual faith and the struggle against it persisted until the beginning of the twentieth century. Despite the millennial domination of the state Orthodox Church, Pagan views remained popular until that time, manifesting themselves in rituals, group dance games, songs, fairy tales, and folk art. Church sermons that insisted that Pagan gods did not exist would seem inconsistent and futile to the people of Rus, so the Orthodox Church made a concession: it declared that the Christian God was the only true god, and the countless gods of the Slavs were demons.

With the help of the tsarist* bayonets, the separation of the Russian Orthodox Church from the state in February 1917 not only deprived the church of its monopoly on religion in Russia, it also made it possible to recall the traditions of the free Slavs and their true Pagan faith. This faith, unlike Christianity, does not enslave the soul of a person by religion but is a special way of thinking aimed at improving a person and raising her to the level of God.

Although the church officially forbade Pagan practices, people continued to organize festivities, folk dances, singing, dressing up, fortune-telling, and so on. They kept building snowmen, dancing around bonfires, and burning scarecrows (symbols of winter). On holidays, you can still hear the cheerful sounds of flutes, pipes, balalaikas, and harmonicas coming from each house, despite the church's prohibition of these celebrations. The joy and liveliness of these celebrations are a stark contrast to religious holidays, with their monotonous services, dim flickering of candles and lamps, endless repetition of "Forgive me, Lord," and a strong smell of incense.

Orthodox churches understood this all perfectly—so they incorporated many elements of folk customs and rituals into their holidays. As Christianity began to spread throughout Rus, it became clear that it would be impossible to introduce a single new holiday without including elements of the Pagan holiday. Failure to do so would mean that the holiday would not be accepted. For the majority of the population of Rus, the conversion to Christianity was formal and superficial. To stamp out the Pagan cult peacefully and unite as many Slavs as possible under the common religion, the church began to "adjust" the calendar to match people's day-to-day lives while also replacing old customs with Christian holidays (see the box for more about the calendar). This practice confused people, who began celebrating church holidays and

---

*Tsarist autocracy, also called tsarism, is a form of autocracy wherein all power and wealth is controlled by the tsar (also spelled czar, tzar, or csar), a title used to designate East and South Slavic monarchs or supreme rulers of Eastern Europe.

honoring Orthodox saints but continued observing the traditions of the ancient religions of their ancestors.

Let's look at the transition from the ancient Slavic holiday of Kupayla to the Orthodox holiday of Ivan Kupala (John the Baptist). During Kupayla, which was originally celebrated June 21, people glorify the God of the Summer Sun, who took control after spring. The celebration of the summer solstice and the full bloom of nature is an ancient Pagan tradition. Nowadays, after the installation of a Gregorian calendar—or new calendar as we call it—the night of Ivan Kupala is celebrated on July 6 through July 7. Unlike the Slavic holiday Kupayla, the day of Ivan Kupala has nothing to do with the God of the Sun. Instead, it is supposed to be celebrated with prayers in the church. But even after the official ban of the day of Kupayla and the introduction of the new holiday, the centuries-old Slavic traditions have remained until today. Though the church condemns them for doing so, people still hold massive festivals, leap over bonfires, release candles and wreaths in the river, and perform other symbolic Pagan rituals.

Changes to the Calendar

World cultures have kept calendars based on astronomical phenomena since time immemorial. The problem arises when they attempt to match up these natural annual phenomena to years that have standard lengths. In 46 CE, the Julian calendar was first developed: it is based on the observation that the Earth completes one circuit around the sun in 365¼ days. Because it is not a whole number of days, one additional day (leap day) is added to the year every four years. This is close—but not exactly—accurate to the astronomical year. If the length of the year is not adjusted, over time the calendar dates will become less and less matched with the natural events they originally were based on.

In the tenth century, with the adoption of Christianity, the Julian calendar was incorporated by the Russian Orthodox Church, and in church institutions—which at that time were considered centers of culture and education—a total rewriting of history began. The mythical date of the creation of the world (the birth of Adam) was used as a "starting point." And only in 1700, by the decree of Peter the Great, Russia and the territories it occupied switched to the chronology system from the birth of Christ. In the same year, the traditional New Year's celebration was moved from September to January.

The next reforms were brought by the victory of the communists. In 1918, the Bolsheviks raised the issue of switching to the Gregorian calendar. The Gregorian calendar accounted for the drift that had been caused by the Julian calendar (because the year is not actually 365¼ days but 11 minutes less than that, which means that in 400 years of the Julian calendar, approximately 3 extra days would accumulate). To address this issue, in the Gregorian calendar certain leap years are skipped, keeping the calendar more accurate. By 1918, the Julian calendar had accumulated thirteen extra days. To "correct" it in the Gregorian calendar, immediately after January 31, 1918, came . . . February 14, 1918.

In 1923, representatives of the Russian Orthodox Church (ROC) also decided to switch to the Gregorian calendar, but Patriarch Tikhon of Moscow (11th Patriarch of Moscow and All Russia; he was canonized as a confessor in 1989) could not attend the meeting in Constantinople, and the ROC continued to live according to the Julian calendar. When Tikhon nevertheless tried to introduce a new chronology system, the believers were very skeptical about the initiative, and the decree had to be annulled.

For another example of a holiday that has Pagan roots, September 22 was when the Slavs traditionally celebrated the day of the autumnal equinox (Ovse) and thanked the God of the Autumn Sun for a generous harvest. As Christianity grew and spread throughout Rus, more and more people began to celebrate a church holiday—the day of the birth of the Most Holy Theotokos, which fell on September 21. Theotokos (Greek: Θεοτόκος, meaning "God-bearer") is a title of Mary, mother of Jesus, used especially in Eastern Christianity. This title is commonly translated into English as "the Mother of God." On this holiday, it was believed that the Mother of God protected farmers, blessed families with prosperity, and helped mothers. Among the Eastern Slavs, this day was also dedicated to the celebration of the end of the harvest. In this case, the Mother of God was simply honored and thanked for the harvest rather than the God of the Autumn Sun.

Many researchers of the spiritual development of Russia have agreed and continue to agree that Russian people are highly polarized. They combine incompatible opposites: Natural, Pagan, and Dionysian elements with ascetic-monastic Orthodoxy. They are constantly at odds with each other, tearing apart our entire reality and leaving deep wounds on our history. Unparalleled searches for God are interspersed with unprecedented examples of schism, anarchy, and sectarianism.

Russia is home to numerous ethnic groups, each with its own distinct culture, language, and traditions. Ethnic minorities and Indigenous peoples maintain their unique identities, including traditional forms of music, dance, art, clothing, cuisine, and religious practices, and have contributed to the country's cultural richness. Russia is home to a variety of religious groups, including Russian Orthodoxy, Islam, Buddhism, and various Indigenous and folk beliefs. Different ethnic and cultural groups may practice different religions or variations of these faiths.

While Russia is indeed home to a variety of religious groups and diverse religious traditions, there have been periods in its history when centralization efforts aimed to promote a dominant religious and cultural identity. During some historical periods, non-Orthodox religious groups, including minority religions and Indigenous beliefs, faced restrictions and discrimination. The state often promoted the dominance of the Russian Orthodox faith over other religions.

Centralization of Russian Orthodoxy has long been closely associated with the Russian state and its rulers. The Russian Orthodox Church has historically played a significant role in promoting a sense of cultural and religious unity among the population. The Russian Orthodox Church has often been used to legitimize the authority of the state, with the church teaching that the monarchy was divinely ordained. This relationship between church and state has been integral to the promotion of centralized authority.

There have been periods in Russian history when the state, in conjunction with the Russian Orthodox Church, sought to suppress alternative religious beliefs, indigenous beliefs, and minority religions. This has led to tensions and, at times, religious persecution. Two centuries of violent procedure led to the formation of a conglomerate of small principalities that were always at war with each other.

Paganism very easily became a victim of expansion, both from the West and the East. History has preserved that concept for us with the unequivocal mandate of Prince Sviatoslav, "the Christian faith is ugliness." Prince Sviatoslav (lived 943–972) was a grand prince of Kyiv famous for his persistent campaigns in the east and south, which precipitated the collapse of two great powers of Eastern Europe: Khazaria (occupying the southeastern section of modern-day Russia, southern Ukraine, Crimea, and Kazakhstan) and the First Bulgarian Empire. His decade-long reign over the Kievan Rus' was marked by its rapid expansion, and by the end of his short life, Sviatoslav carved out for himself the largest state in Europe. Though his mother had converted to Christianity, Prince Sviatoslav remained a staunch pagan all of his life. However, due to his abrupt death in ambush, his conquests, for the most part, were not consolidated into a functioning empire.

Christian expansion continued: the temples of the ancient gods were desecrated, and one of the first Christian saints, Gleb ("Holy Passionate Gleb," Prince Gleb Vladimirovich of Murom, who was canonized together with his brother Boris) took part in the Pagan massacres, killing followers with his hands. Therefore, the thesis about the divinely revealed acceptance of a new religion does not stand up to any criticism; this grandiose rhetoric arises wherever people want to hide the facts. It is known, for example, that Russian epics were not written down until the eighteenth century purely for ideological reasons. Literature that expressed criticism of the Orthodox principles of the Christian religion was utterly absent in prerevolutionary Russia. It is shameless and absurd to assert that Orthodoxy has always been organically inherent in the Russian people.

HISTORICAL HERESIES

Starting from that first baptism, from one century to the next, Russia was filled with heresy after heresy, resisting the official state church with all its might. Strigolniki, Nontrinitarianismists, Judaizers, and many other movements that have sunk into oblivion, as well as formalized consistent teachings, were brought to life. And what is remarkable is that each land, each region, brought its own unique local flavor into this thousand-year struggle based on the ancient Slavic views on nature, morality, and the afterlife. So, for example, iconoclasm, one of the most stable freedom-loving trends, took the form of numerous practical manifestations, which consisted of the desecration of icons, creation of so-called Hell icons, and mockery of crosses. However, it was also reflected in detail in theoretical works: the dogma of the Trinity of God, the supernatural origin of Christ, the Mother of God, and miracle workers.

Strigolniki are a heretical movement that arose in the middle of the fourteenth century in Novgorod and Pskov, Russia. They rejected the church hierarchy and monasticism, calling the clergy corrupt and ignorant; they believed that the sacraments of communion, penance, and baptism could not be accompanied by extortions in favor of the church; and they demanded that the laity have the right to preach the religion. Supporters of heresy were townspeople and small clergy. In the middle of the fifteenth century, Strigolniki disappeared.

Nontrinitarianism is a broader term that refers to monotheistic belief systems, primarily within Christianity, which reject the mainstream Christian doctrine of the Trinity; namely, that God is made up of three: the Father, the Son, and the Holy Spirit, and yet is also indivisibly one essence.

Judaizers (Russian: Zhidovstvuyuschiye) may be loosely translated as "those who follow Jewish traditions" or "those who think like Jews." Judaizers appeared in the fourteenth century. This sect received its name from ideological opponents, representatives of the Orthodox Church, who believed that the teachings of the Judaizers continued the traditions of secret Jewish sects and implanted Judaism in Russia. Members of this sect rejected church authority, the sacrament, icons, and priests. Supporters of heresy rejected the outward manifestations of the Christian cult; denied the church hierarchy, fasts, holidays, temples, veneration of icons, all sacred objects, services and rituals; denied the dogma of the Holy Trinity, the deity of Jesus Christ and his resurrection from the dead. They insisted that Jesus is not God, but a simple man. The Judaizers kept their faith in secret; therefore, no written original texts and testimonies explaining their teachings have survived. By the verdict of the church council, the members of this sect were declared heretics and were severely oppressed. But these beliefs spread rapidly, and fans appeared all over Russia (including some high church officials).

Even back then, our ancestors, who are now commonly called "illiterate savages," were able to conduct a detailed philological analysis of sacred texts, analyzing the contradictions between the Old

Testament and the New Testament. The religious opposition was at one time so strong that Ivan III Vasilyevitch, also known as Ivan the Great, personally provided his support. Ivan III, Grand Prince of Moscow and Grand Prince of all Rus, first served as the coruler and regent for his blind father Vasily II; Ivan ascended the throne in 1462. His rule is marked by vastly expanding the territory of Moscow. His first enterprise was a war with the Republic of Novgorod, with which Moscow (as a northern district of Golden Horde) had fought a series of wars stretching back at least a hundred years, and he used the people's heresy as one of the most powerful tools in the political struggle.

CHRISTIAN BY BAPTISM AND A PAGAN BY WORLDVIEW

Death gives rise to natural fear and frightens those of little faith. It is everywhere, "waiting in the wings." It is shrouded in a veil of secrecy. Still, it seems to show its nearness through hints (signs in folklore, wisdom of the old faith believers). A person who is unstable in faith and religion is shallow and lives a life shrouded in fear. He is both a Christian by baptism and a Pagan by outlook. He lives on the border-line between church teachings and the primitive elements of mytho-logical ideas, borrowing from the church and remembering old beliefs, worshipping the saints, and fearing house spirits (Domovoy) or forest spirits (Leshy).

> "A woodpecker pecks at moss in a cottage—death will follow."
> "The garden blooms late—its owner will die."
> "A raven caws in the church—there will be death in the village; a
>   raven caws in a hut—there will be a death in the yard."
> "If the house spirit chokes you at night," an old believer would say,
>   "ask this: Is it for better or for worse?"
> "If a dog howls down (into the ground), someone will die."

"Mice gnaw clothes—death is coming."

"Flies in the hut in winter, someone will die."

"If crumbs fall out of someone's mouth, death is coming."

"If straw gets stuck to the tail of a hen, someone will die."

"If you misidentify someone on the street, someone will die."

"If a saint icon falls—someone will die."

There is a long list of folklore superstitions that old believers prescribed to—many people continue to do so to this day.

With the first forced baptism of Kievan Rus', Orthodoxy acted, as it does today, as an integral part of the tradition. That "tradition" in folk culture is where custom replaces belief itself. Over time, religious traditions, rituals, and practices become deeply ingrained in the culture, even if the original religious beliefs and meanings behind those traditions fade or evolve. This concept can be applied to the Christianization of Kievan Rus' and its cultural impact.

Integration of Orthodox Christianity. The forced baptism of Kievan Rus' led to the integration of Orthodox Christianity into the daily lives and culture of the population. Christian practices, rituals, and symbols became integral parts of the tradition and customs of the people.

Cultural Adaptation. Over time, the religious beliefs and practices may have evolved and adapted to the cultural and social context of the region. People incorporated Christian elements into their existing customs and beliefs, creating a unique blend of folk culture and Christianity.

Customs and Rituals. As generations passed, certain customs and rituals associated with Christianity may have become disconnected from their original religious significance. These customs persisted and evolved, and people may have continued to observe them without necessarily adhering to the original religious doctrines.

Cultural Heritage. The traditions and customs influenced by the forced Christianization became an integral part of the cultural heritage of the region. They played a role in shaping the identity and values of the people and contributed to the rich tapestry of Russian culture.

Continuity and Change. While some customs remained consistent over time, others evolved or were adapted in response to changing social, political, and cultural dynamics. The coexistence of Orthodox Christianity and traditional folk beliefs has been a characteristic feature of Russian culture.

In summary, the forced baptism of Kievan Rus' introduced Orthodox Christianity and its associated traditions into the region's culture. Over time, these traditions became deeply embedded in the folk culture of the people, even as the original religious beliefs and meanings may have evolved or diminished. This phenomenon reflects the dynamic interplay between religion, culture, and tradition in the historical development of the region.

Christian ritualism based on popular religiosity, both in the past and current era, coexists with other Pagan and magical belief systems. In some Slavic villages to this day, if a man becomes ill, for example, he will go to a church to light a candle. Still, he may also visit a "grandmother" (a witch) or a healer. If he sees a black cat, he spits over his shoulder or knocks on wood. He can pray according to the Orthodox prayer book yet follow astrological forecasts and pray to the gods for good crops and a successful harvest. There are many such examples of dual faith in Russia in the contemporary world. Even church activities are subject to superstitious misperception in popular understanding. For instance, when a priest enters a sick person's house to read the last rites, a superstitious person will try to observe which foot the priest crosses the threshold of the house with first; if right, the patient will recover; if left, he will die. There are many similar superstitions:

"The ember fell out of the censer when the priest used incense around the deceased—soon another person will die."

"If, during the unction, the candles fall with their butt to the threshold, then the patient will die."

"If they are waiting for a priest to come to the home of a dying person with the Holy Sacraments, then they should put a knife on the table to ward away death."

3
Our Roots

Fish are born in the ocean, but a fish is not made of salt.
Just because your surroundings are chaotic doesn't mean
you must also be. It's not the condition you're in that shapes
your reality, but your will and how you perceive it.

NATASHA HELVIN

Many people renounce their ancestors. Yet, renouncing one's roots is the worst thing a living being can do. Just imagine a tree that "renounces" its roots! Your roots define your existence. They shape your world and actions. They are what make you act in a certain way, say certain things, and hold on to certain beliefs. No matter how you try to escape your roots, you are forever anchored to them. It's like trying to run away from yourself. You will always be you, no matter how much you try to reject your core origins. Attempts to disavow your forebearers will only serve to enslave your subconsciousness and consciousness to someone else's doctrine, which will never be in your favor. You will never know and embrace your true self. Instead, you will find yourself restricted by your own actions. You are you; you are the main reason for your existence. You must be your own source of inspiration. Allow yourself to be at one with your ancestors and all the forces that exist with them.

What happens when you reject the help of your ancestors? You ignore thousands of years of the learning, values, and experiences of those who came before you, who lived, loved, and gave you life, who sacrificed their lives for you to be here today. Do not blindly convince yourself that your ancestors and spirits will simply disappear should you attempt to turn your back on your heritage and legacy. Don't blame them for the illusory person who was planted in your brain to fear or ignore your ancestors' efforts. I often hear people describe their ancestors using words such as *satanic* or *evil* and progress to declare that they are very different from their ancestors. For example, some of you may believe that ancestors who offered sacrifices to the gods were "evil." If your ancestors were evil, then who are you?

Your ancestors are always there to guide you, whoever they were in their past lives. Either accept your reality, your legacy, or you allow other people to manipulate you forever. After all, if the root of a tree is bad, so is the tree.

The spirits of your deceased relatives are always there to give you strength. To teach you how to cope with challenges, steer you away from making mistakes, and help you achieve your goals and desires. When people ignore the experience, teachings, and help passed down by their ancestors, they lose the power to embrace those learnings in their lives. Your ancestors are a rich source of energy, strength, wisdom, and experience. Water enters the tree from the soil through the roots to support its life and keep branches healthy and strong. Your clan is the same. We all have roots; the descendants are leaves on the many different branches nourished from the first ancestor.

You can ignore or reject your ancestors for many reasons. Whoever these people were during their own lifetimes, they are now behind the veil. They had an opportunity to learn from their experiences when they were alive. It is not to say that they are more spiritually developed because they have passed on to another realm, but they can now see the bigger picture and have experienced spiritual elevation. This elevation can aid the spiritual evolution of the people who reject their ancestors for any reason. However, the unresolved problems associated with their ancestors tie them to the past, preventing them from moving forward. You can never wholly free yourself from our past, even though it has already come to pass. You need first to reflect on the world in which your ancestors lived and try to understand their past actions, not in an attempt to justify these actions but to enable you to move forward and teach your children a better way.

Sometimes, a person may naively believe they are better educated, more intelligent than their uninformed ancestors. How little they know! Yes, reading books and attending university can make you smart, enlighten you, and give you knowledge. But just because your ancestors could not read or write does not mean they aren't smart or wise. They are real. They are pure. They are survivors. The people who "weren't smart" and were "illiterate" sacrificed themselves for you to be here today and live your life, to hold your children in your arms, and to continue your bloodline.

Meeting our basic needs today is virtually effortless—we have everything we need at our fingertips. We can drive to the grocery store to pick up food and visit a physician if we feel unwell. To get a glass of water, all we need to do is turn on the tap. It doesn't require an education. Your ancestors had to *survive*. Some ancient cultures still try to stay alive today; on the coast or forest, prairie or mountain, desert or tundra—some inhabitants of the Earth continue to rely on ancient survival skills. These people live what we perceive to be primitive lives; however, their basic survival skills keep them alive and, most importantly, happy. Each particular form of land and surroundings requires specialized knowledge; survival relies on leveraging the resources given to us by Mother Nature, not exploiting them. How many of you could survive in primitive conditions? You may have a good idea of what to do in theory, but could you survive in practice? Even with a university education. Many of the primitive people who continue to adopt the lifestyles of ancient cultures are not educated in the sense that you might be familiar with, but they are nonetheless the most compassionate people you will ever meet in your life. They live communally, which is the main reason they haven't starved to death. And that is what I call true freedom—the opportunity to live freely within ourselves and our community, respect each other, be productive, creative, supported, and validated. Of all the people I have met, so-called primitive civilizations are the friendliest and, most importantly, the happiest people in the world.

Natural instincts and being close to nature are in your genes; the genes passed down by your ancestors. Without this connection and communication, you are missing something fundamental, and you are losing yourself. Many people can't move forward with their spiritual practices because they are surrounded by barriers; roads, highways, asphalt, and electronics all serve to block our ability to connect with real nature. Yet, our modern civilization teaches us to build more and more barriers as we embrace material goods, pleasures, and self-indulgence. People turn away from their history, roots, and, therefore, themselves, creating a perpetual craving and emptiness in their souls that forms a dark hole.

By disregarding the power, energy, and wisdom that has been passed down through generations, it is akin to blocking a river with a dam. Despite having access to abundant water, they allow themselves to suffer from thirst. The solution lies in quenching their thirst with the gifts bestowed by their ancestors: nourishment from the mother, wise guidance from the father, blessings from the grandmother, and direction from the grandfather. This knowledge, which is instinctively understood by all living beings on this planet, is something that only humans dare to ignore. This concept is described in detail in Anne Ancelin Schutzenberg's book *The Ancestor Syndrome*, which I have used as a resource.

It is useful for everyone to know their ancestry, learn how to draw power from their descendants, and leverage and strengthen these valuable connections. After all, your clan can provide you with a healthy family, a career, prosperity, elevated social status, and successful personal realization. However, those same ancestors can take away or destroy what someone has, make them "re-live" their own mistakes, or pay their debt.

Suppose you don't understand what is causing your problems, why your life is the way it is. A problem that cannot be understood cannot be solved. There is a belief that a person's fate is "determined by nature." But, as with everything in this world, someone else came first, before you. A clan, like all life on Earth, must change and adapt to stay alive. And these changes should always be for the benefit of the members of that family. A person's environment largely depends on the actions of her ancestors.

Human life itself is linked directly to psychology. And psychology, in turn, is inextricably linked with the family, parents, children, and so on. It is no coincidence that all psychological theories (for example, systemic family organization, which we will discuss in chapter 4) ultimately emphasize an individual's connection with her family and parents. Many modern psychological techniques are similar to shamanic practices. Everyone needs to understand the mechanism by which a person's ancestry influences her—it's essential for those who have magical abilities (psychic) or ambitions.

In the shamanic tradition, for example, the first thing a practitioner must do is to establish a relationship with an ancestor's spirit. As one of the earliest forms of religion, shamanism most likely arose during the Stone Age in societies characterized by an economy based on hunting. Shamanism has survived among many ethnic groups of the world—in Africa, North and East Asia, among the Native American tribes, and more—at different development stages. The word *shamanism* comes from the Evenki language,* where *shaman* or *saman* means an "excited,

---

*Evenki, formerly known as Tungus or Solon, is the largest member of the northern group of Tungusic languages. It is spoken by Evenks or Ewenkī in Russia and China.

exalted person." The main characteristic of a shamanic worldview is animism: everything that surrounds a person—objects, plants, animals, and so on—are viewed as "soulful." Followers of shamanism believe in numerous evil and good spirits capable of influencing the life and death of a person, expelling and attracting diseases, providing good luck, and dooming some to misfortune. Being in a state of ecstasy, the shaman performs a special rite of communication with the spirits, called *kamlanie*, to influence the spirits and act as a mediator between them and the people.

Let's explore shamanism in more depth using an example of one of the most developed forms that have survived to this day among several ethnicities found within contemporary Siberia. The worldview of the followers of this particular form of shamanism believe that the universe consists of three worlds: the Upper, where only spirits live; the Middle, where people, animals, and plants live along with the spirits; and the Lower, where the souls of the dead go. Each shaman has helper spirits and patron spirits to whom he turns during a ritual. Spirit-helpers predominantly take the form of wild animals, fish, and birds, and the spirit-patrons, as a rule, are the spirits of the deceased ancestors of the shaman. All shamans have their receptacles—vessels of the spirits.

Most shamans use a tambourine during the ritual, which after a special rite of revival (animation) is considered a mode of traveling to the Upper World, like a horse or a deer may gallop in the physical world. Through the music played on the tambourine, the shaman enters into a trance that enables him to travel to the Upper World, chasing the animal with a tambourine's mallet, which is interpreted as a whip. Some shamans do not have a tambourine—it is replaced by a special rod called a *vargan* (a specific musical instrument).

As a rule, shamans wear specially designated ritual clothes that include a headdress, cloak, and shoes, which are used for ceremonial purposes only. During the ritual, which is usually performed for medicinal reasons in the presence of the patient and his relatives, the shaman, having entered a trance, summons the spirit-helpers and beats the tambourine, thereby traveling to the world of spirits to force evil spirits to leave the patient and heal him. While chanting incantations, often very poetic, the shaman informs others about the difficulties and struggles of his journey and vividly describes the battles he encounters with evil spirits along the way.

Shamanism is usually hereditary. It is believed that after a shaman's death, his spirit passes to his descendants, and the spirits themselves choose the people with whom to connect from the relatives of the deceased shaman. The beginning of shamanic activity is associated with a mysterious mental distress that manifests itself during the puberty of the future shaman. A person begins to hide from people, often fleeing into the taiga (Siberian forest). At this time, he eats almost nothing, starving himself to the point he may even forget his name. This condition indicates that the spirit of a deceased ancestor-shaman has entered his body and spirit. In such cases, a sick shaman, without even wanting to, becomes a shaman. Relatives make him a tambourine and the clothes he needs to perform shamanic rituals. Having received these gifts, the shaman begins his ritualistic activity. The most amazing thing is that in the process of treating his patients, the mental health of the shaman is also restored, and all obvious manifestations of any serious mental distress he suffered from in the recent past suddenly disappear.

Scientists and travelers who observed shamanic rituals in the nineteenth century unanimously concluded that shamans have neurological disorders and a special mentality. The concept of a "special mentality" in the context of shamans and spirit communication typically refers to a unique mindset or state of consciousness that enables them to connect with spirits, access altered states of awareness, and navigate the spiritual world. This mentality may involve altered perceptions, heightened intuition, and a deep understanding of the spirit realm, making shamans distinct from the average person in their ability to interact with and interpret spiritual entities and energies. This point of view subsequently became widespread among researchers of shamanism. However, in recent decades, many scholars have argued that the so-called shamanic disease is just a kind of initiation by which the future shaman consciously performs the rituals prescribed to him in accordance with the role assigned by his tradition.

Arguably, the hereditary nature of shamanism is the result of a process of multigenerational selection by a tribal collective of people with certain mental characteristics, above all, the ability to induce a regulated state of trance that is accompanied by deep hallucinations. The hallucinations lead to the chosen shamans inheriting some of the fundamental psyche's features, allowing them to perform actions that their relatives use as a mechanism to communicate with spirits.

Haitian Vodou exhibits some characteristics that are very similar to the shamanic phenomenon: the *houngan*, a Haitian Vodou priest, communicates with the spirits. As the head of his temple, he has no superiors. He represents a priest, healer, spiritual advisor, exorcist, magician, choir leader, organizer of Vodou ceremonies, and even a judge in his community. But one cannot become an houngan simply by aspiration alone. Anyone who actively pursues the role of houngan initiates a war with the *lwa* (Haitian Vodou spirits) and, thus, becomes the victim of misfortune and failures. In the Haitian tradition, devotees believe that the houngan plays a central role because it is his calling, the call from the spirits, from which he has no right to hide or refuse.

Sometimes a person called by the spirits does not feel attracted to this profession and may even rebel against the idea of becoming a Vodou devotee. In such cases, conflict arises within that individual. The lwa will haunt him until he finally surrenders to his calling.

ANCESTRAL GODS FOR SLAVIC PAGANS

For Slavic pagans, Rod is the supreme god. He is the whole universe. He is above all Pagan gods. The gods are the forces of nature, and all of them together constitute nature. From this point of view, all monotheistic gods are nothing more than people's creations (or fantasies) and, accordingly, will disappear with the end of humanity. On the contrary, the Pagan gods will exist as long as the universe exists. It is also very important to note that Pagan philosophy allows one to perceive Rod both personally (as a god\personality) and impersonally (as the Universe or Nature). According to most scientific studies, Rod arose from a first ancestor. He is the East Slavic spirit-patron of the descendants, the house, the clan and fate.

Paganism is based primarily on Rodolubiye (love for the family and love of the family). Rod literally translates as "the clan" and is understood by us in the indissoluble unity of three elements. These are Essence:

Rod as Itself (Rod the All-Existing All-God All-Holder—the unified all-penetrating spiritual beginning)
Heavenly Rod (power of the ancestors)
Terrestrial Rod (the kinship of relatives)

Ancestral gods are the essence of the faces of the unified Rod and his creative powers, as we comprehend them through our own spiritual experiences. These forces are manifested both all around us in nature and in ourselves. So, for example, the Power of God Perun in Nature is a thunderstorm, and in the human heart it is the will to overcome trials. We reunite the inner and the outer through a ritual of ancestral blessing, thereby gaining spiritual harmony, mental integrity, and bodily health.

Heart teaches us to love. Reason teaches us what is just. Ancestral and clan law teaches us the wisdom of our ancestors. But the highest wisdom is acquired through harmony. To be in harmony with oneself, with the ancestors, with nature, and with your relations means finding your place in life—finding your true self.

Paganism is a natural spirituality inherent in a person from birth. Man is born a Pagan; he does not become one. It is also a philosophy. As such, it is impossible to understand Paganism without philosophical reasoning.

This reasoning also begins with the fact that we directly perceive our gods from birth without a religious institution's intervention. And our leaders then teach us this exact direct perception of the divine in the universe. The gods are directly behind natural phenomena. They are here with us in this world. Therefore, the earthly world is holy and eternal, and people live in the temple of the gods, nature.

Humans largely determine the future of the Earth. The gods have made us responsible for the ecological safety of our world. We are also responsible for the lives of our descendants. Since we are descendants of the gods, the end of our lineage is like the death of the gods. Paganism places great responsibility on individuals but also gives them many joys. Our mythology gives us the answers to what a person should do on Earth and the meaning of life on Earth. These answers can also be viewed as a life philosophy.

The fundamental philosophical concepts inherent in paganism are the meaning of existence given by the gods; the law of morality in the existence of the world; the law of the balance of the opposing forces of the universe (good and evil in particular); the law of the fullness of the Pagan faith (we have been given everything that is required); the concept of Nav (the afterlife) and Yav (the world of the living)—a duality similar to yin and yang in Taoism; and Darwin's principle.

The concepts of tradition and Paganism are composed of a highly developed philosophical and ethical system. Paganism is traditional folk culture, an ancestral belief system, a combination of worldviews that strives for the harmonious development of a person in nature and the acquisition of the necessary abilities to benefit an ancestral tribe. This is something our modern society is sorely lacking. It is poisoned by a disregard for the planet's integrity/body and our own living bodies.

The traditional Pagan worldview played the same role for our ancestors that dialectics performs for science today. Suppose dialectics essentially acts as a method of scientific knowledge, the language of interdisciplinary communication. In that case, Paganism is the same language, a system that unites the knowledge of the entire clan (tradition), a structure that permeates all societal spheres of life that our ancestors had.

Folk culture has preserved and passed rich folkloric songs, fairy tales, riddles, and more down to us that share the heritage of our ancestors. In some areas of the world, the traditional "primitive" way of life has preserved the symbolism of embroidery and wood carving, which also contains ancient Pagan meaning. However, Orthodox Christianity itself in Russia has so absorbed our ancestors' Pagan symbolism and rituals that the Jewish and Greek components have long faded into obscurity. But the ancestral memory of our people has preserved something that neither conquerors, baptizers, nor persecutors can destroy—the Slavic spirit, mysterious for some and inexpressible in words, the spirit of eternal Paganism.

4

Energy of the Family System

Within efforts to study how energy circulates among people and the forces of life and death work, it is advisable to start with what you can closely and carefully observe: your family and, if possible, your ancestral system. We can get all the power we need from our own family, our ancestors, to live a fulfilling and happy life. We don't have to look for some magical, mysterious powers, turn to other traditions, collect initiations worldwide, and worship someone else's gods. We don't need to enslave ourselves to the doctrines of others. All we need is within us. I believe that the psychological theory called systemic family constellations can provide much insight and direction regarding our family relationships. These concepts fit in with the Slavic beliefs about the family as I understand them. For this topic I draw on information from Anne Ancelin Schutzenberg's book *The Ancestor Syndrome.*

For any system to operate correctly, it's important to know the rules and the consequences of violating these rules. The family system is no exception. The three most important rules in a family system are related to the correct flow of energy and are described in more depth below.

The first rule: All family members have the right to be members of this family. This rule is often violated in a situation where a family doesn't recognize one of the members because she doesn't behave as is customary in that family, did something terrible, or went against her parents' will. Afterward, it's easier for relatives to pretend that she never existed at all and delete her from the family's official history. But the flow of energy in the family has a memory that cannot be erased. Therefore, the very place in the family that this "excluded" person once occupied will attract energy, changing the lives of the rest of the family.

There is the memory of an individual and the memory of the entire family system as a whole. A system's memory is something like a magnetic field that affects all the people who enter the system, even if the people themselves don't realize it. For example, when a woman renounces her unsuccessful son, and the family stops talking about him, this affects his fate and the fate of this woman's other children. Her son's children (grandchildren) may be condemned to the same fate of that excluded relative, even if they are unaware of the events of the past. It is as though they are drawn to fill his vacant spot. Or they will live as if they can't find a place for themselves in their lives. This is one of the manifestations of the call of blood and unconscious love for all relatives. Blood can force a person to take on someone else's fate if this fate has been deprived of the right to exist and be respected.

One may ask: Is it really necessary to respect and accept absolutely everyone in your family, even those who have done something terrible against their family? What if the lineage is weak because of those family members? What if instead of giving power to the descendant, it takes it away? There may be suicides in the family, murderers, family estrangement, violence, parental rejection, abuse, and so forth. In this case, a person often doesn't seem to live her destiny and endlessly deals with the problems handed down to her from her ancestors. It becomes an endless cycle in which issues and illnesses repeatedly appear: lack of joy in life, suicidal thoughts, physical or mental illness, difficulties in building relationships, infertility.

Only a person whose spiritual level is already progressive can understand that everything that has happened is the result of actions taken by a specific family member in order to create his destiny and the destiny of his descendants based on the energy flow in the clan. Most of the time, this happens when a person pays someone else's debt. It can run in the family for many generations; until it gets fixed, it will continue to exist in your clan.

You're here to find the reason and change the direction of negative family flow to progress, grow spiritually, understand the complicated family map, continue to improve, and create a better future for generations to come. You are here to correct past mistakes and pass a better family system down to your descendants. It is very hard to understand those family members, but in order to move forward and create a perfect space for future generations, you have to work hard within yourself to fix the broken parts of your family history.

The universe doesn't make mistakes; it gives us exactly what we need. Everyone encounters a period in their lives when the universe tests how well they have learned a life lesson. You must overcome these tests to reach a certain stature or confirm you have earned your stature in life. And one of these tests is to honor your ancestors. Maybe in one of the previous incarnations, you created the "knot" that led to difficulties in the family. Maybe it was you who was the "bad" relative; your task now is to atone for your mistake by correcting it. If you fail to do so, you will continue to suffer from it. It is difficult, almost impossible, to escape negative ancestral programming all by yourself. It can be difficult to forget, forever etched in memory; however, it can be healed and presents a valuable learning opportunity.

I want to emphasize once again that it is necessary to recognize everyone as a family member, even the people who are perceived to have let the family down. But this does not mean you need to give them the best and pretend nothing terrible has happened. It only means that they have their place in the family's structure, and it is necessary to recognize this. Mention them and remember them as a part of your clan. Respect should be shown to each family member; it is very important. No black holes should be left. See it this way: You are in a boat full of holes, and water starts to pour in. You need to seal all of those holes so the water will stop coming in, and you won't drown. Bad relatives are like one of those holes; if you leave even one hole unsealed, open water will still come through, and you will eventually drown.

Second rule: the hierarchy of family structures and the direction in which energy flows are very important. You must remember that the energy of life must flow toward the future. What you received from your parents (strength, care, attention) must not be given back to them but to your own children. Of course, if there was hate, pain, and suffering, this is something you don't want to pass on to your offspring. The law of hierarchy states that if you begin to treat your parents as you treat your own children, you will reverse the flow of energy and turn it into a backward circle.

When starting a young family, the connection with the parental family should gradually fade into the background. Children also have a hierarchy: the first child has an advantage over the second, the second over the third, and so on. It is very important to be respectful of elders and their experiences. To do this, the family must have a hierarchy of seniority that all its family members respect. This helps to ensure the younger members of the family (for example, the children) can easily adapt to the older ones' experience and knowledge. And this will happen when you teach children to respect their elders, which builds a perfect hierarchy family system where energy flows smoothly and healthily. Elders possess more energy than us, and we possess more energy than our children; it's all based on experiences and knowledge. These are the universal laws, laws of nature.

The third rule: the correct balance of energy distribution is important. When it comes to energy circulation between people, someone always gives it, and someone accepts it. Roughly speaking, within a family setting, there is always someone who acts as an energy vampire (I will talk more about energy vampires later) and someone who acts as her donor. In a healthy situation, these energy flows are multidirectional; that is, the "vampire" and "victim" are constantly changing places. Each gives the other what she is happy to share because she has an excess of energy. In response, the other gives slightly more energy back to her, making their relationship stronger, warmer, and closer. The same is true in the opposite direction. When energy is taken away from a person, in response, he must give a little less energy to maintain the overall energy balance. If the energy balance is not restored, if one person constantly takes all the energy for himself and another person constantly gives it (even if a person does so voluntarily), it will almost inevitably lead to the destruction of the entire system of energy circulation, which leads to the destruction of the entire family. An energy imbalance often occurs in single-parent families and families where male or female energy obviously dominates the household (for example, in a family where there are several women and one man, or one woman and several men).

If drama and resentment plague the family, something is wrong with the flow of energy. Pessimism, hopelessness, and despair are also symptoms of an incorrect flow of energy. If you do nothing about this situation, it will turn into a real problem, perhaps not in your life, but in your descendants' lives; they will have to solve it for you to find peace and happiness. Sometimes, a soul incarnated in the family must act as a purifier of the clan and atone for the clan's mistakes. In some cases, at the cost of their own life, health, or well-being. Fate constantly confronts these people with the problems that exist in the family. Until they solve them, their fate will be denied them. Some omens indicate that someone must first solve all of the family's problems—for example, when a person often sees one of her deceased relatives (or several relatives) in a dream. Dead ancestors often come to people in dreams when they want to remind them of the need to perform one of the family's tasks. Another omen is a very large external resemblance of a person to one of the ancestors or a detail of appearance repeated in several generations (for example, a similar birthmark). An important sign will be the birth of a child on a date that's important for one of his ancestors, such as a birthday or the day of someone's death.

In addition to individual members of the clan, the clan as a collective can influence its own development. Spouses who came into the clan from the outside are often chosen and called upon by the family lineage. The clan attracts spouses who can somehow help solve the problems in the family lineage. It doesn't mean that this person possesses some power. Sometimes it can be even a person with the same family problems. In such cases, the combined problems become so aggravated that they become impossible to ignore. Hence, people start recognizing problems and trying to solve them after leaving them on the dark shelves for so many years. This is one of the reasons why inbreeding ultimately leads to degeneration. The clan loses one of the mechanisms that regulates its development. All the mistakes and ancestral problems accumulated in the line begin to "rot," poisoning the atmosphere and lives of the clan members.

But it is within your power to change and improve your program, to become an ancestor whose descendants will remember him with gratitude.

ENERGY FLOW IN THE FAMILY

People constantly exchange energy with each other. When a person is interested in something or experiences emotions or feelings, she gives the object of her attention some of her energy, thus, nourishing it. Energy is one of the most important forces; thanks to energy, true human communication, mutual help, and love are possible. If the flow of energy from person to person is disrupted, the fundamental interaction system is destroyed, leading to conflicts and resentment. If there is no energy between people at all, the relationship ends. Of course, most energy is transferred between people who are close to one another—relatives.

A family in which energy flows correctly forms a shared energy field. This field protects the family from the negativity that can damage it and synchronizes people who enter the field. A couple who have a solid and harmonious energy field feel like two halves of a whole. Their bond is such that the death of one of them may even lead to the death of another. I should note that by "family," I don't mean "Dad, Mom, and me," but all the people with whom you are connected by blood ties. If your great-great-great-grandfather died many years before your birth and you haven't heard anything about him, he is still a member of your family and influences your destiny. And if you have any information about him, you can influence your destiny through him.

Surprisingly, our unborn relatives also have a strong influence on us. A child who was aborted, miscarried, or died in the womb can play a crucial role in the life of its future living sisters and brothers and the lives of the whole family. Even if your great-uncle lives on the other side of the world and you have never seen him, he is a member of your family; although, of course, he has less effect on your day-to-day life than your immediate ancestors. Therefore, by keeping in touch with all of your family members, you increase the life energy that is available to you.

Of course, your parents play the most significant role in your life. Even if they didn't directly raise you, you know very little about them, you have disavowed them, they have disowned you, or you were conceived with the help of modern fertilization technologies, biological parents remain the roots that connect the person with reality. Parents who adopt a child obviously also play a crucial role, but it is usually weaker than the role of his biological parents.

The most important energy you have is your life force—that stream of life that you received from your parents simply through birth and existence on Earth. Life itself is questionable if you experience problems with this energy: You suffer in the absence of spiritual and physical strength, which hold the meaning of your very existence. People who experience problems with their life force often try to find a replacement for vitality, be it by engaging on a spiritual quest, withdrawing into the world of dreams and fantasies, or succumbing to alcohol or drugs.

You receive energy from your father and mother in different ways. From ages four through to about twelve years old, a child feels the need for the energy of the parent of the opposite sex. A boy feels the need for his mother's energy, and a girl craves her father's. At this age, the basis of relationships with the opposite sex and erotic preferences are usually forming. From about eleven or twelve years old, the child tends to switch to the parent's energy of the same gender. At this age, a person begins to align with the behavior of their gender. Boys have an interest in traditionally masculine topics, and girls have an interest in the feminine. It is no coincidence that in many traditional cultures throughout the world, it is at this age that the ceremonial processes by which a child is transitioned into adulthood occur.

Of course, apart from the family relationships in your life, other important relationships also strongly influence your destiny. For example, someone who saved your life, who took the life of a person, one of your ancestors (and if this situation is hushed up, it runs the risk of repeating itself in a family's history over and over again), or someone who gave you lots of strength and energy (for example, a nanny who has practically become a family member). Your destiny is also affected by those people who were seriously harmed by you or one of your ancestors; this is especially true if your ancestor committed murder, in which case your family members should recognize the victim and mourn that person as a relative.

Energy connects our world to another. People form and maintain energy connections with both living loved ones and those who have passed on to another world (be it recently or long ago). It is often more difficult to work with such connections because they are difficult to comprehend and challenging to change, and the work takes place, not in ordinary space, but the sacred.

The sacred dimension has always been present in traditional society. Historically, many cultures have believed that people with special abilities (shamans, witches, sorcerers) touched the other world and ordinary people. Of course, they could not directly influence reality based on their desires, but they regularly performed rituals, manipulating the energies that influenced their existence and the world around them. Many members of contemporary society may find these practices strange. How, for example, could spring rituals—such as those that called for the early arrival of the sun's heat—influence reality? After all, spring is always destined to follow the patterns of Mother Nature. However, the key to understanding the sacred dimension is understanding that these rituals were required for spiritual and psychological reasons; they were not intended to focus on physical reality.

We all know that a person's physical and biological reality is not everything and that, sometimes, faith and confidence in one's spiritual strength can work real miracles. The rituals aimed to harmonize human beings with the entire universe and harness its strength and power. I used to say: When you have a problem, change the energy around it, and the problem will disappear.

The greatest power is the power of life and death, and every person has it. We were all born, and we will all die at some point. We all carry the energies of life and death within us. We are connected with our ancestors and relatives via a life-and-death relationship. Therefore, it is crucial to have the correct flow of energy throughout the family system.

In Slavic tradition, the sacred is woven into ordinary life. At the same time, these two worlds, the world of the living and the dead, are separated. Touching the other world is regular but regulated, and many rules and norms need to be observed and met. All fundamental changes in a person's life are made when the boundaries of the two worlds are open because there is a sharp change in energy exchange and immense energy flow. These boundaries are wide open when a person goes through specific stages in life. As such, when going through fundamental stages of change, the person herself and those around her need to be incredibly attentive and careful to maintain control, if not over physical reality, then over her inner state, both psychological and spiritual.

ENERGY VAMPIRES

One way the energy exchange in a family can be disrupted is through what's called "energy vampirism." The normal flow of energy in a family occurs when people take turns to absorb each other's energy; however, an energy vampire absorbs excessive energy levels and fails to pass it on to other people. He loves only himself and recognizes the flow of energy in only one direction—toward himself. This kind of person constantly drains others' life forces without giving anything in return.

Energy vampirism is something a person develops during his childhood. It most often happens when the flow of energy and love is distorted between a child and his parents. When a child doesn't receive genuine love from his parents, he misbehaves and receives attention in the form of their irritation and anger instead. Gradually, he gets used to receiving energy in this way and does this with his parents and other people through moodiness, tantrums, stubbornness, aggression, rudeness, and bad habits.

Among adults, vampirism can take many forms. One of these is jealousy, and this jealousy can manifest from either direction: Either the person is continually jealous of his spouse for no reason, makes her justify herself, starts arguments, keeps his spouse in a constant state of psychological stress, or he goes out of his way to orchestrate situations to make his spouse jealous, ostensibly to fan the flames of passion in their relationship; but in reality, to siphon energy from his spouse.

In another case, energy vampirism may look like constant reproaches and nagging. With this method, the energy vampire drains people's energy by trying to make them feel guilty, irritated, or resentful.

Another form of energy vampirism is making use of one's energy bond with a child. In this case, even though a child has grown up, a parent may not want to part with her or the energy that he receives from her. The parent unconsciously strives to keep the child from moving away and becoming independent. For example, this type of parent will display a negative attitude toward any of their child's potential romantic partners, so she stays single until the end of her days. They may also keep their adult child in a position of financial dependence, preventing a child from providing for himself and learning to take responsibility for his own life.

How can you protect yourself from energy vampires? In general, the best approach is to refrain from interacting with them. But unfortunately, if you have one in your family, this won't work. The main rule when dealing with an energy vampire is to refrain from playing his games. His goal is to get you to focus all your attention on him and prevent you from feeling calm and collected. A vampire cannot feed on "pure or good energy"—that is to say, love, faith, and goodwill.

The energy that the vampire wants to evoke stems from irritation, resentment, guilt, and fear. Energy vampires come in two varieties: active and passive. Active vampires openly incite a conflict, provoking a person to rash emotions, words, and actions. The best strategy for dealing with this type of energy vampire is to stay calm. You need to maintain an even mood, avoid drama, speak quietly, and reduce your voice to a whisper if an argument starts. It will be very effective to pity the vampire (at least silently, in your mind). But do not try to "fix" him; after all, he will feed on any energy you expend doing so. If possible, in potentially critical situations, it's a good idea to leave the house or at least go to another room. Some people believe you can also protect your energy field by crossing your legs or arms, as believed in my family.

Passive vampires don't usually act openly. They can be recognized only by the state in which you find yourself after communicating with them: You will feel weak, low on energy, and full of guilt and irritation. Most often, these vampires drain your energy through complaints and nagging.

Try not to take what they say to heart, or you will be filled with a storm of negative emotions. Treat this kind of energy vampire with humor: After all, energy vampirism and the ability to laugh at yourself are incompatible things. The best defense strategy against any energy vampire is maintaining your inner harmony and loving yourself and life. After all, it is challenging to harm a person who is full of healthy, positive energy.

Suppose the energy vampire is a relative of yours. In that case, you can try to help them transition their method of replenishing their energy to a healthier one. For example, encourage them to spend more time in nature (nature is one of the most powerful batteries for energy and spiritual recharge) to experience more positive emotions.

After interacting with an energy vampire, it's best to take a cool shower and replenish your energy. To do so, spend some time in nature or do some of your favorite activities. Always keep in mind that the victim of an energy vampire can often unconsciously become a vampire himself when trying to replenish his own energy by, for example, taking it out on someone from his own family.

Energy vampires can also become a couple. In such cases, they become codependent. While they technically form a single whole, their influence on each other is harmful and destructive.

Of course, the energy of a family in which vampirism exists can hardly be called healthy. It's a disruption that negatively affects all the family members, especially the children. It will be challenging for children who grow up in this kind of family to learn harmonious, healthy ways of exchanging and absorbing energy. To be sure the family's energy flow stays healthy, you need to take every opportunity to harmonize it, including invoking the spirits of your ancestors, seeking advice from psychologists or other family relations specialists, and resolving family conflicts as soon as they arise.

5
Seven Generations of Contact

W hen you look in the mirror, you're looking at that perfect reflection of yourself! The reflection has been traveling down from generation to generation. Each time, it has been reshaping and getting better and better. This face of ours is perfection within its highest form. From the time of our very first ancestors to that of our mothers and fathers today, it has been reshaping to this very face. Take a look at your face and ask yourself, Why should you show honor and respect to the ancestors that came before you or all of the sacred spirits? Now, think of your children, or those who will be here, in this place, where you are standing right now after you've transcended to the hereafter. Would you like them to forget this image that you're looking at?

Ancestral tradition is at the core of all spiritual teachings and religions. It could be called "home religion" (or "family religion") because it is the veneration of the dead ancestors of a particular family. Ancestral spirits are those inhabitants of the other world who are initially benevolent toward a person and ready to patronize her. As the most important guardians of the family, they can give their descendants help and protection using the power inherent in the spirits. You must accept this help; this is something people learn by performing rituals of reverence for ancestors—showing the correct behavior and attitude toward their families. In addition to my own beliefs, I draw on the works of O. N. Sharaya and D. A. Samsonov in this chapter (see the bibliography for details).

The tradition of venerating ancestors represents a holistic world-view through which a person is part of a unified system, part of nature. Knowing this can save people from many mistakes and benefit them greatly. After all, the great importance of ancestors can be understood from a basic biological perspective—our ancestors are present (one might say resurrected) in us in the form of genes. We are made of their flesh and blood. Everything they experienced (actions, sensations, thoughts) is transmitted to us and, subsequently, our children. And we must pay tribute to our ancestors at least for the fact that they survived and gave us life; after all, if they had not existed, we would not have come into existence.

A person's connection with the spirits of his kin represents one of the strongest connections and "energy shields." It protects a person from external energies (including witchcraft and sorcery) that can become destructive and eradicate his energy. Suppose a person has a weak or no connection with his ancestors. In that case, he becomes defenseless in the face of harmful energy. Many people who practice magic ask me how they can protect themselves against other people's energies, both from their clients and their competition. Sadly, they don't understand that all you need is a good connection with your ancestors.

Suppose a person doesn't feel like he is a part of his lineage. In that case, he will most likely feel like an orphan throughout his life. He will strive to make up for this "psychological orphanhood" in some other way. After all, every creature needs to belong and have a shared space with his kin. Each ancestral spirit has a fundamental characteristic that sets it apart from all others. This kind of culture develops from one generation to the next: family traditions, rules, and family rituals that have been refined to protection via hundreds of years of culture and lived experience. The shared culture unites the family and allows it to preserve its integrity. An ancestral spirit's particular characteristic represents an amalgamation of the spirit of every person who has ever been a part of the clan. Its strength depends on its efforts and the time during which the family exists.

Initially, a family is a clash of different energies: the energies of childbirth from the sides of the husband and the wife. Even if a husband and wife are very similar people who belong to the same race and social environment with shared professional outlooks, hobbies, and interests, they still come from different clans, each of which has its distinct characteristics and family traditions. And in certain situations, they will have to reconcile their behavior with the conflicting requirements of these energies.

In some cases, the contradictions between the energies of the clans are so great that people never manage to find a common language. This phenomenon can be observed between spouses and generations. For example, let's say a child is born into a family of hereditary thieves yet chooses to pursue a career in law enforcement. She may become ostracized within her family and feel unsupported by family members who brand her a traitor. Her children will feel the influence of her upbringing and the "call of the blood." They will feel the temptation to follow the path that many generations of their ancestors had taken, even though they have never been told the stories of previous generations. People subconsciously remember their clan's history. There have been many instances where a person repeats an event that happened to his ancestor, even in the absence of any prior knowledge of it.

The strength of a clan's spirit feeds on the memory and attention of the clan's descendants. Therefore, it is appropriate to keep photos of ancestors and know your ancestry. The clan's strength increases when relatives maintain good relationships and are ready to help each other; when they are aware and are working together to correct the history of previous generations. Ancestors exist as long as they are remembered.

And if you don't remember them or arrange a memorial meal or celebration in their honor, your connection with your ancestors will gradually weaken, as too will the clan itself. The very concept of "ancestral tradition" suggests we should hold regular ceremonies and rituals that are dedicated to the commemoration and veneration of ancestors.

It's important to note that the need to respect, honor, and value our ancestors is not isolated to any particular religion. It is a common human situation that is interpreted differently in different cultures. Everyone is free to pursue their own beliefs within the framework of any tradition: the one you have inherited, the one you choose because it is close to you in spirit, or even none at all. After all, even if you are an atheist, a materialist, you can't deny that your behavior in the current world is influenced by your ancestors because their genes are within you. And when you become aware of this influence, it will be easier for you to work with this energy and direct it beneficially.

Although ancestral spirits can come at any time, proper communication occurs only when a particular order is observed. If you want to connect with your departed ancestors and the whole clan, you need to pay your respects regularly. It's advisable you do so in special periods when the forces of nature are most active. The Pagan tradition follows the logic of the living—the cycle of alternation of life and death. Traditionally, people believed that time is nonlinear and the most important events repeat every year. In many traditions, it is believed that a person should know seven generations of his lineage—that is, all 126 ancestors up to the seventh generation. It is believed that each generation of ancestors is responsible for some part of our lives. Therefore, to understand how our family affects us, we need to know what all seven generations of our ancestors were like, what they did, and what happened in their lives.

Some may think that the more distant the ancestor is in time, the weaker her influence will feel on a person; but that's not the case. As time passes, our ancestors become enormously powerful! I want to note again that, in any case, you can't denounce your ancestors, any of them, no blank spots. Descendants who condemn, resent, or have contempt for their ancestors further complicate future events and impede clan flow. You must remember that all your ancestors are your teachers, and the clan brings you up through them. Do not rejoice if their problem has bypassed you: After all, it may still manifest itself in your future or that of your descendants. Suppose there are "fallen" ancestors in the family. In that case, you need to behave with humility and work to ensure their mistakes will not become yours and those of your children.

THE SACRED NUMBER SEVEN

Slavic belief systems are rich in folklore and mythology, and they often involve the concept of seven generations, which represents a significant and sacred cycle of time. In these belief systems, it's understood that the actions and decisions of an individual can impact not only their immediate descendants but also their ancestors and descendants for seven generations. This belief emphasizes the interconnectedness of family and the importance of living in harmony with nature and one's ancestors. Rituals and ceremonies are sometimes performed to honor and seek guidance from these ancestral spirits throughout the seven generations. It's a fundamental aspect of Slavic folklore and spirituality.

The choice of seven generations in Slavic belief systems is rooted in the significance of the number seven in many cultures, including Slavic folklore. Seven is often considered a sacred or mystical number with various symbolic meanings, such as completeness, perfection, and spiritual significance.

In Slavic mythology and folklore, the number seven is associated with cycles and patterns in nature and the cosmos. It represents a complete cycle of time and is often used to express the idea that one's actions can have far-reaching consequences over an extended period. By emphasizing seven generations, Slavic belief systems underscore the idea that one's deeds can influence their family and descendants through several cycles of life. Ultimately, the use of seven generations reflects the belief in the interconnectedness of past, present, and future, with the number itself holding cultural and spiritual significance.

The number seven is associated with various symbolic meanings.

Completeness: Seven is often seen as a number that represents completeness or wholeness. It signifies the idea of totality, implying that something is full and perfect.

Sacred Cycles: The Slavs, like many other cultures, believed in cycles in nature and the cosmos. Seven was considered a number that marked the completion of a cycle, such as the seven days of the week, seven phases of the moon, or seven seasons in some Slavic calendars.

Spiritual Significance: Seven is often linked to spiritual or mystical concepts. It was associated with the idea of transcending the physical world and reaching a higher, more spiritual level of understanding.

Protection: The number seven was sometimes believed to have protective qualities. In Slavic folklore, it was thought to ward off evil spirits and bring good fortune.

Rituals and Traditions: Many Slavic traditions, rituals, and folklore incorporate the number seven. For instance, weddings and other celebrations might involve seven rounds or steps, emphasizing the sacred nature of the occasion.

Connection to Nature: Seven was tied to natural rhythms and cycles, such as the seven days of the week corresponding to different celestial bodies (e.g., Sunday for the sun, Monday for the moon), which were significant in agricultural and calendrical activities.

Overall, the significance of the number seven in Slavic culture mirrors its importance in various aspects of life, from spirituality and folklore to the organization of time and the understanding of the natural world.

The concept of seven seasons in the Slavic calendar is part of the traditional agricultural and folkloric understanding of time in some Slavic cultures. These seven seasons are different from the four-season calendar that is more commonly used in modern times. The Slavic seven-season calendar was adapted to the agricultural needs and natural cycles of the region. Here are the seven seasons:

1. Early Spring (*Raná jaro*): This season typically represents the very beginning of spring when the snow starts to melt and the first signs of new growth appear.
2. Spring (*Jaro*): Spring proper, when the weather becomes milder, and the land begins to awaken. It's the time for sowing crops.
3. Pre-summer (*Předjaří*): This season falls between spring and summer, marked by warmer temperatures and more abundant plant growth.
4. Summer (*Léto*): The warmest and most productive time of the year, associated with the peak of agricultural activities and the growth of crops.
5. Harvest (*Dozrávání*): This season represents the period when crops ripen and are ready for harvest.
6. Autumn (*Podzim*): After the harvest, the weather begins to cool, and the leaves change colors, marking the transition from summer to winter.
7. Winter (*Zima*): The coldest and darkest time of the year, when nature rests and preparations are made for the coming spring.

These seven seasons were closely tied to the agricultural calendar and the activities of rural life in Slavic communities. They helped people plan their farming activities, festivals, and rituals, which were often linked to the changing of the seasons. While this concept is not used in modern calendars, it provides insight into the traditional Slavic way of understanding and living in harmony with the natural world.

The number seven is also significant in Russian folklore and is considered a magical and mystical number. It is associated with powerful and transformative events, as well as with mystical creatures and phenomena. In Russian fairy tales and folk stories, magical quests or trials are often structured around the number seven. For example, a hero may have to complete seven tasks or overcome seven obstacles.

Here are some examples of how the number seven is important in Russian mythology:

1. Seven-Headed Dragon: One of the most famous sevenfold figures in Russian mythology is the seven-headed dragon. This dragon appears in the folk tale of Dobrynya Nikitich, a heroic warrior who defeats the dragon and saves a princess. The dragon's seven heads represent a formidable and magical challenge.

2. Weekdays and Celestial Bodies: In Russian mythology, each day of the week is associated with a celestial body. The seven days correspond to the sun, moon, and five planets known at the time (Mars, Mercury, Jupiter, Venus, and Saturn), and each of these days has its own set of traditions, beliefs, and activities.

3. Seven Winds: Russian folklore often references the "Seven Winds," each representing a different direction and having specific qualities. These winds are sometimes personified and play roles in various tales and beliefs as well as many occult rituals and witchcraft.

4. Magical Properties: The number seven is associated with magical properties in Russian mythology. For example, charms, spells, or rituals may involve repeating actions seven times to invoke protection or good fortune.

5. Seven Sisters (The Pleiades star cluster): Known as the Seven Sisters, this start cluster is often associated with a group of seven sisters who are magical or celestial beings. Their appearance is sometimes linked to important events or prophecies and to stories of love, beauty, and celestial events.

6. Lucky Number: In Russian culture, seven is generally considered a lucky number, and it often plays a role in various customs, rituals, and superstitions as a symbol of good fortune. Many Russian rituals and traditions involve the number seven, particularly in celebrations like weddings and the honoring of important life events.

7. Seven Wonders: Similar to other cultures, Russian folklore may reference the seven wonders of the world, signifying extraordinary and awe-inspiring phenomena.

These are some of the ways the number seven is woven into the fabric of Russian mythology, adding depth and symbolism to the stories, beliefs, and traditions of the culture.

In various occult and esoteric traditions, including those associated with witchcraft, the number seven is often regarded as significant due to its mystical and symbolic properties. While the interpretation of this number can vary among individuals and groups, the following are some general associations with the number seven in the context of Russian occult and witchcraft traditions.

Spiritual Wholeness: The number seven is often seen as a symbol of spiritual completeness and perfection. It is associated with the idea of achieving a higher level of consciousness and spiritual enlightenment.

Magical Powers: In Russian folklore and occult practices, the number seven is sometimes connected to the belief in the magical and mystical properties of certain objects, rituals, or spells that require seven repetitions or seven days of work to achieve their desired effects.

Lunar Phases: The phases of the moon are significant in many magical traditions, and the lunar cycle typically spans about 29.5 days, which is approximately four seven-day weeks. The number seven may be associated with moon-related magical practices.

Seven Chakras: Some practitioners of Eastern-based esoteric traditions, which have influenced Russian occultism, work with the concept of the seven chakras, which are energy centers in the body. Each chakra corresponds to a different aspect of consciousness and well-being.

Seven Planets: In astrology and Western esotericism, there are seven classical planets (including the sun and moon), each associated with different qualities and influences. This can play a role in magical and astrological practices.

It's important to note that nowadays, the interpretation of the number seven in Russian occult and witchcraft traditions can vary, and different practitioners may have their own unique perspectives and applications. Additionally, Russian occultism may draw from a variety of sources, including Western esoteric traditions, Indigenous beliefs, and Slavic folklore, contributing to a diverse range of interpretations and practices.

In Russian tradition, as in many other Western and Eastern astrological traditions, the concept of the seven planets is often recognized. These planets are the following (with Russian names in parentheses):

Sun (*Solntse*)

Moon (*Luna*)

Mercury (*Merkuriy*)

Venus (*Venera*)

Mars (*Mars*)

Jupiter (*Yupiter*)

Saturn (*Saturn*)

These seven celestial bodies have played significant roles in Russian astrology and are often associated with different astrological and esoteric attributes such as personality traits, elements, and planetary rulerships. Astrologers and practitioners use these planets to interpret birth charts, predict astrological influences, and gain insights into various aspects of a person's life.

The concept of the seven planets in astrology is rooted in ancient traditions and is related to the visible celestial objects in the night sky. In traditional astrology, these seven celestial bodies were considered the most prominent and influential, and they were associated with specific qualities and attributes. In antiquity, people observed and tracked the movements of celestial objects without telescopes or other modern instruments; therefore the seven planets were those that were readily visible to the naked eye. Each of the seven planets was associated with specific qualities and attributes, and these associations formed the basis of astrological interpretation. While modern astronomy recognizes additional celestial objects and celestial bodies beyond these seven (such as Uranus, Neptune, and Pluto), traditional astrology continues to use the original seven planets as they have been historically significant and continue to hold astrological meaning. Astrologers often incorporate these seven planets into natal charts, horoscopes, and astrological readings to provide insights into a person's character, life events, and destiny.

SEVEN GENERATIONS OF THE CLAN AND HOW THEY AFFECT YOU

In Russian spiritual belief systems, particularly those rooted in shamanic or Indigenous traditions, the concept of seven generations is often associated with a spiritual and ecological perspective on the interconnectedness of generations and the impact of human actions on the environment. Each of the seven generations is believed to represent a particular aspect or quality, and their significance may vary among different Indigenous groups. Here is a general understanding of what each generation may represent:

The Present Generation: The current generation, which holds the responsibility for making decisions and taking actions that affect the well-being of the environment and future generations.

The Past Generation: The generation that came before the present one, often seen as the source of wisdom and the repository of traditional knowledge and values.

The Three Generations Behind: These generations encompass the grandparents, great-grandparents, and ancestors. They are revered for their wisdom and are believed to provide guidance from the spirit world.

The Seventh Generation Ahead: This represents the future generations and is a central focus in this concept. Decisions and actions taken by the present generation are believed to have far-reaching consequences for the well-being of the environment and society seven generations into the future.

The idea is that individuals should act in a way that ensures the well-being of the environment and society not just for their immediate benefit but also for the benefit of future generations. This concept emphasizes sustainability, responsible stewardship of the land, and a deep respect for nature and the interconnectedness of all life.

It's important to note that the specific interpretations of the seven generations may vary among different Indigenous groups and individuals, but the general principle of considering the long-term impact of one's actions on the environment and future generations is a common theme in many Indigenous spiritual belief systems.

The First Generation

The first generation is you. You are the culmination of the entire family tree, and it is you that carries on the hopes of your ancestors. You are the connection between the past and the future. You are responsible for yourself and to the universe for your will. You are responsible for your soul and all the choices you make in your life. This is an important philosophy to carry with you as you decide how you will approach the challenges that inevitably arise in your life. Knowing what an important point you represent on your family tree, ask yourself whether you're choosing an appropriate action.

The Second Generation

The second generation is the parents: the father and the mother. This generation consists of two people. They are responsible for your direct upbringing, including your behavior in the family and the wider community, your habits, and your attitude about your physical, mental, and emotional health, and about life itself. You should work with your parents for mental health, substance use disorders, or disability issues. This might be as simple as asking them about the issue and then honoring their response, or it might be more complex as the situation requires.

The Third Generation

The third generation is the grandparents (four people). This is the generation where talents most often originate.

Numerology is an essential component of many occult practices, including Russian witchcraft and spirituality. The number three can also be associated with spiritual growth and transformation, reflecting the stages of purification, illumination, and union with God in the spiritual journey. The number three may symbolize the spiritual connection between the living and the deceased. It represents the idea that the spiritual realm, the earthly realm, and the realm of ancestors are interconnected. The triangle is often considered a symbol of strength, stability, and balance, and it may be associated with the idea of connecting with and drawing strength from one's ancestors. The number three is connected to the idea of balance and harmony. It is seen as a stable and harmonious number, reflecting the balance between opposing forces or elements.

The number three also has religious significance in Russia. It represents the Holy Trinity, one of the most significant and central aspects of Russian Orthodoxy, which consists of God the Father, God the Son (Jesus Christ), and the Holy Spirit. The number three also represents Divine completeness and perfection, the unity and the interrelationship between the three persons of the Holy Trinity. In Russian Orthodoxy, during the Sacrament of Baptism, the child is traditionally baptized three times, each time in the name of one of the persons of the Holy Trinity. In addition, the divine liturgy and many other liturgical activities in Russian Orthodoxy often feature a repetition of prayers, chants, or actions three times. And, finally, the cross, a central symbol in Christianity, often has three horizontal crossbeams. The top beam represents the sign that was placed above Christ's head on the cross, the lower beam represents the footrest on which Christ's feet were nailed, and the central beam represents the main part of the cross. All of these examples underscore the spiritual significance of the number three in worship and spiritual practice.

In terms of your ancestors, the third generation is responsible for your thinking, abilities, and how you realize your talents in life. They are accountable for your communication, contact with other people, activity, energy, and reaction speed. Often, this generation is responsible for your profession or hobby.

Grandparents hold a special role because communication with them teaches the child to communicate with the whole clan. A young child thinks his parents have always existed only as his parents, not as part of an ancestral line. The grandparents show the child that his father and mother also have parents. Thus, he sees the chain of his lineage going back into the past and knows he must continue it. The third generation is excellent to work with if you have communication problems or breakdowns in marriage and relationships, wish to make your enemies at peace with you, experience job and career-related problems, and anything related to a quick and successful healing from injuries or accidents. For example, you might be struggling in your career and looking for your next step. If your grandparents have passed on, you could focus on their memory or on an item that was important to them and explain the problem that you're having. You might be able to feel the answer that they give you, or it might come later as a sign that you'll recognize.

The Fourth Generation

The fourth generation is the great-grandparents (eight people). In our times, it is sadly not so common for people to meet their great-grandmothers or great-grandfathers. The symbolism of the number four is associated with creativity, joy, or other positive attributes. Therefore, this generation, and the ones that came before it, are extremely important.

The fourth generation is responsible for forming a person's attitude toward love, intimacy, joy, creativity, and material well-being. They teach their descendants how to make money, manage it correctly, harmonize their space, and see beauty. Great-grandmothers and great-grandfathers protect you energetically and create your ability to focus and achieve what you want according to your desire. If you have problems in this generation, you might become isolated, distrustful, emotionally repressed, and unable to enjoy life. If you need help with love or marriage-related problems and spiritual protection, you should work with this generation. They offer tremendous protection when you deal with witchcraft or the occult, need to protect yourself from a sorcerer, or believe someone is trying to harm you. They key word for this generation is *protection*, and they can give you all you need.

The Fifth Generation

The fifth generation consists of the parents of the great-grandparents (sixteen people). This generation helps you achieve results! The fifth generation is responsible for strength, strong character, decisiveness, energy, ability to act, achieve success, and have military-related victories (back in the day, we called them great warriors). If there are problems in this generation, an individual may have trouble finding success in her endeavors. She might become cruel to others, or she might suffer from cruelty, cowardice, and lack of will. This generation is excellent to work with to help you improve your psychic abilities, mediumship, and achieve the desired results in a field. If you have an important decision to make and find yourself at a crossroads, they are the generation to turn to for advice. They can help you "see" the future.

In Russian folklore and belief systems, the number five holds specific and well-defined symbolic significance (as do some other numbers, like three or seven, which are more prevalent in various cultures and belief systems). In some Russian traditions, the number five is associated with protection and warding off evil forces. For example, the hand gesture known as the *figa* or *hamsa*, which is a fist with the thumb sticking out between the index and middle fingers, is used to protect against the evil eye and negative energy. It is believed to have the power to deflect harm and bring good fortune.

The number five is also associated with balance and harmony in nature. The belief that everything in the natural world should exist in equilibrium is a recurring theme in Russian folklore and spirituality. This idea extends to the balance of the elements, seasons, and the cycles of life.

In some Russian folk traditions, the number five is known to be associated with the five classical elements, which include earth, water, fire, air, and ether (or spirit). These elements are seen as fundamental building blocks of the universe and are sometimes integrated into cosmological and metaphysical beliefs. The number five can also represent the cycle of life, including birth, growth, maturity, aging, and death. This cyclical aspect is often reflected in various folk tales and rituals.

It's important to note that the symbolism of numbers can vary widely and can be deeply rooted in specific cultural, regional, or spiritual traditions. The significance of the number five in Russian belief systems can differ among different groups and may be subject to interpretation.

The Sixth Generation

The sixth generation is the grandparents of the great-grandparents (thirty-two people). Because this generation has almost always already passed into the ancestral realm before the first generation was born, the sixth generation is considered sacred and a source of spiritual guidance. Grandparents of great-grandparents form your attitude toward customs and established laws, including the customs and laws of the clan. This generation is responsible for the spiritual heritage you receive and your ability to act as a spiritual mentor for other people. They are also responsible for your physical health, sickness, mental and physical diseases . . . everything related to health and healing. They cure all kinds of conditions and bring good spirits to the house to keep you and your home protected. They are great to open doors to crossover to communicate with people who died a violent death (suicide, murdered, etc.).

The number six also represents cyclic nature. The concept of the cyclic nature of life in Russian witchcraft is deeply rooted in the belief that life, nature, and the spiritual realm operate in recurring cycles, and that these cycles are interconnected. The number six can be used in rituals within this belief system to align with and symbolize these cyclical beliefs. The following is an explanation of how the number six may be employed in such rituals.

Changing of the Seasons. Russian witchcraft often revolves around a reverence for the changing of seasons and the elements. The number six may come into play here as a way to represent the cyclical nature of these seasons. For instance, six phases of the moon might be incorporated into a seasonal ritual, emphasizing the transitions from one season to another.

Harmony. Russian witchcraft emphasizes the importance of living in harmony with the natural world and its rhythms. The use of the number six can serve as a way to align with the cycles of nature and to harmonize one's spiritual practices with the changing seasons. This alignment is believed to promote balance and prosperity.

Amplify Energy. The number six may also be employed in rituals that emphasize repetition to amplify the energy and intention. In Russian witchcraft, repeating actions or incantations six times can be seen as a way to harness the cyclical energy of life and channel it into a specific magical goal.

Russian witchcraft often if not always, includes practices related to ancestor veneration and communication with the spirit world. The number six could be used to symbolize the connection between the living, the deceased, and the cycles of life and death. Rituals that involve honoring ancestors or seeking their guidance might incorporate the number six to strengthen this connection.

Just as nature undergoes cycles of growth, death, and rebirth, personal and spiritual growth is also seen as a cyclical process. The number six may be included in rituals related to personal transformation and self-discovery, highlighting the cyclic nature of one's spiritual journey.

The Seventh Generation

The seventh generation is the great-grandparents of the great-grandparents (sixty-four people). This generation forms the foundation of the individual's whole clan. If you can enlist the help of ancestors from this generation, you will be able to handle any task and influence destiny. The seventh generation is associated with your life's duty, retribution for all the mistakes and mischiefs of the family, justice, legal matters, the fate of the family, and the possibility of your transformation, magical power, and everything to do with the power of change, manipulation, and healing the clan. This generation can help you become a great sorcerer. They teach you the art of sorcery and share truth, dreams, and visions. This generation is the best to work with when you are seeking spiritual protection. They can protect you against spiritual attacks, sorcery, manipulation of any level and any kind, and possible spirit attachments and possessions (spirit attachments may happen when one is working with the dead). It's great if you know something about the ancestors of this generation. Any information about them will make your connection with the clan stronger and more successful.

The concept of the seventh generation symbolizes a strong connection to one's ancestors and a sense of continuity. Practitioners believe that their magical and spiritual traditions have been passed down through seven generations, emphasizing the importance of preserving and honoring their ancestral knowledge. Similar to the concept in Indigenous belief systems, the seventh generation is seen as a reminder of the responsibility to make choices that positively impact the future and preserve magical and spiritual practices for future generations. The seventh generation is associated with the accumulation of wisdom and knowledge over seven generations. Practitioners believe that the insights and magical techniques passed down through the generations are particularly potent and meaningful.

In Russian witchcraft, the seventh generation may symbolize the culmination of a cycle, where the wisdom and magic of previous generations have reached a pinnacle. In some magical rituals or spells, the concept of the seventh generation might be incorporated to tap into the cumulative power of generations and ancestral spirits. It can represent a connection to ancestors who have practiced similar magic.

The seventh generation could be invoked or called upon for protection and blessings in magical workings. Practitioners may seek the assistance and guidance of their ancestors from the seventh generation to help them in their magical endeavors.

It's important to remember that Russian witchcraft is a diverse and often highly individualized practice. The significance of the seventh generation in Russian witchcraft may vary among different practitioners and traditions, and its importance can be deeply rooted in personal beliefs, regional customs, and the specific goals of magical workings.

LOCATION OF THE ANCESTORS AND POINTS OF CONTACT IN SLAVIC TRADITION

Suppose that the light of another dimension is everywhere, in parallel with ours, separated from us by some barrier. The light is the World of Dreams, which is undoubtedly evidenced by the content of Slavic lullabies. That light *is* everywhere, just like our world, and it's just beyond the borderline. The barrier itself can act as a communication channel.

For example, if water acts as a barrier between the world of the living and the world of the dead in a funeral rite, in the future (after burial), it becomes a method for communication. After the burial of a loved one, it is common in many cultures to have rituals that involve sending offerings or objects downstream in a river or other body of water. This act is believed to allow for communication with the spirits or ancestors in the afterlife. Offerings may include items like food, flowers, or symbolic objects. Rivers and flowing water are often associated with the passage of time and the continuous cycle of life. It can symbolize the flow of life and the journey of the soul beyond death.

Fire also acts as a traditional channel of communication. "You are a holy light and gray smoke, rush to the sky, bow down to my parents, tell them how we are all doing here" (quoted by Dmitry Zelenin, "A folk rite"). In Slavic mythology, in general, and in relation to the tradition of honoring ancestors, fire is, in many ways, equivalent to water. Fire has been used since ancient times as a channel of communication with the ancestors, and it is the upward movement of both fire and smoke that proves to be the connection point between Earth and the sky. Upward movement itself is also used in Slavic tradition to connect with the ancestors; hanging ritual objects on trees or throwing them on the roof were ways to send them to the "Upper World."

The flames and smoke rising upward are seen as a means of connecting the earthly realm with the heavens or the world of the spirits. Fire rituals, such as lighting bonfires, candles, or lamps, are common in various cultures to invoke the presence of ancestors, offer prayers, and seek guidance from the spiritual realm. The act of lighting a fire is believed to serve as a bridge between the physical and spiritual worlds, allowing communication and reverence for the departed.

Both fire and water are integral elements in the spiritual and cultural practices of many societies, and they serve as mediums for connecting with the spiritual realm, honoring ancestors, and maintaining a sense of continuity between the living and the deceased. These traditions reflect a deep understanding of the interconnectedness of the physical and spiritual worlds and the enduring presence of the ancestors in the lives of their descendants. Fire is also considered protective. In Slavic folklore, it is believed that fire has the power to ward off malevolent spirits and protect homes and individuals from harm. People may light fires or torches to create a protective barrier.

In some rituals, sacrifices are made by burning offerings in fires. These offerings are presented to ancestral spirits or deities as a means of communication and veneration. The smoke rising from the fire is believed to carry these offerings to the spirit world. The associations between fire and the spirit world in Slavic culture are deeply rooted in the belief in the interconnectedness of all realms of existence. Fire is regarded as a powerful and sacred element that facilitates communication, protection, and the maintenance of a relationship with the spirit world and ancestors.

These traditions are an integral part of Slavic spirituality and folklore. There are some similarities with the concept of Ginen (also spelled Guinée) in Haitian Vodou. Ginen refers to the spiritual realm, often understood as the heavenly or ancestral realm. While it is a common belief in many spiritual and religious traditions that heaven is located above the sky, in Haitian Vodou, there is a unique perspective that associates Ginen with being located under the water, particularly the waters of the sea. Ginen is believed to be the dwelling place of the ancestral spirits, the *lwa* (spiritual beings or deities), and other supernatural entities. The concept of Ginen under the water reflects the belief that the spirits and ancestors inhabit a realm that is accessible through water, such as the sea. This connection with water is also evident in various Vodou rituals and ceremonies, where water is often used for purification, offerings, and as a means of communicating with the spiritual realm.

Another point of contact is all sorts of holes in the ground—caves, pits, hollows in roots, or wells, are used as communication channels with the "lower world" or Underworld. These natural features are believed to serve as channels or gateways for communication with the spirit world or the realm of the dead. The concept of an Underworld or lower world is common in many cultures and represents a distinct spiritual realm often associated with ancestors, spirits, and the afterlife.

Caves are significant in many mythologies and belief systems. In Slavic folklore, caves are often depicted as entrances to the Underworld or the realm of spirits and ancestors. These caves may be seen as portals to the otherworld, and rituals or offerings might take place at these locations to seek communication or guidance from the spiritual realm. Pits, holes in the ground, or hollows in tree roots are also viewed as potential connections to the Underworld. These natural depressions in the Earth are seen as points of access for the spirits of the deceased or other supernatural entities. Wells are often associated with water, and as mentioned earlier, water has symbolic significance in bridging the gap between the living and the spiritual realm. Wells may be used as places for offerings, divination, and communication with the lower world.

Various rituals and offerings may be conducted at these natural formations to establish a connection with the spiritual realm or to seek guidance, blessings, or protection. These rituals can include lighting candles, burning incense, and offering food or other items to appease or honor the spirits.

A similar belief system can be observed in Haitian Vodou tradition when we bury specific items or offerings to the ancestors or spirits under a tree or in a hole, or when we hang offerings from a roof, and so on. Placing offerings or items in specific locations is a way to establish a connection with ancestral spirits, deities, or other supernatural entities. It is believed that these items serve as offerings to honor and communicate with the spirits. The act of burying or placing items in a designated spot is an expression of reverence and respect for the spiritual world. It demonstrates a willingness to maintain a relationship with the spirits and to seek their guidance and blessings. The specific locations chosen for these offerings often have symbolic significance. For example, a tree might represent the axis mundi, linking the earthly and spiritual realms. Hanging offerings from a roof can symbolize reaching toward the heavens. These practices are often passed down through generations as part of cultural and spiritual traditions. They help maintain a sense of continuity and connection with the beliefs and practices of ancestors.

In the Slavic tradition as well as in Haitian Vodou one can also make contact with the Underworld through boundary (or liminal) spaces. These liminal spaces are gaps in the fabric of being, where one space ends and the other has not yet begun. For example, the threshold of a house acts as a place in which the "home" has ended, but the "space of the outdoors" has not yet begun. Our world can be figuratively represented as a collection of ice floes floating on a river of another world. There are gaps between the ice floes through which we can see the water underneath. Crossroads, borders, gates, thresholds, corners, windows— all represent points at which we can contact the dead.

The practice of burying departed family members in specific locations, such as borders, roadsides, fields, or under the threshold of a house, to ensure the protection of their descendants and to establish a connection between the living world and the world of the dead is a belief found in various cultures and has been part of the folklore and spiritual traditions of different regions, including Russia.

This practice is rooted in the belief that the spirits of ancestors can act as intermediaries between the living and the deceased, offering protection, guidance, and blessings to their descendants. Placing the deceased in these specific locations is believed to facilitate communication with the spirits and to keep the ancestral connection strong. While such practices may vary in the specifics of their implementation and the cultural context in which they are observed, the common thread is the belief in the continued presence and influence of ancestors in the lives of their descendants. These customs are a testament to the enduring significance of ancestral connections and spirituality in various cultures around the world.

An indisputably significant contact and communication channel with the ancestors is the cemetery where they are buried. It should be intuitively clear that all other things being equal, physically visiting the graves of our loved ones is the best thing we can do. Within the tradition of honoring our ancestors, one can distinguish those ancestors we still remember and those we revere as a collective entity. This division in Slavic mythology is fundamental. Among other things, it also affects when we contact our ancestors. We visit the individualized life cycle of the ancestors we remember at nine days, forty days, birthdays, and on their anniversary. We visit and pay our tribute to all other ancestors on calendar holidays.

Here, by the way, lies the line that separates a Pagan from an ordinary person. Most people, as a rule, remember and even honor those who died, naturally associating their memory with their dates of birth and death. This, I stress, is something that still cannot be knocked out of us by any religion or atheism. It is too embedded in the foundations of our psyche. However, a Pagan must strive for more. Pagans must endeavor to honor and respect even those ancestors we have no name for or memory of. The faceless force that is neither good nor evil. Simply—power. This perspective is ingrained in Haitian Vodou doctrine and African-based traditions.

It's important to understand that ancestors extend beyond your grandmother and grandfather, mother and father. There is also that faceless multitude who stand behind the people who directly influenced your life—the clan! So, the contact points with the ancestors and the days on which they are celebrated occur at liminal points during the calendar year—both purely solar events (like solstices and equinoxes) and the moments of the change of seasons as determined by natural signs (i.e., when crops mature or birds migrate).

The significance of the tradition of honoring your ancestors is almost impossible to overestimate. Along with the customs of honoring the gods and reverence for nature, the tradition of honoring our ancestors is one of the pillars on which the entire construct of Slavic Paganism rests. Moreover, I believe that the ancestral tradition serves as a kind of litmus test that allows one to judge the depth and seriousness of various modern Pagan trends. The less dedication that is given to the ancestors in a modern form of Paganism, the less "Pagan" it is, and the more likely it is to be some role-playing or protest subculture that operates under the guise of Paganism.

Alas, in the age of the triumph of scientific knowledge, many do not regard the gods with any respect. However, celebration of our ancestors remains a force (on an intuitive level) that even the most inveterate atheists take seriously. In the Slavic tradition, the connection between the living and deceased members of the clan never ends. Furthermore, the well-being of the living depends on their ancestors.

6

The Pagan Calendar and Its Connection to Our Ancestors

Human life is not solely human existence but a part of the life of the entire universe and its cosmic harmony. Living in harmony with nature means harmonizing human cycles with the natural cycles of the Earth. When winter is coming, you need to prepare for frost. When spring is approaching, you should cultivate the land. There is a time of hope, a time of waiting, a time of accomplishment, a time of harvesting fruit, and a time of death. However, nothing is gone without a trace; water returns as rain, the effort is the result you harvest, youth turns into old age, and old age nourishes childhood. In the Pagan tradition, people believed that Mother Earth and Father Sun were also their ancestors. After all, they give people energy, food, warmth, light—life itself. As a resource for this chapter, in addition to my own experience and beliefs, I used Dmitry Nevsky's book *Slavic Rituals of the Ancestral Cycle*.

GODS, ANCESTORS, AND THE PASSAGE OF TIME

For Slavic Pagans, the cycle of the year is overseen by the gods of the sun. Dazhbog or Dazhdbog is a solar deity associated with the sun and its life-giving qualities. He is often depicted as a radiant and benevolent figure, symbolizing light, warmth, and prosperity. Dazhbog's name is derived from the Slavic words for "give" and "god," emphasizing his role as a giver of blessings and abundance. He is the father of four gods who represent the sun at different times of the year: Kolyada (the newborn sun), Yarilo (the bright summer solstice sun), Kupylo (the spring equinox sun), and Avsen (the autumn equinox sun).

Dazhbog's wife is the Luminous Dawn, often referred to as the Red Maiden or Zorya. The Zorya are a group of mythological sisters who are often associated with the morning and evening stars, as well as with the sun and moon. There are typically three Zorya sisters: the Morning Star (Utrennyaya Zvezda), the Evening Star (Vechernyaya Zvezda), and the Midnight Star (Polunochnaya Zvezda). The Zorya are often depicted as celestial beings who guard and control the movements of cosmic bodies. They play a role in opening and closing the gates that allow the sun and moon to rise and set. While their individual names and attributes may vary in different versions of Slavic mythology, they collectively represent the forces of light and celestial order.

Celestial order also depends on the god Khors, who was revered by the Slavs as the ruler of a chariot that carries the solar disc across the sky. The well-known Slavic group dance *khorovod* that progresses in a circular counterclockwise pattern comes from the name Khors because it resembles that movement of the sun across the sky.

There is a legend: Once, in ancient times, when everything was just created, Svarog, the God of the Sky, said to Rod, the creator of all the living, "Father, Kin to All, we need to put things in order in the sky, so that Khors can't ride his chariot around whenever he pleases. The sun comes and goes at the most unexpected times for the Earth." Rod agreed with Svarog's concern, and together they decided to create four solar breaks: two solstices (summer and winter) and two equinoxes (spring and autumn). They subsequently agreed to appoint a god to watch each year's period and tell Khors how much light to shine down on the Earth and what degree of strength to use. And so, they appointed the god Avsen as the god of the change of seasons. From that day, they called him the God of the Autumn Sun and honored him on the holiday of the autumnal equinox.

These eight points of the solar cycle at which the intensity of sunlight changes (the solstices, equinoxes, and the cross-quarter days between them) hold symbolic meaning in almost all world cultures. Astrologically, these points show the sun's passage through certain degrees to cardinal signs and the middle of fixed signs. Symbolically, they represent the passage through the eternal opposition of light and darkness. These days are energetically charged and have different meanings and feelings depending on the astrological position of the sun. Even someone who has nothing to do with agriculture or any connection to any magical or occult system feels that his state on the darkest day of the year—the winter solstice—is different from the state on the vernal equinox. In Eastern Slavic traditional culture, it is believed that on these days reality converges with the mythological era that existed at the dawn of time. During such moments—at the junctions, borders, and turns of time—the other world opens to a person invisible in ordinary time.

There is a common misconception that the tradition of honoring your ancestors is tied only to some specific holidays within the Pagan calendar. This is not true. All Pagan holidays, absolutely all of them, involve the veneration of the ancestors. Of course, some involve more veneration, some less. In my personal opinion, there is an obvious connection to the agricultural cycle. The summer period is likely marked by the lowest level of veneration, and when grains stop flowering to harvesting is the period associated with the veneration of the ancestors. Historically, there were no special holidays during the summer period, as people were very busy working in the fields. However, starting with the harvest, each of the significant holidays is somehow connected with the veneration of the ancestors—not with a specific funeral or someone's death, but with a category of ancestors.

During the transition to Christianity, the ancient Pagan holidays, which, despite being prohibited, continued to be celebrated by people, were shifted to merge with Christian holidays. Centuries later, most places adopted the Gregorian calendar, but the Orthodox Church continued to celebrate according to the Julian calendar, meaning the Christian holiday dates are different from when other groups celebrate.

In addition, the dates of the holidays vary depending on the location and climate (they coincide with the actual harvest, moon phase, etc.). And even though all of these occasions are opportunities to honor the entire clan, each of these days symbolically corresponds to one of the generations of the clan, so special attention should be paid to that generation.

While the specific customs and rituals can vary by region and individual practices, here are some examples of how certain celebrations may be associated with honoring different generations of the clan in Russian pagan traditions, but I will talk about them later in detail.

Kolyada and Kupala: These are two of the most prominent Pagan celebrations in Russian folklore. Kolyada is typically associated with the winter solstice, while Kupala is celebrated around the summer solstice. Both festivals often involve rituals related to the generational cycle of life, including the passing of knowledge and traditions from one generation to the next. Special rituals and offerings may be made to honor ancestors of past generations, seeking their blessings and guidance for the present and future generations. Many Pagan celebrations in Russia involve family gatherings where multiple generations come together to participate in rituals, share stories, and pass down cultural and spiritual traditions. Some may include rites of passage ceremonies, such as initiation rituals or coming-of-age ceremonies. These events mark the transition from one generation to the next and serve as opportunities to honor the changing roles and responsibilities within the family or clan.

Seasonal celebrations often include rituals that recognize the contributions of different generations in the clan to the cycle of life, growth, and renewal. For example, the spring equinox and autumn equinox may be occasions to acknowledge the generational cycles within the family. These customs may involve offerings, prayers, songs, and other rituals that express gratitude to ancestors and respect for their roles in the family's history.

The specific practices and beliefs associated with honoring different generations within the clan can vary, as Pagan traditions in Russia are diverse and can be influenced by local customs and regional variations. Nevertheless, the common thread is the importance of maintaining a strong connection with one's ancestors and recognizing the roles and contributions of each generation in the continuity of family and cultural traditions.

Ancestral Associations with the Days of the Week

In some Slavic and Russian traditions, each day of the week is associated with a specific family member or type of activity. This tradition, known as "naming days of the week," has been a part of Russian and Slavic folklore and superstition for centuries. The associations vary among different sources and regions, but here is a common list of associations:

Sunday (Voskresenye): Sunday is often associated with God or the Sun. It is a day of rest and prayer. In some traditions, it may also be associated with the father of the family.

Monday (Ponedelnik): Monday is often associated with the Moon and is considered a day for women and mother figures in the family.

Tuesday (Vtornik): Tuesday is associated with Mars, and it is often seen as a day for men and father figures.

Wednesday (Sreda): Wednesday is associated with Mercury. It is a day for communication and often represents siblings or other family members.

Thursday (Chetverg): Thursday is associated with Jupiter and is often linked to extended family members and grandparents.

Friday (Pyatnitsa): Friday is associated with Venus, and it is considered a day for love and romance, often connected with children.

Saturday (Subbota): Saturday is associated with Saturn and is often a day for reflection and solitude. It may be connected with ancestors and the deceased.

It's important to note that these associations are rooted in folklore and superstition and may not be universally observed or strictly followed in modern Russian culture. Some people may still adhere to these traditions, while others may not pay much attention to them. The significance of these associations can vary between regions and individual families. The associations between days of the week and family members are part of the rich tapestry of Slavic and Russian folklore.

THE CYCLE OF THE YEAR

Russian Paganism, like many Pagan and nature-based belief systems, emphasizes the cyclical nature of time and the interconnectedness of humans with the natural world. The changing of seasons, the cycles of nature, and the movements of celestial bodies play a central role in this worldview. Time is often seen as a continuous, cyclical process with no true beginning or end.

We choose to begin the story of the wheel of the year with the holiday of Korochun, the time of the death of the Old Sun and the birth of the Infant Sun, which symbolizes the transition from one phase of the annual cycle to another.

KOROCHUN

Korochun is the winter solstice (December 21–22), the shortest and darkest day of the year (in other Pagan traditions this holiday is called Yule). Korochun is the day on which the sun passes through its symbolic death. From this day on, sunlight gradually increases in length of time each day in the Northern Hemisphere until the summer solstice (June 20–21).

Korochun is symbolically associated with the cycle of rebirth. The holiday itself consists of two parts: The onset of pitch darkness due to the extinguishing of the old sun and the appearance of a new, very young sun, which will become stronger day by day. On these days, the ceremony of extinguishing and lighting the fire is traditionally held. This period is associated with immersion in the depths of the history of the clan, and it also celebrates the personal will of an individual and her destiny; it is an end and a new beginning. Like the sun that has to die before it can be born anew, this period is associated with a deep transformation of the personality, an internal change in consciousness, and an understanding of the world. On these days, it is good to conduct rituals associated with the past's immersion or to predict the future.

Many rituals associated with Korochun involve protective actions, such as the making of charms and amulets to ward off negative influences and protect against evil spirits during the darkest part of the year. These objects are often believed to possess magical properties that can shield the wearer from harm or bring good fortune. They can take the form of jewelry, talismans, or small objects with inscriptions or symbols. Specific herbs and plants believed to have protective qualities are used in rituals and charms. For example, garlic and juniper branches are sometimes hung in homes or worn as garlands to ward off evil spirits. Verbal or written prayers, chants, or incantations may be recited as part of protective rituals. These invocations are thought to invoke divine or ancestral protection. Doorways and thresholds of homes are often regarded as places where spirits can enter. To protect against unwelcome spirits, rituals may involve marking thresholds with symbols, salt, or other protective substances. To seek favor and protection from benevolent spirits or ancestors, offerings of food, drink, or other items may be made. This reciprocity is believed to strengthen the bond between the living and the spiritual world. Protective rituals and talismans are an important aspect of Pagan traditions, as they reflect the belief in the existence of both positive and negative spiritual forces and the desire to maintain a harmonious relationship with the unseen world.

The day of the winter solstice is traditionally considered a particularly dangerous time when the world of the living and the world of the dead are in contact with each other; therefore, it is advised that only knowledgeable people (witches or sorcerers) perform magical rituals. The rest of the people usually celebrate the holiday later, a few days after the longest night, when the sunlight has already become a little brighter, and the danger of coming into contact with the world of spirits and the dead has passed.

KOLYADA

Kolyada is traditionally celebrated on or around December 21 or 22, following the Julian calendar, which is used in some Slavic Orthodox traditions. However, the Kolyada festivities may extend beyond that date and continue until January 6 or 7, which corresponds to the Orthodox Christmas Eve and Christmas Day. Kolyada may vary in timing depending on regional traditions and cultural variations. Some Slavic communities may celebrate it a few days earlier or later, and customs can differ between regions. In some areas, Kolyada celebrations can last for several days, with different rituals and festivities taking place on various dates.

Kolyada's connection to the winter solstice reflects its role in celebrating the return of the sun's light and the promise of longer days as winter begins to wane. The customs and rituals associated with Kolyada are a way to welcome the sun's return and seek good fortune for the coming year. While Kolyada is not typically linked to the concept of a "baby sun" in the same way that some other traditions might reference a "sun child" or solar deity, it does celebrate the rebirth of the sun and the lengthening of daylight hours. That is, you may find symbolism related to the sun and its return, but the imagery of a baby sun is not a central theme. Instead, Kolyada typically involves caroling, bonfires, divinations, and rituals that emphasize the renewal of the sun's power and the hope for the return of warmth and light as winter transitions into spring.

Kolyada is a very ancient Pagan holiday that wasn't originally associated with Christmas at all. With the arrival of Christianity on Slavic lands in the early Middle Ages, Christian holy days replaced Pagan celebrations, including Kolyada. According to the church, Jesus Christ was born during the winter solstice—and thus this became the main "reason" for the celebration. As such, it's not surprising that the Kolyada is associated with Christmas and has adopted many Christian traditions.

This holiday is celebrated cheerfully and noisily to drive away any unkind spirits that can prevent the birth of the new sun. People burn fires and sing and dance around them. Costumed young people wearing masks depicting terrible monsters symbolize the spirits who came from the world of the dead to visit their descendants. They walk around the courtyards and sing special carols, demanding food and respect from the

Fig. 6.1. Young people dressed in traditional Kolyada costumes
(Photo by Aladjov, cc by 3.0)

hosts, or else there will be "devils in your yard, grubs in your garden."

Eastern Slavs celebrate Kolyada as a complex of sacred rituals, including those that can be performed with figurines molded from snow and ice. First, during this time, when the destructive forces of nature are strong, it is possible to destroy or freeze problems. You can concentrate all the negativity a person has or the image of the enemy in a figurine made of snow or ice. Second, you can mold a picture or any personal item using snow. When it melts into water in the spring, it will nourish the sprouts of the desire that it embodied. Those types of spells are good for emotional healing, ridding people of sickness, and so forth. Overall, this time of year is a great one for all types of divination.

It is believed that during this time of the year, with its deep darkness and longest night, the boundary between the living and the spirit world is thin, allowing for increased contact with ancestral spirits. As a result, Kolyada often includes rituals and customs designed to honor and seek blessings from ancestors. The divination practices during Kolyada are intended for seeking guidance, predicting future events, or understanding one's prospects in matters such as love and marriage. This time period is symbolically associated with the sacred seventh generation, the founders of the clan, and it is a time when a person can change his destiny with their assistance. The divinations might involve using everyday objects like mirrors, apples, or candles, and the goal is usually to gain insights into the future or to uncover hidden truths.

MASLENITSA

Maslenitsa, also known as Pancake Week or Shrovetide, doesn't have a specific date because its timing is determined by the date of Easter in the Eastern Orthodox Christian calendar. Easter is a movable feast (meaning it's based on a lunar calendar) and is celebrated on the first Sunday after the first full moon that follows the vernal equinox. Maslenitsa begins seven weeks before Easter Sunday and lasts for a week.

Maslenitsa symbolizes fertility and the arrival of spring. The holiday is associated with the end of winter and the beginning of the agricultural and growing season. Several customs and symbols within the celebration reflect these themes of fertility and renewal. Pancakes, or *blini* in Russian, are a central feature of Maslenitsa. Their round shape and golden color symbolize the sun and its warmth. Eating blini is believed to bring a fruitful harvest. Blini are traditionally cooked by unmarried girls who then do divinations over them regarding their marriage prospects. If the first pancake is lumpy, there will be no wedding that year. Pancakes also hold a special meaning for pregnant women. When the pancakes are served, the women carefully watch who takes the first one. If a man takes it, then the unborn baby will be a boy. If a woman takes the first pancake, then the baby will be a girl. One of the rituals during Maslenitsa involves constructing and then burning a straw effigy, often representing a lady or the winter season. This act is seen as a way to symbolize the banishing of winter and the welcoming of spring. People engage in various outdoor activities, such as sled rides, games, and contests, to celebrate the return of warmer weather and the growing season.

Maslenitsa is a time for singing, dancing, and general revelry. These activities are believed to encourage fertility and good fortune in the coming year. Overall, Maslenitsa is a joyful celebration that marks the end of the cold, dark winter and the beginning of a more fertile and fruitful season. It embodies the hope for a bountiful harvest and the renewal of life in nature. In some regions, rituals are performed that are associated with calling for blessings from ancestors or seeking their protection during the changes of spring.

Maslenitsa includes various divination practices that are traditionally performed to predict the future, seek guidance, and to change your faith. These divinations often reflect the hope for a bountiful year ahead as winter gives way to spring. The following are some common Maslenitsa divination practices.

Mirrors and Candle Divination: In this divination, a mirror is placed outside under the moonlight with a lit candle. People then gaze into the mirror and try to catch a glimpse of their future spouse or learn about their future. The moon and candlelight are believed to reveal hidden truths.

Apple Divination: Apples are used in various divination rituals during Maslenitsa. One common practice involves peeling an apple in one continuous strip and tossing it over your shoulder. The shape of the fallen peel is said to reveal the first letter of your future spouse's name.

Dream Divination: Some people use Maslenitsa as a time to focus on their dreams. Before going to bed, individuals may set an intention to receive guidance or insight through their dreams. Dreams during this period are believed to be particularly meaningful.

Egg Divination: Eggs are also used in divination. One method involves placing an egg in front of an icon, saying prayers, and then cracking the egg open to reveal symbols or shapes that may offer insights into the future.

Kolyada Wheel: While not divination in the traditional sense, the spinning of the Kolyada wheel, a symbol of the sun's journey through the sky, is performed as part of the Maslenitsa celebration. This ritual is believed to bring good fortune and favorable outcomes for the coming year.

Divinations during Maslenitsa are often organized and carried out in groups, which adds to the festive and communal spirit of the celebration. Friends and family members may gather to participate in these divination rituals together. Group divinations are not only a way to seek insights into the future but also a source of fun and shared experiences during Maslenitsa.

Traditional Slavic songs called *vesnyanki* are sung during Maslenitsa, often on mountain tops and hills, as a way to invoke the arrival of spring and welcome the changing of the seasons. These songs are meant to celebrate the rebirth of nature, the return of warmer weather, and the awakening of life after the cold winter months. Vesnyanki are typically joyful and filled with optimism, and the spring rituals associated with them play a significant role in Slavic cultural and folk traditions, reflecting a deep connection to the natural world and the spiritual realm.

In the Caucasus (the region between the Black Sea and the Caspian Sea, occupied mainly by Armenia, Azerbaijan, Georgia, and parts of Southern Russia) there remains a custom to polish all bronze and copper dishes on the day of the vernal equinox and put them out in the yard; it is thought that the bright radiance of their shine will invoke the sun. By polishing and displaying these metal dishes, people are essentially harnessing the radiant qualities of bronze and copper to symbolically call upon the sun to shine brightly. It is a beautiful way to celebrate the changing of the seasons and to encourage the return of warmth and light after the darkness of winter.

Another important part of the Maslenitsa festival is to create a figure made of straw that represents Lady Maslenitsa or Mistress Maslenitsa. This straw effigy symbolizes the personification of winter. The figure, often dressed in feminine clothing, is constructed with a smiling face and is usually seated in a sledge. The sledge is sometimes pulled through the streets by participants in a festive procession. On the last day of Maslenitsa, which is called Forgiveness Sunday or Cheesefare Sunday, the straw effigy is taken to a designated location, and a ceremony is held where it is set on fire. The burning of the Lady Maslenitsa effigy is a symbol of bidding farewell to winter and welcoming the arrival of spring and warmer days.

In addition to celebrating the arrival of spring, Slavic traditions often involve rituals related to honoring the dead during the springtime. This includes visiting the graves of loved ones, leaving offerings, and paying respects to ancestors. The connection between the celebration of spring and the remembrance of ancestors highlights the cyclical nature of life and the belief in the interconnectedness of the living and the deceased in Slavic folklore.

The "warm the dead" rite is observed in some regions of Russia, particularly in Siberia and the northern areas, during the winter months. This custom is rooted in the belief that the souls of the deceased need to be cared for and kept warm during the harsh winter. Family members prepare food, such as bread, porridge, and vodka, as offerings to the deceased. These offerings are believed to nourish and comfort the spirits of the dead. A table is set with the prepared food, and a place is designated for the spirits of the deceased. This place setting is often arranged in a specific manner, with an empty chair and utensils for the spirits to "eat" the offerings. Family members may gather around the table and invoke the names of their deceased loved ones. They may speak to the spirits, sharing news and updates from the living world. In some variations of the rite, a fire or candle may be lit to represent the warmth and light offered to the spirits. The offerings are then symbolically "warmed" by the fire.

According to tradition, people need to eat well on these days. If they do, the future harvest will be good and people will live in abundance throughout the year. For this reason, everyone has to be fed, especially orphans, poor people, and domestic animals. It is also important to spare the heels of the bread and place them in the dark corners of the home for the Domovoy.

And here is another reason for the main ritual dish of pancakes: On this day, it is believed that the spirits of ancestors who visit their relatives feed on the smell of fat or oil in which the pancakes are cooked; your house should have a "frying pan smell"! Tradition dictates that people are not supposed to eat the first pancake; rather, they put it on a windowsill in the attic as an offering to the spirits of the ancestors. The ancestral spirits fly "on bird's wings" to visit their descendants and rejoice with them during this time.

The time of Maslenitsa is considered auspicious for seeking blessings and assistance from ancestral spirits. It's a time to request their help in various aspects of life, such as career, studies, personal abilities, and prosperity. Maslenitsa is seen as a favorable period for rituals associated with energy, intelligence, and the pursuit of wealth and prosperity. The customs and rituals of Maslenitsa, including the preparation of pancakes, are a way to align with these goals.

The most important connection to focus on during this time is the one with the sixth generation of the clan. Connect with them with by remembering them with a special attention. While the specific focus on the sixth generation can vary by region and family, it highlights the deep reverence for the interconnectedness of family and the spiritual significance of ancestral connections during this important Russian festival. By paying special attention to the sixth generation, Maslenitsa serves as a time to reflect on the collective wisdom and heritage passed down through the family line. It's a reminder of the enduring presence of one's forebears and the role they continue to play in the lives of their descendants. It also serves as a way to ensure that the legacy and wisdom of the past are carried forward into the future.

RADONITSA

Radonitsa is traditionally celebrated on May 1. In other Pagan traditions this holiday is known as Beltane. Radonitsa is a holiday of the Earth's fertility and people, the forces of the Earth, the forces of matter, and love. This holiday is especially focused on matters associated with women; for example, fortune-telling rituals to predict whether a woman will marry, how many children she will have, and the gender of her offspring. Rituals are also performed to ensure a good harvest the following summer. During this time, the rituals must involve the "maypole"—a living tree decorated with ribbons, beads, flowers, and so on, symbolizing the awakening of nature and the World Tree. Traditionally, young men and women are excited to celebrate this holiday: It is believed that those who stay home during this time and do not participate in the festivities will have an unsuccessful marriage in their future.

In general, the entire period from Radonitsa to the summer solstice is a series of holidays associated with fertility, female energy, and love. The gradual flowering of life in nature makes the invisible world of spirits stronger day by day. As such, Radonitsa rituals are related to fertility of all kinds (i.e., conception and childbirth, future harvest, or material wealth). Rituals for improving health and rituals for beauty can be performed at this time as well. It was believed that for a girl to become beautiful, she needed to wash her face with dew at sunrise on the morning of May 1, or even completely roll around in the dew. This is also the best time for rituals related to love, marriage, and relationships in general.

This period is associated with the fifth generation (the parents of the great-grandparents). It is very useful to remember them, talk about their lives, and address them with requests during this period. It is a good time to ask them for protection, enhance your connection with the spiritual world, and strengthen your relationships with people in the physical world: your family, friends, or coworkers.

The night of May 1 is traditionally known as Walpurgis Night. In the Middle Ages, it was believed that the boundaries were erased between worlds on this night, and all the evil spirits and witches of the world went to the Sabbath. Ordinary people were warned to be especially careful and, with the help of rituals, protect themselves and their homes against dark magic.

In ancient Rome, "Lemuria" (or "Lemuralia")—the holidays of the dead—were celebrated during this period. It was believed that souls could roam the world in the form of ghosts or vampires (*lemures*) on these days. At midnight on the appointed days, the head of the household, typically the father, would perform a ritual to exorcise the lemures. He would walk through the house barefoot and toss black beans over his shoulder while reciting incantations. This act was symbolic and served to placate the spirits. The belief was that the spirits would be attracted to the beans and gather them, leaving the household in peace. After scattering the beans, the father of the family would wash his hands and feet in running water, symbolizing purification. This step represented the transition from the interaction with the spirits to the cleansing of the household. To further drive away any lingering spirits, the head of the household would make loud noises, often by banging a copper basin or other loud instruments. This was done to ensure that the spirits left the premises and did not return.

During this time, Siberian Tatars celebrate Tsym Payram, the Day of Remembrance of Ancestors. Tsym Payram, also known as Tışmek, typically falls on the sixth day of the month of Sha'ban in the Islamic lunar calendar. It is an occasion for family gatherings, where relatives come together to share a meal and exchange stories about their ancestors. On this day, families visit the graves of their ancestors, where they clean and maintain the burial sites. They may offer prayers and recite verses from the Quran in memory of the departed. Food and offerings are made at the gravesites, including traditional foods and items of sentimental value. Special prayers, supplications, and recitations from the Quran are an integral part of the Tsym Payram observance. These prayers are offered for the well-being of the ancestors' souls.

In the Slavic tradition, Krasnaya Gorka or St. George's Day is also celebrated during this period, marked by several days of joyful commemoration of ancestors (one of the variants of the name is "Joyful Grandfathers"). This is a national public holiday during which people bring memorial food and visit the cemetery, and this demonstrates yet again the valuable role of the ancestors in all types of celebration.

SEMIK (RUSALIA)

Semik (Rusalia) is the only major Slavic holiday that does not coincide with any point in the annual solar cycle; it is celebrated on the seventh Thursday after Easter. People are forbidden from performing any physical work at this day (such as cleaning the house, doing laundry, cooking, etc.) due to the belief that doing so would bring bad luck. This holiday is one of the most important memorial days among the Slavs. People arrange a memorial meal for their ancestors the night before, and then on the day itself they visit the graves.

Semik is the only time of year when the "living dead" (those who died before their time) are commemorated. It is believed that, in comparison with the ordinary deceased, the living dead are more demanding; for an ordinary dead person, the smell of food is enough (i.e., the frying pan smell on Maslenitsa) but the living dead need real food intended for the living. Ordinary dead people are satisfied with the clothes that were put in their coffin, but the living dead quickly "wear out" the clothes and require new ones, and so on. On this day, the living dead seek to harm their living relatives who have forgotten them and not paid their respects. Therefore, during the Semik memorial rites, people try to appease the souls of the living dead by holding a memorial feast on their graves so they will not harm the living.

People have to be especially careful during this time because there is a high probability of encountering otherworldly beings—in particular, mermaids.

Mermaids

Mermaids in Slavic mythology are spirits are associated with water. They were believed to be protectors of fields, forests, and waters. They were portrayed as young, pale-skinned girls with loose hair, who were often either naked or wearing torn dresses. It was believed that mermaids were once maidens who committed suicide, drowned in water due to an unhappy experience or unrequited love, or who were murdered in the water. In Russian demonology, mermaids were considered living dead or "lost dead"—that is, those who died before their time, and would wander between the worlds of the living and dead until they reached the age that they were meant to die. After Christianity came to Russia, it was believed that unbaptized girls, as a rule, became mermaids.

Mermaids were considered dangerous for humans, especially for men. It is said that when a mermaid desired a man, she lured him into the water, where he would be drowned. But girls also had to be vigilant. Mermaids are said to dislike human girls and would drive them out of the forest however they could—frightening them and stealing their clothes and food. Mermaid behavior can be unpredictable, but it is not all bad, and they can be helpful to humans as well. In some cases, mermaids loved children and protected them in every possible way, including saving them from wild animals and leading them out of the forest if they got lost. Sometimes, mermaids rescued a person who was drowning. They were often described with cheerful characteristics: at night, they tumbled, played, performed circle dances, danced, and laughed. And they were good for the land: it was believed that where the mermaid runs, "the grass grows thicker, and the harvest is rich."

It is believed that during this holiday period, "Mermaid Week," mermaids come out of the water (lakes, rivers, seas) to comb their hair, swing on tree branches, and sometimes lure passersby, "Men, come swing with us!" to play and frolic on the ground, dance in circles with songs, make jokes, and laugh; they can be seen at crossroads, in cemeteries, in fields, in flowering meadows in the forest, and on tree branches (most often on birch trees).

Customary beliefs held that, sometimes, during their dances, mermaids performed a ritual that protected the harvest. However, they could also punish those people who treated them disrespectfully (for example, if they worked on Semik) by sending locusts to destroy their crops, causing droughts, prolonged downpours, or frosts to their fields, or killing livestock. Traditionally, it was believed that meeting a mermaid could bring a person good luck and wealth, or, on the contrary, could lead to his death, depending on where and how she was seen. Therefore, it was advisable not to go to the forest or near water alone, not to stay there after sunset and, of course, not to swim, especially at noon or midnight (times when the veil between the worlds is thinnest).

People also believed it was necessary to appease the mermaids so they won't harm the living. Therefore, they would go to the tree branches near rivers and lakes and leave bread crusts, old clothes, embroidered towels, mirrors and hair combs, and skeins of thread.

The ceremony of "seeing the mermaid" is usually held on the Sunday of Mermaid Week (although it could also take place on the Day of Souls, Pentecost Saturday, or during the celebration of Ivan Kupala). The ceremony takes place in the evening, often at midnight, and its main participant is a person dressed like a mermaid, who, with shouts and songs ("I will lead the little mermaid to the forest, I myself will return home,") leads everyone out of the village and into the field, forest, or river.

After being exiled, the mermaid hides for some time and then secretly returns to the village while the festivities continue. There is sometimes a similar rite called a "mermaid funeral," in which a mermaid is symbolically burned or drowned in the river. The meaning of these rituals is to remove mermaids (as malevolent spirits, the living dead) from people's homes at the end of spring and leave them in places where they can reside without causing harm to people.

It is during this time (before Pentecost) that female initiation rites

Fig. 6.2. The Kumlenie
custom
(Painting by D. O. Osipov,
c. 1860–70)

are traditionally held. Young girls are formally recognized as adults who
have reached marriageable age. A respected woman from the village
gathers up the girls and take them to the forest (usually a birch forest). There, the girls sing chants, dance in circles, and perform the rite
of Kumlenie. Kumlenie is an initiation rite performed during spring-
summer holidays for the Eastern and Southern Slavs, as well as a form
of youth union. Two female friends walk under an archway made of
birch and exchange kisses on the cheek and small gifts. However, the
prevailing hypothesis is that, during this ceremony, the girls do not
become bonded with each other but, for a time, with the mermaids to
appease them and have their future foretold. This time of the year is
associated with the fourth generation. You may ask them for stability
in your life, such as emotional or financial stability, a stable home, or a
stable future.

PENTECOST

Pentecost is a Christian holiday that is celebrated on the seventh Sunday after Easter. It commemorates the descent of the Holy Spirit upon the apostles and other followers of Jesus Christ, as described in the New Testament book of Acts, specifically in Acts 2. Pentecost is often regarded as the birthday of the Christian Church.

The ritual called "driving the bush" or "walking the bush" is held on that day. Walking the bush is a ritual that combines elements of both Pagan and Christian traditions, as well as a reverence for nature. In rural areas, the transition from Pagan beliefs to Christianity led to the blending of older customs with new Christian traditions. The use of greenery and natural symbols in the ritual reflects a connection to the natural world and the changing seasons, which was important in many Pagan belief systems. This blending of traditions allowed communities to maintain cultural and spiritual practices that had deep historical roots while adopting Christianity. Walking the bush is a fascinating example of how cultural and religious traditions can evolve and adapt over time, creating a unique and meaningful blend of customs.

This ceremony is perhaps the oldest of the Pagan Slavic rituals that have been passed down to us (it is still preserved in Belarus and Ukraine). During this holiday, a girl ("bush"), dressed up in greenery and branches, walks around the village with other women, singing as they go. They wish the owners of each house good health and prosperity. In response, people give them money or treats in the form of a variety of homemade foods. In this rite, the bush symbolizes not only the power of nature and fertility, but also the spirit of the clan: among the Slavs, it is believed that the souls of their ancestors may be hidden in fresh greenery (remember that the tree is often a symbol of the clan).

Also on this day, all over the village, houses and churches are decorated with green branches and flowers. The use of green branches and leaves represents the vitality and growth of nature during the spring and early summer. It's a way to connect the natural world with the religious significance of the holiday. The decorations symbolize the presence of the Holy Spirit and the renewal of faith. The green branches may also be seen as a representation of the "Green Sunday" or the Pentecost theme of new life and spiritual growth. Green branches and flowers represent the vitality and beauty of the natural world. They serve as a way to connect with the spirits of the land, forests, and fields, which were often considered sacred in Slavic Pagan beliefs. Decorating houses and churches with greenery and flowers often involves the participation of the entire community. Families and individuals may contribute to the decorations, and it's a way for people to come together to prepare for the celebration.

For some Slavic pagans, these decorations may also be seen as a way to honor and welcome the spirits of their ancestors. The vibrant, living plants can symbolize the presence of ancestral spirits, who are believed to be closely connected to the natural world and its seasonal changes. Just as the arrival of spring and the blossoming of flowers represent renewal in nature, these decorations can symbolize spiritual renewal and growth in one's connection to the spirit world. It's a way to seek blessings from the spirits and ancestors for a prosperous and harmonious future.

This time of the year is associated with the third generation. In addition to the importance of the Holy Trinity in Slavic Orthodox Christian beliefs, pre-Christian Slavic Pagan beliefs include triple deities or goddesses associated with various aspects of life. For example, the Zorya sisters are a trio of goddesses who govern celestial bodies and the passage of time. The concept of generations is important in Slavic culture, and the number three often symbolizes three generations: ancestors, the present generation, and future generations. All ancestors are honored, the current generation carries on traditions, and rituals may involve seeking blessings for the future. At this time of year, you can especially ask for focus, protection, and success.

Fig. 6.3. A young girl dressed up in greenery in
the walking the bush custom
(Rivne regional state administration, cc by-sa 4.0)

Fig. 6.4. The inside of the church is decorated
with greenery and branches

KUPAYLA (IVAN KUPALA)

Kupayla or Ivan Kupala (June 21–22, Gregorian calendar July 6–7) is the summer solstice, a midsummer holiday. Kupayla is a Pagan holiday that became associated with the Christian holiday Ivan Kupala (John the Baptist); a mixture of influences now can be seen in this celebration. This night is the most powerful of the year and a time when both good and evil spirits are equally active. It is considered one of the best times for divination.

The holiday's name is derived from the Slavic word *kupati*, which means "to bathe" or "to swim," as water-related rituals are an integral part of the festivities. During this time, as is the case during the spring holidays, the elements of water and fire are very important; it is when the sacred marriage of fire and water takes place. People often gather near rivers, lakes, or other bodies of water to participate in water-related rituals. These rituals may include swimming, diving, or washing one's face to purify and rejuvenate the body. In the old days, people believed that all the evil spirits left the seas on the night of Ivan Kupala.

Fig. 6.5. Kupayla khorovod around the bonfire
(Photo by Vladimir Lobachev, cc by-sa 4.0)

Therefore, the water was considered healing and possessed magical power, helped cleanse people from evil, healed from diseases, and promoted good health. In honor of this belief, it is still customary to pour water over everyone you meet on that night. It is believed this helps a person cleanse her soul.

Bonfires are a central element of Kupayla celebrations. People bathe in a dew at night and rivers in the daytime, and jump over bonfires until the next day's sunrise. Using the friction of dry sticks, people produce what we call "live fire" and make a huge bonfire. A pole with a burning wheel is positioned in the middle of the fire—the symbol of the sun. The fires are also believed to have purifying and protective qualities. According to tradition, whoever jumps the highest without touching the flame will be happy. Those who jump over the fire set intentions for what they want to receive: success, bravery, beauty, attractiveness, improved health, and more. Mothers burn clothes taken from their sick children in the bonfires so that the sickness will dissipate. It is also customary to set fire to the wooden wheel, which is subsequently rolled down the mountain, symbolizing the solstice.

Fig. 6.6. Jumping over the fire

Fig. 6.7. Kupayla wreath
(Photo by zlatoust100.gmail.com)

Floating wreaths with lit candles on the water is another common practice. On the day of Kupayla, the girls insert lighted candles into woven wreaths and release them into the water in the evening. If the wreath drifts away from the shore quickly, it means that girl will have a happy and long life or a good marriage. If the wreath sinks, it means she will not get married this year, or she will have problems in love. The best outcome is for the girl whose wreath drifts the farthest away or whose candle burns the longest.

The gathering and use of various herbs and flowers are an important part of Kupayla celebrations. Herbs are believed to have special powers on this day, and people may collect them to make wreaths, sachets, or decorations. On this day it is customary for people to dress themselves in sashes of flowers and wreaths, dance in a circle (khorovod), and sing special songs. Herbs and flowers are often associated with the holiday's themes of love and protection. A popular Kupayla tradition involves the search for the elusive "fern flower," which is believed to bring good fortune to those who find it. However, the fern flower is considered magical and can only be found on this special night. If you do find it, it may fulfill your deepest desires and grant you magical capabilities, including the ability to speak the language of nature (birds, animals, plants), predict the future, remove obstacles, and find buried treasure.

Kupayla is associated with romantic themes and the idea of love. Young couples may participate in rituals to determine the strength of their relationships or seek out their future partners. Girls cast love spells using the Kupayla dew. The most powerful love rituals are performed during Kupayla night.

The rituals of this time are associated with the strength and fullness of life. These rituals should help people gain courage, achieve their goals, realize their abilities, show what they are capable of, accomplish a good position in life, achieve good health and happiness, find love, and build a loving, healthy family. Ivan Kupala is associated with a person's all seven generations. You can honor them all and ask for their support and assistance.

SPAS

During August, farmers see the fruits of their hard work ready to be harvested.

Slavic Pagan tradition includes three harvest celebrations, Honey Spas, Apple Spas, and Nut (or Bread) Spas—which take place around August 14, 19, and 29.

First is Honey Spas (August 14), when beekeepers remove the first honeycombs from their hives. The first honeycombs are donated to the departed spirits in commemoration of deceased parents. A piece of honeycomb should also be given away to children and the poor. It is customary to bake honey cakes, pancakes with honey, and many other goodies with honey and poppy seeds on this holiday. Honey Spas traditionally acts as the farewell to the summer.

Apple Spas is a harvest festival (August 19), and Slavic Pagans believe that apples are endowed with a special power on this day—they bring health, beauty, strength, and happiness. According to traditional beliefs, Apple Spas herald the onset of autumn and the transformation of nature. The Eastern Slavs were the only ones on this day who were supposed to eat apples and dishes made from the fruits of the new harvest.

The Eastern Slavs also believed that deceased children whose parents had not eaten apples until that day were given gifts in the Underworld, and those children whose parents who had tried apples did not. Women who had lost their children in the morning of this day had to take several apples and put them on their children's graves.

The third, Nut Spas (or Bread Spas), is celebrated at the end of August, on the 29, and marks the commencement of the nut harvesting season and the completion of the harvest of grain crops. It is customary to bake nut bread, pies, and rolls from the flour of the new harvest.

All three Spas holidays are very revered by Russians to this day. They combine the customs and rituals of the Pagan culture of the people with church holidays. In places where the customs of our ancestors are still followed, you can witness the same rituals that our ancestors performed. In other places, they are heavily mixed with church services.

The rituals of this time are associated with strength and prosperity of life. These rituals should help people gain courage, prosperity, love, peace in their homes, good health, and strong cleansing.

This month is associated with a person's second generation, your parents. Asking for blessings and expressing love and gratitude to your parents is a heartfelt and meaningful gesture on this day. Share your feelings openly and honestly. Tell your parents why you love and respect them. Allow your parents to share their thoughts and feelings as well. Listening is an essential part of a meaningful conversation.

Remember that this is a personal and intimate conversation, so be sincere and speak from the heart. It's a beautiful way to strengthen your family bonds and let your parents know how much they mean to you.

OVSE

Ovse is a term that represents the autumnal equinox in Slavic traditions. The autumnal equinox typically falls around September 22 or 23 in the Northern Hemisphere, marking the transition from summer to autumn when the day and night are of approximately equal length. In Slavic folklore and culture, the changing of the seasons, including the arrival of autumn, is often associated with various rituals and customs. While there may not be a single, widely recognized Ovse holiday, there are many regional and local traditions that take place during the autumn equinox and throughout the autumn season.

Many Slavic cultures have harvest festivals during the autumn equinox to celebrate the successful gathering of crops and to give thanks for the year's bounty. These festivals may include feasting, dancing, and other communal activities. Some traditions involve rituals intended to protect the harvest and ensure a good winter. People may create protective charms or perform rituals to ward off negative forces.

Autumn is a time when the natural world undergoes changes, and it is also a time when people may honor their ancestors by leaving offerings at gravesites or performing rituals to connect with their forebears. Ovse is a time for family reunions and gatherings. Families come together to share stories about their ancestors, keeping the memories alive and passing down family traditions and history.

People create small ancestral altars within their homes, featuring photographs of deceased family members and offerings. These altars serve as focal points for meditation and reflection. Special rituals or

Fig. 6.8. *Reaping,* painting by Nikolay Bogatov, 1896

prayers may be performed to invoke the guidance and protection of ancestors during the changing seasons and in the face of the upcoming winter. This may include lighting candles or incense and reciting prayers. Ovse is often associated with harvest festivals, and during these feasts, some may set an extra place at the table for their ancestors. It's a way of including them in the celebration.

This is the last "bright" holiday of the annual cycle. It is believed that good spirits leave the world of the living during this time and are replaced by their opposites at the beginning of winter. This holiday marks the time when the leaves fall, the harvest ends, and people fortify themselves for the winter and the new year. Historically, it was also the time when Slavic women span wool and produced needlework.

On this day, appreciation and gratitude are given to Mother Earth; the harvest is completed, which is intended to ensure the family's well-being for the rest of the year and the beginning of the next. On this day, the harvest of vegetables begins—onions are harvested first. Usually, a meal is arranged and the whole family gathers. Beer is brewed, and a sheep is slaughtered especially for the celebration. A cake is baked from the flour of the new crop, and people glorify Mother Earth for giving birth to bread and other sustenance.

It is believed that the goddess Zhiva—the personification of fertile strength, youth, and beauty of all nature and man—leaves the Earth on Ovse. Zhiva reigns when fields and forests, orchards and vegetable gardens turn green and bloom; her reign is like waking up from a dull winter dream and seeing—for the first time—the beauty of blossoming nature, youth, love, and tenderness. But by Ovse, spring leaves are slowly replaced by the frost and cold of winter. The harvest is coming to an end, and people thank Zhiva for not allowing them to starve to death and sending fertility to Earth.

During this period, birds start to migrate to warmer lands. Many Slavs believe they fly to the Upper World where the souls of the dead live. As the birds fly across the sky, people look up to them and ask them to bring back news from their dead ancestors or friends.

According to the legend in the land of the Eastern Slavs, there existed a heavenly paradise called Iriy. This paradise was believed to be a place of eternal summer, abundant gardens, and a great Tree of Life that stood at its center. The Tree of Life was said to be a towering birch or oak tree, with branches that reached high into the heavens. In this heavenly realm, the souls of the deceased found their eternal rest and happiness. However, there was a disturbance in Iriy. A raven had taken residence in the branches of the Tree of Life. This raven, with its loud and raucous cawing, disrupted the peace of the souls of the dead. Their eternal rest was disturbed by the noisy raven, and their tranquility was shattered.

Svarog, the God of Light, the guardian of Iriy, and the protector of the heavenly garden, saw the unrest caused by the raven. He decided to intervene and bring balance and harmony back to Iriy. Svarog ordered the raven to give up the keys to the gates of Iriy, the keys that allowed access to the paradise, and to transfer them to a more peaceful and melodious bird, the swallow. The raven didn't dare to disobey the god, but he kept one key to the secret door for himself.

The swallow began to shame him. In his anger, the raven tore several feathers from her tail; since then, the swallow's tail has been bifurcated. Having learned of the raven's outrage, Svarog became so angry he condemned the entire raven tribe to peck dead corpses until the end of time.

On the day of the autumn equinox, the borders between worlds are thin, and the people who have preserved all the knowledge of their ancestors are well aware of this. That is precisely why Slavs love to honor their ancestors on days like this. People usually prepare protective magic at this time; they gather fallen bunches of red mountain ash berries and hang them outside the windows of their houses. To this day, people believe that these berries protect the home from all kinds of darkness and disease. You can also use an ash branch to draw a circle on the window or around the entire house.

In Hinduism, this time of year also marks one of the most important holidays for the remembrance of ancestors and working with one's clan: Pitr-Paksha (from about mid-September to early October) when the Hindu people honor their ancestors, especially through food offerings.

The time for festivals begins on the day of the autumn equinox. Even those who are usually cautious about sharing their achievements or talking about their health (for fear of being jinxed), can and should brag about their harvest and praise their children during these ancestral holidays to avoid bad luck. The autumn equinox day is suitable for rituals related to health, social status, education, spiritual practices, and travel. This period is associated with the sixth generation, the grandparents of the great-grandparents.

VELES'S NIGHT

Veles's Night, which falls on the night from October 31 to November 1, is a significant and mystical celebration in some Slavic Pagan traditions. It is closely tied to the worship of Veles, the Slavic god of the Underworld, who holds sway over the gateway between the world of the living (Yav) and the realm of the dead (Nav). The celebration of Veles's Night has some similarities to the widely known holiday of Samhain, celebrated in various Pagan traditions.

Veles's Night is a time to remember and honor deceased ancestors. It is believed that the boundary between the living and the dead is particularly thin during this time, allowing for easier communication with those who have passed on. Like Samhain, Veles's Night is a festival of the dead. People may set up altars or make offerings to their ancestors, seeking their guidance and blessings. Bonfires are often lit as part of the celebration. The flames symbolize both the hearth of the home and the transformative power of fire. Similar to Halloween customs, some people may wear masks or disguises during Veles's Night. This tradition can be traced back to the belief that spirits or supernatural entities roam freely during this time, and wearing masks serves as protection from them. It is a common practice to engage in divination or fortune-telling during Veles's Night to gain insight into the future, seek answers to questions, or connect with the spirit world.

Veles's Night is the beginning of the darker half of the year. Night gains more and more power on Earth and makes us think about the inexorable course of life and the fact we have no control over one thing—death. On this night, the gate is wide open until dawn, when the first rooster sings. Veles's night is a night of great power when the spirits of our ancestors and those who will live after us appear as an integral whole. This is a family holiday. It is also believed that on the Veles's night the spirits of the ancestors return to their descendants to teach them wisdom and bless the whole family. Before dark, people light a fire; it was once a rite of cleansing and liberation from evil forces to jump through the fire and walk with bare feet on its burning coals. That is why the celebration of Veles's night for the Slavs is of particular importance. Along with understanding these phenomena, an unexpectedly new perception of folk holidays, customs, and the opposing unity of the elements arises.

According to popular belief, on this night the souls of ancestors visit their descendants living in Yav for the last time in the year, after which they fly to bright Iriy garden until next spring. Veles's night is a magical night of trial and initiation. On this night, you are encouraged to go down into the dungeons of your subconscious and gain power if you can overcome your fear. This is the time for purification, comprehension, understanding, and transition to a new level. At night, a plate with a treat for the souls of the dead is put in the backyard. A candle is placed on the windowsill to light the way for the souls who are ready to come to you. Apples, pumpkins, zucchinis, and autumn flowers are placed on the altar. We remember the departed loved ones, friends, and relatives without regret.

The Slavs sacredly revere the days of commemoration of ancestors, and they take care to make their ancestors welcome. Before the festival, they clean their houses and wash in the bathhouse, where they leave a bucket of clean water and a new broom for the souls of their ancestors. They lay a festive table, and the owner of the house makes a speech, inviting dead ancestors to the table to dine with them ("Grandfathers come, drink with us, eat . . ."). All doors in the house are opened so that the ancestors can enter and sit at the table. Before putting food on a dish for the family, the first dish has to be put on a special plate for the spirits.

The solemn memorial dinner lasts quite a while; everyone remembers the best in their deceased relatives, whose actions more than one generation of this kind can be proud of. During the festive dinner, people speak only about their ancestors, their lives, individual cases, character traits, wisdom, wise advice, and good deeds. The conversation begins with a story about the oldest and most famous ancestor and ends with a recollection of the recently deceased. At the end of the celebration, people say their good-bye with the words, "Farewell to all my ancestors, go, take with you (trouble, illness, etc.), wait for us for when the time will come."

On November 1, all the food that was left on the table overnight is taken to a natural body of water or left in the forest, and bread is crumbled on the roof for the birds in the belief that every bird on this day contains the spirit of a deceased ancestor who eats before they leave.

Many other traditions have holidays around this time of year that highlight the ancestors and the thin veil between the worlds. Both Halloween and the Day of the Dead originated from traditional Pagan cultures and, although influenced by Christianity, still retain their original characteristics. Unlike Halloween, in which the fear of the other world comes to the fore, the Day of the Dead (which originates from the customs of the Indigenous peoples of the Maya and Aztecs) is a time to remember the dead with joy and laughter. It is believed that the souls of the departed return to Earth during the day on the Day of the Dead to see their relatives and enjoy earthly experiences that they are deprived of in the afterlife. This holiday is widely celebrated throughout Latin America with carnivals, candy skulls, and, of course, visits to ancestors' graves. The Aymara Indians in Bolivia celebrate the Day of Skulls around this same time of year; they decorate the skulls and bones of their deceased relatives, which they store in their homes, and carry them in a festival procession to the cemetery. In their worldview, this is a time when the denizens of the other world (spirits, deities, the deceased) to connect with the living.

The Haitian Vodou tradition holds an annual celebration known as Gede around the same time as the Veles's Night or Samhain celebrations. The Gede celebration is dedicated to honoring the Gede spirits, who are revered as the spirits of the dead and ancestors in Haitian Vodou.

This festival typically takes place in late October to early November and aligns with the broader concept of honoring and communicating with the deceased. During the Gede celebration, participants engage in various rituals and ceremonies to pay respects to the Gede spirits. These rituals often involve music, dance, and offerings, including rum, food, and other items that are believed to please and appease the spirits. The Gede spirits are known for their mischievous and irreverent personalities, and participants in the celebration may dress in elaborate costumes and masks to mimic their behavior.

Similar to the Veles's Night and Samhain traditions, the Gede celebration in Haitian Vodou emphasizes the connection between the living and the dead. It is a time to seek guidance and blessings from the spirits of the ancestors, to remember and honor those who have passed away, and to acknowledge the cycle of life and death. We will discuss more about Haitian Vodou traditions later in this book.

Veles's Night rituals are associated with magic, wisdom, secrets, and getting rid of all bad and negative energy. On this day, rituals can be carried out to dispense with something or someone: unnecessary things, connections, bad habits, negative character traits, offenses, obstacles, negative people, and diseases. Even ordinary cleaning takes on a magical meaning: Along with the garbage you throw away or burn, the things you no longer need in your life will disappear. But pay attention. The line between the worlds is very thin to nonexistent during this time, and even one small action not correctly carried out can have very bad consequences.

This period is best suited for self-reflection; just as nature freezes, so people should reduce external activity and turn to their essence, origins, ancestors, and history. Symbolically, this period is associated with the seventh, most sacred generation: the great-grandparents of your great-grandparents. If you know your seventh-generation ancestors, you can turn to them for advice on the very foundations of your destiny and your path in life. You can also learn more about your family and immerse yourself in its history. It is an especially great time to address any painful experiences that faced your ancestors, such as loneliness, mental health issues, wrongful death, and any other secrets that lurk in the shadows.

But as the dark of the year comes, so does the light. The wheel turns from Veles's Night toward the winter solstice, and just after that moment of deepest darkness, the light of the new year creeps in. The cycle, as always, begins anew.

7

Color Symbolism of the Slavs

In Slavic tradition, ornaments held significant cultural, spiritual, and symbolic meanings beyond their role as mere decorations. All signs held a particular meaning and, in this sense, ornaments represented ideograms, a kind of writing. The symbols involved were not simple, but sacred, and were primarily intended not for people but for the higher forces on which people depended. Therefore, the meaning of the ornament was predominantly magical. An ornament is a spell—not a verbal spell (which is temporary) but a visually represented form that acts constantly.

Ornaments were an integral part of Slavic folklore, and each design, pattern, or symbol carried its own unique significance. Many Slavic ornaments featured protective symbols that were believed to ward off evil spirits, protect the wearer, or safeguard the household. These symbols often drew from ancient Pagan beliefs and were later incorporated into Christian motifs. Some ornamental patterns were associated with fertility, abundance, and prosperity. These designs were used in various contexts, from clothing to home decor, to invoke positive energy and blessings for a fruitful life.

Ornamentation was a way for Slavic communities to express their cultural identity. Different regions and ethnic groups had their own distinctive ornamentation styles, reflecting their unique heritage and traditions. Ornaments were frequently used in rituals and ceremonies, such as weddings, funerals, and other life events. They played a role in symbolizing transitions and marking significant moments in a person's life. Many Slavic ornaments drew inspiration from nature, incorporating elements like plants, animals, and celestial bodies. This connection to the natural world symbolized the interdependence between humans and their environment. In both Pagan and Christian contexts, ornaments were imbued with spiritual significance. They were believed to bridge the gap between the earthly and the divine, serving as conduits for spiritual energy and blessings. Some ornamental patterns were thought to possess mystical qualities. For example, certain geometric shapes and motifs were believed to hold hidden knowledge and secrets accessible to those who understood their significance.

Ornaments often convey stories and legends. Through their intricate patterns and designs, they could tell tales of heroes, mythical creatures,

Fig. 7.1. Slavic symbolism on textiles at the Museum of Folk Architecture and Ethnography in Pyrohiv, Kyiv, Ukraine
(Photo by Maksym Kozlenko, cc by-sa 4.0)

and important historical events. Some ornaments incorporated the "evil eye" symbol, believed to protect against malevolent glances or envy. The use of ornamental patterns on clothing, household items, and even architecture was seen as a way to elevate the everyday to the spiritual. It was a reminder of the sacred within the mundane.

Slavic ornamentation is a rich and complex aspect of their cultural heritage, and it continues to be celebrated and cherished as a reflection of their history and beliefs. The symbolism and meanings associated with these ornaments have been passed down through generations, connecting the past with the present and serving as a reminder of the enduring cultural and spiritual significance of these traditions.

These ornaments and patterns appeared all over in the lives of the Slavs, in their homes and on their bodies. The patterns that adorned the clothes of Slavs held deep meaning, and their location on the garment was also significant. The Slavs divide the world into the world of the dead and the world of the living: Nav and Yav. The shoulders and neck symbolize divine light; the hem, the Underworld; and the sleeves,

Fig. 7.2. The author wearing a traditional shirt with symbolic patterns on the neckline and sleeves

the world of the living. Each pattern reflects the process of movement and development, a combination of masculine and feminine, light and darkness, earth and sky. The meaning of the symbol varies according to where it is painted on the dress or shirt. The craftsmen honor the universe and the gods when they create the ornament. The sacred meaning is the basis; aesthetics always takes second place.

Let's turn our attention to the meanings of color. Consistent associations with one color or another have been handed down over the years and are indirectly explained by the physiology of the human brain. For example, it is widely accepted that red has a stimulating effect that can result in the release of latent aggression. Green, on the contrary, is calming. However, the fact that different people attach different connotations (sometimes completely opposing) to different colors suggests that mythological reasons play a greater role in giving color to a particular meaning than psychophysiological aspects. For example, the traditional color of mourning for Europeans is black, while for the Japanese, it is white. Europeans associate the color yellow with impurities, while it is a holy color for Buddhists. From all the variety of colored phenomena, man selected only a few. It is difficult to determine what factors influenced this choice. In this section, I will limit my discussion to the symbolism of color among the Slavs.

RED

Red is the color of a burning flame, blood, sunrise, and sunset, and is associated with the idea of life and sacrifice. Red symbolizes not so much the phenomena themselves but the state of transition from one world to another. In this sense, the color red expresses an active principle, the idea of perpetual motion, the cycle of the universe from birth to death and, again, to resurrection. Individual human life is likened to a flame. Death is the extinction of the last spark of life, turning into ash. But, just as the flame ignites again when the flint hits the chair, the person will also rise.

Rod—the main deity of the Slavs, is associated with red. Slavs believe that all humans are descendants of Rod; Rod gives life to humans. Therefore, there is a connection between red and human life as a transition from Nav to Yav.

Red is the color of celebration, luxury, love, and passion. So, in ritual activities and particularly in the Slavic costume, red is the dominant color, and Slavs typically wear red belts, boots, dresses, and shirts during rituals. The red accent on holiday clothing is essential since this color is prevalent in the world of reality, the world of people. Slavs believe that the gods will not hear you if you are not wearing clothes with a red element in them. Red in Russia has always been synonymous with the word *beautiful*. Traditionally, girls wore red-colored blush made of berry juice, red beets, or other vegetable dyes. It was believed this gave them a unique beauty.

Vladimir the prince of Kyiv was called the "Red Sun," a name that emphasized the ruler's relationship with the gods. There is a long tradition among Indo-European people to identify the importance of people in power to justify their right to the throne. All solar deities of the Slavs had the symbolism of red and a clear tie to the people who called on them, their power, and their patronage in assistance to the ritual. A good example is the Slavic god Yarilo, which means "bright, Sun-like."

Blood is red, and its sacredness should never be underestimated in a philosophical sense. Traditionally, Slavs believed that their blood was from the Gods. The (red) blood was sacred, and the kinship bond of blood was sacred and important for clan unity. Sometimes, blood was used to seal business contracts and other important transactions.

When the god Rod was addressed on special occasions, blood acted as the transmission of information. It is worth quickly reviewing the origin of those incredible sacrifice myths. People often cut the palm of their hand with a knife and allowed their blood to drip onto the altar when the believer addressed God. When two people cut their hands and touched palms, they secured the deal in heaven, as if they passed their oath to the supreme God through their blood.

Red flames and fire in the sacred sense represent an integral attribute of any Slavic holiday. Through a fire, by offering treasures (various grains, honey, etc.), red also acts as a messenger of thought from a person to the gods. Red is also a common sight during funerals, and the deceased is often wrapped in red cloth or red is painted onto her clothes. According to some, red is a marker of ritualism and demonstrates the importance of what is happening. However, it's not mourning the dead that is emphasized. Red is the symbol of celebration and, as I mention above, resurrection.

Red is a symbol of transferring information between man and the gods. These are all strong indicators that the red color in the funerary tradition was only a link, transmitting the human soul to the sun gods. It is key to understanding the sacred activities of our ancestors, and realization of its depth and scope gives us an awareness of many cultural aspects of Slavic Paganism in the era when beliefs in the sacred power of the clan were dominant.

BLUE

Blue is a symbol of water. Water represents life (crops, fish, spiritual cleansing, etc.). It is believed that women are sacred since they are birth givers. The child resides in the water in a woman's womb for nine months before being born and returns to the water after death. Haitians hold a very similar belief about returning to Ginen, the underwater realm of the spirts and ancestors. Some Slavic people believe that blue merged with brown, the color of the Earth, and both women and Earth are symbols of fertility. Traditionally, a pregnant woman would wear a belt in blue tones. Blue was also associated with funeral rites; the dead were sent in the boat along the river. The boat was set on fire with an arrow, so the deceased met Marena (the Goddess of the Afterlife), who delivered him to the ancestors and gods.

Blue is also associated with marriage. During weddings, two colors are intertwined, blue and red, masculine and feminine. The feminine represents water, and the masculine represents fire—complimentary elements that neutralize each other. The woman pours, the man boils and burns, allowing, in the combination of these principles, a new family, a new life to be born.

Blue is also the color of lightning, and Slavic ancestors perceived lightning to represent a weapon of the God Perun. Therefore, in some epics Russian vigilantes used the metaphor of lightning. Perun is the patron saint of the defenders of the homeland; lightning is a strong image of the manifestation of divine power, greatness, and strength. It was precisely with such qualities that Perun endowed the warriors with divine power. Blue was considered a masculine color that protected people against the elements. In addition, wearing blue represented a sign of readiness to protect a woman. If a man gave a woman a blue gift, it symbolized that he was willing to protect her throughout his life. Wearing a dress of this color also could mean that a person had embarked on the path of self-improvement.

GREEN

Green is the calmest of all the colors. This color predominates in nature during spring and summer and causes joy, a good mood, and positive emotions. It represents the departure of the cold winter and the arrival of warmth. There is a whole layer of Slavic concepts associated with green. In mythology, river and swamp inhabitants were endowed with green attributes, which meant that this color was close to the symbolism of water. Green, in general, is a representation of youth. Nature and the forest, in particular, are full of green, especially in the spring. This is how nature comes to life. This is how we observe the ancient magic of the birth of a new life. Therefore, the color green is clearly comparable with the symbol of the sown field—the sign of birth and new life.

Green is one of the most powerful Slavic symbols. The magic of green nature is divine; millions of people try to spend their summer holidays surrounded by green. People often find peace, an escape from the city, and a break from their personal problems when they are planted into a green environment. Green literally heals the human soul. Green in Slavic mythology is the favorite color of the forest spirit, mermaids, and other creatures living near bodies of water. According to the Russian oral folk tradition, mythology, and belief system in general, green symbolizes youth. The young wine was called "green." This epithet could also be applied to a child who tried to do something "adult-like" and failed. Immature, young, unprepared, the list of synonyms for the use of the word *green* is extensive.

In the south, Slavs believed that green was associated with healing and cleansing properties; it could drive out evil spirits on the "green grass," "green tree," and "green mountain." The use of green color in national clothes is more inherent among the Belarusians. For example, the use of this color in amulet clothes, such as belts, shirts, and sundresses, suggests that the owner is in a good mood, full of optimism and life. His natural energy overflows, and he is tuned in to a positive perception of life in all its diversity. Green is life-oriented, which means it only brings good emotions.

BLACK

The God Chernobog (literally, "Black God") personifies the forces of evil and darkness and represents a collective image of everything underground, dark, gloomy. In addition to these images, Chernobog is the patron of magic. The Slavs believe evil is not an absolute concept, nor is good. If, with the help of magic, you could remove the evil eye, this represents a good deed, even if dark methods are used. Behind Chernobog, there is a whole lineage of dark gods who have different preferences and "occupations."

For the Slavs, black represents the night, darkness—a time of sleep, and a temporary void. Black is also associated with underground motives. The black color is rarely used during every day or festive and ceremonial activities. Many researchers stubbornly consider it the color of mourning. This is a Christian tradition that has nothing to do with the era when Paganism dominated. Slavs tried to comply after the implementation of Christianity. However, they couldn't dress in full black clothes for the commemoration, as it represented the equivalent of calling upon death. Slavs also perceive the black color as Earth. This is a complex image. In combination with red, it enhances the protective effect of the ornament. Black is the fertile Mother Earth; this color was assigned to protect women from infertility.

YELLOW

The color yellow itself is considered a sacred color, a powerful one since it is the natural color of the sun. The yellow color is often used in military paraphernalia to denote a direct connection with the gods. Yellow, like red, is perceived to be a noble color. Both colors can often be found on the ornaments that adorn clothing, arms, and the neck. Yellow is bordered by another shade, gold. Traditionally, the nobility could afford gold.

Yellow is also associated with the solar cult. It was a solar symbol of the sun's energy, healing, honey, and wheat, which signifies wealth, prosperity, and well-being. When used in a sacred pattern, embroidery represents the material wealth of the owner. The sunflower is also considered a solar plant, and its references are always solar. Yellow is also the warm color of wood, and wood is perceived as a building material and the primary source of heating. The sacred role of a log home and a source of warmth in winter is difficult to underestimate. It represents home, comfort, and completion. In clothing and embroidery, yellow is worn mainly by married women. In ritual activities, yellow can only be used in combination with red and is worn mostly by the priesthood. Yellow is the color of wealth, autumn harvesting, and the color of gold. It represents dignity and nobility.

WHITE

White is an exciting concept to talk about. The most significant binary opposition in Slavic mythology was between white and black. This was expressed primarily in the Slavic Gods—grandfathers Belbog ("White God") and Chernobog ("Black God"). It was believed that these two monoliths led the branches of two pantheons: the first, the good and light gods, the second, the dark gods.

The main element of Slavic ritual clothing is a white sundress or a long shirt made of flax, nettle, or hemp thread. These clothes represent a person's bright thoughts, her desire for good deeds. On any Slavic holiday, a person will appear in a white shirt. In the wedding tradition, white is a symbol of purity and innocence.

Traditionally, Slavs buried deceased loved ones in white ceremonial cloths, and the people who came to say good-bye to the dead always wore white clothes. It was believed that the person has departed the Earth to feast with the light gods, which was something to celebrate. Essentially, the funeral was a "farewell" celebration with songs and dances. Interestingly enough, as I mentioned earlier, in Japan they still see the departed off in white clothes. Additionally, white snow has always symbolized the death of nature. A correct understanding of white is essential for cultural studies, including a complete and accurate understanding of Slavic mythology. White is a strong cultural marker, and its symbolism is interesting and multifaceted.

GRAY

Gray is an "unremarkable" color; it stands on the verge between white and black, and herein lies its duality. Gray is considered a strong color. Psychologically speaking, it is the color of fatigue, detachment, even depression. It disguises a person in a crowd, making him insensitive to the environment and merging him with reality. This duality factor is one of the main motifs in Slavic folklore: the hare and the wolf, the two most famous heroes of the Russian fairy tales, are both often referred to as "gray," but their habits are fundamentally different.

The duality between the hare and the wolf in Slavic folklore represents contrasting qualities and characteristics. Although both the hare and the wolf are often referred to as gray in folklore, the hare is specifically associated with the epithet "gray." The hare (*zayats* in Russian) is typically portrayed as a clever and resourceful character. In many tales, the hare outsmarts larger and more powerful foes using wit and cunning. The hare is often a symbol of quick thinking, agility, and intelligence. Its ability to outwit predators aligns with the idea that brains can overcome brawn.

The wolf (*volk* in Russian) is often portrayed as a more powerful and cunning antagonist in Slavic folklore. It may also symbolize danger, threatening the story's protagonist. In some stories, the wolf may also represent the darker, more aggressive aspects of human nature. The wolf can symbolize danger, strength, and the untamed forces of nature.

In the context of Slavic folklore, these animals serve as archetypal characters that embody certain qualities and lessons. The duality between the clever hare and the formidable wolf may reflect the complexity of human nature and the challenges individuals face in navigating a world that requires both intelligence and strength.

In Russia, gray was historically considered a color suitable for wearing when traveling, since dust is less noticeable on gray. In the spiritual circles of the Slavs, the deep gray color was considered a symbol of philosophical maturity and wisdom. Pagan priests often wore gray robes for very important ceremonies, such as naming a child and initiation.

Gray is sometimes seen as a neutral color, balancing between the extremes of black and white. It may symbolize harmony and equilibrium in nature and life. In some contexts, gray is associated with wisdom and maturity. It represents the accumulation of experience and knowledge over time, suggesting a seasoned or mature perspective. Gray is a versatile color that can adapt to different surroundings. It may symbolize the ability to navigate through various situations and environments with flexibility.

Gray is often found in the natural world, such as in the colors of stones, clouds, and certain animals. In this context, it may be associated with the Earth and natural elements. In some spiritual traditions, gray represents a state of transcendence or a merging of opposites. It suggests a connection between the material and spiritual realms.

And of course, duality: As mentioned earlier in the context of the hare and the wolf, gray may symbolize the duality present in nature and human nature. It reflects the coexistence of contrasting qualities and can evoke a sense of ambiguity and mystery. It exists between light and darkness, and this in-between quality may be linked to the unknown or hidden aspects of life.

The association of the color gray with Stribog aligns with the symbolism of gray in Slavic tradition. Stribog holds a prominent place in the pantheon of Slavic mythology, and his attributes often include aspects related to the natural elements, especially the wind. The connection between the color gray and Stribog can be interpreted in the following ways:

Wind and Air: Gray, as a color, may evoke the imagery of the sky, clouds, and the movement of air. Stribog's role as the God of Wind aligns with the atmospheric and ethereal qualities associated with the color gray.

Wisdom: The gray color's association with wisdom may complement Stribog's role as a deity associated with knowledge and insight. Wisdom often implies a nuanced understanding of the complexities of life, much like the subtle variations within the color gray.

Neutrality and Balance: Gray's neutral quality can be linked to the idea of balance, and Stribog's role as a wind god may involve maintaining equilibrium in the natural world.

Transcendence: The color gray's representation of ambiguity and mystery may reflect Stribog's connection to the unseen forces of the wind, which can be felt but not always seen.

It's important to note that interpretations of symbolism can vary, and the association of gray with Stribog may have nuances specific to certain regions, myths, or individual beliefs within the diverse tapestry of Slavic folklore. Gray clothing may be chosen specifically for ceremonies, rituals, or religious observances dedicated to Stribog. The act of wearing gray could be part of a larger ritualistic expression of reverence. Gray, as a color associated with Stribog, becomes a visible marker of one's identification with the divine realm.

The choice of specific colors for different deities and spiritual practices is a common phenomenon in various cultures, including Slavic traditions. Colors often carry symbolic meanings, and their selection is intentional, reflecting the attributes, characteristics, and energies associated with particular deities or aspects of spirituality.

8

The Ancestors in
Haitian Vodou

People often ask me how and why I came to practice Haitian Vodou. Vodou and Slavic traditions, seemingly disparate at first glance due to their geographical and cultural origins, share striking similarities rooted in their historical experiences and spiritual foundations. Both traditions have endured the challenges posed by external forces such as colonialism, slavery, and oppression, shaping their resilience and adaptive nature. Furthermore, the oral transmission of knowledge plays a pivotal role in both Vodou and Slavic practices, emphasizing the importance of storytelling, memorized songs, proverbs, and legends in passing down cultural and spiritual heritage through generations. The reverence for ancestors is a common thread that runs through both traditions, underscoring the significance of familial and ancestral connections in shaping individual spiritual paths.

Both Vodou and Slavic traditions share a profound emphasis on honoring and respecting ancestors. In both belief systems, the ancestors are regarded as integral figures whose influence extends beyond the temporal realm. The practices of Vodou and Slavic traditions involve rituals, ceremonies, and prayers dedicated to the veneration of ancestors, recognizing their role as mediators between the spiritual and earthly realms. The ancestral connection serves as a foundation for cultural identity, shaping the spiritual paths of practitioners in both traditions.

Additionally, the syncretic nature of Vodou, blending Catholicism with Indigenous African beliefs, echoes the syncretism observed in Slavic traditions as they absorbed influences from various cultural and historical contexts. Furthermore, the Christianization of the Slavs led to a syncretic blending of Pagan and Christian elements. Despite the distinct cultural landscapes that birthed Vodou and Slavic traditions, their shared emphasis on survival, oral tradition, and syncretism highlights the universal themes that unite them on a profound spiritual level, and parallels can be drawn in terms of the syncretic blending of Indigenous and Christian elements, cultural resilience, and adaptations made by communities in the face of religious and cultural transformations.

I do not want to mix up their respective practices when serving the lwa, but I can syncretize Vodou and my ancestral practical aspect of the work. In my personal experience, being a Haitian Vodouisant requires more self-discipline than being an adherent of many Pagan deities by today's Neopagan standards. I have adopted the principles of the Haitian Vodou faith because I fundamentally disagree with much of modern Paganism and new age witchcraft, which lack a clear focus on ancestors. In comparison to those traditions that have kept their pedigrees for centuries, this is a serious mistake for those who created the modern Pagan religious practices.

THE HISTORY OF HAITIAN VODOU

To understand Haitian Vodou as a culture and religion, you need to understand its history. Haitian Vodou is a syncretism of Catholicism and traditional religions from various regions of Africa. The forced migration of Africans through the slave trade to the West Indies, where they brought their traditional religious practices, and the attempts by European slave owners to convert them to Christianity, particularly

Catholicism, set the stage for the blending of these diverse belief systems. The fear of slave uprisings and the desire to control the enslaved population influenced the way Christianity was imposed on the slaves. The superficial and vague form of Christianity presented to them aimed to limit the potential for rebellion by avoiding teachings that emphasized human dignity and personal worth. The restriction on gatherings, including religious services, further illustrates the attempt to suppress any form of collective organization that could pose a threat to the existing power structures. In this challenging environment, the enslaved people demonstrated resilience and creativity by incorporating elements of their African religious heritage into the Christian framework they were exposed to. The resulting syncretism, as seen in Haitian Vodou, reflects a complex interweaving of Catholicism with traditional West African beliefs, shaped by the unique experiences of the Haitian people.

This syncretic process allowed for the preservation of core beliefs and practices within an oral tradition, highlighting the adaptability and survival of cultural and spiritual elements despite the oppressive conditions of slavery. The parallels between Vodou and traditional West African religions underscore the continuity of a shared religious identity, albeit with variations influenced by syncretism, creativity, and diverse experiences.

The deliberate strategy of slave owners to separate enslaved individuals from similar linguistic and cultural backgrounds was a method employed to prevent the formation of cohesive groups that might resist their oppressors. By dispersing people with diverse languages, customs, and traditions, slave owners aimed to disrupt potential unity and alliance among the enslaved population. This practice not only hindered effective communication but also created an environment where individuals from different African regions coexisted with varying belief systems and cultural practices.

In this context, the enslaved people faced the challenge of maintaining a sense of identity and community amid the intentional fragmentation imposed by slave owners. The shared experience of oppression, coupled with the diverse cultural and religious backgrounds, contributed to the development of a unique syncretic religion like Haitian Vodou. The amalgamation of Catholicism with the diverse African traditions became a way for enslaved individuals to express their spirituality, retain a sense of cultural heritage, and foster a collective identity.

The syncretism in Haitian Vodou, blending elements of Catholicism with African religious practices, can be seen as a creative and adaptive response to the oppressive conditions of slavery. It allowed enslaved people to forge a spiritual system that resonated with their collective experiences while incorporating elements of their varied African cultural backgrounds. This syncretic process not only served as a form of cultural resistance but also provided a framework for community building and solidarity among the enslaved population in the face of adversity.

After Haiti gained its independence in 1804, the Vatican severed ties with Haiti until 1860. During this period, few Catholic priests lived in Haiti, and the last chapter of syncretism of the Haitian Vodou tradition emerged. Upon the return of Roman Catholicism to Haiti in 1860, the church began a long, but unsuccessful, campaign against Vodou, which culminated in an all-out war up until the 1940s. In the 1950s, particularly after the Second Vatican Council, the Catholic Church incorporated Vodou music, drumming, and dancing into the Catholic liturgy and worked to unite, rather than defeat, Vodou ministers.

Since 1970, fundamental Protestant sects, almost exclusively from the United States, have increasingly opposed Haitian Vodou, accusing its adherents of devil worship, suggesting cannibalism, and demanding that Catholic converts be completely severed from their Vodou connection.

In Haiti, most of the people practice Catholicism and Haitian Vodou at the same time. There is a well-known saying that Haitians are 80 percent Catholic and 100 percent Vodou. People usually attend mass at the church and then stop at the peristyle or other spiritually significant places for ceremonies on certain holidays. For the people of Haiti, mainly as a byproduct of a complex colonial history, this practice is considered natural. In recognition of this fact, in 2003, Catholicism and Vodou became Haiti's two national official religions.

RITUALS IN HAITIAN VODOU

Haitian Vodou has many things in common with Roman Catholicism. These similarities are ritual gestures, prayers, worship, and veneration of spiritual entities and saints, including colors and song rhythms associated with specific spirits. In Vodou and Catholicism, it is believed that help from the spirit world is much more likely if needs and desires are requested through a joint public ministry, because many harmonizing voices and intentions are considered stronger than individual ones. Thus, Catholicism and Vodou pursue the same goal of communication or other participation in deep mystical, collectively organized communication with spiritual beings.

Therefore, the two religions demonstrate more similarities in basic fundamental beliefs and practices than differences. It is striking how deeply rooted Catholicism is in the Haitian Vodou tradition. This connection also can be observed in the opening prayers of the Haitian Vodou ceremonies. Our Father, Hail Mary, and the Apostolic Creed are always pronounced in French in the same order. Universal Catholic gestures are also used in Vodou ceremonies, such as the sign of the cross accompanied by the recitation of the phrase (in French): "Au nom du père du fils et du saint esprit. Ainsi soi-t-il" (In the name of the Father, Son, and Holy Spirit. Amen). The purpose and meaning of these prayers are the same in both the Haitian Vodou ceremony and the Catholic mass.

In Christian religions and the Vodou tradition, baptism is a cleansing ceremony that marks the beginning of a new life and, for children and babies, brings a person to faith. Particularly in Vodou, it is more about looking at faith with new eyes, empowering and spiritually aligning a person. Phrases from the Priye Ginen (Prayer of Africa) are recited or chanted in a call and response method. It is similar to the Catholic responsorial, or "responses" of the community to the word of God.

The Priye Ginen is a very long prayer that loosely follows the framework of Catholic devotion known as the Litany of the Saints. It is sung to "open the ceremony" at the beginning of celebrations. The houngan (priest) or mambo (priestess) leading the ceremony will sing a verse, and then the congregation will repeat it responsively. The Creole character of prayer can be seen in the transition between languages and spiritual entities. The reception begins in French, transitions to Creole, and ends dramatically with *langaj*, or African words that have no known translation. Langaj is considered the ancient language of the lwa (the Vodou spirits, which are based on African deities and often syncretized with Catholic saints), and it acts a powerful direct connection with the spirits. Its correct use in ceremonies helps to *fe choffe* (warm up the spirit). It is believed that as a result of the evolution of the Creole language, the exact meaning of African words has been lost.

The early French portion of the Priye Ginen evokes the rhythms of the Catholic prayers and chants recited during mass. This part of the Vodou ceremony is solemn. There are no drums or dancing, and the congregation can usually sit face-to-face with the *hougenikon* (song leader) or mambo or houngan who is performing the ceremony. In a particularly formal setting, such as the final *kanzo* (initiation), a ritual known as baptism, worshippers do not sit but stand behind newly arrived initiates awaiting baptism as a sign of reverence and respect.

Vodou practitioners, known as Vodouisants, engage in a diverse range of rituals and ceremonies that involve the worship of various lwa, each possessing distinct characteristics and roles in their interactions with humanity. The inclusion of lwa that serve as rulers of the unnamed dead reflect the reverence for ancestral spirits, connecting practitioners to a broader, collective heritage. The emphasis on honoring both the unnamed dead, who are seen as ancestral figures for all, and the specifically named dead, which may include the practitioners' own ancestors, underscores the importance of ancestral veneration in Haitian Vodou. Ancestral connections provide a link between the living and the deceased and offer a source of guidance, wisdom, and support.

The practice of welcoming the dead during Vodou rituals and celebrations is notable. Through visions and possessions, practitioners believe they can receive knowledge and experiences from the spirit world. This interactive aspect of Vodou reflects a dynamic relationship between the living and the spiritual realm, fostering a sense of continuity and connection with the past.

Vodouisants believe that every person has a soul, in which there is both *gros bon ange* (great guardian angel) and *ti bon ange* (little guardian angel). Ti bon ange is the element that contains the individual qualities of a person. In other words, her character, personality, and willpower. The Vodou concept of the ti bon ange seems to correspond to the Roman Catholic doctrine of the soul, for Vodouisants believe that it "appears before Bondye to stand before the heavenly tribunal where it is arraigned for its misdeeds and must suffer the appropriate penalties," as written by Leslie Desmangles (*Faces of the Gods*, 69). The gros bon ange is the part of the soul that animates the body and keeps it alive; it is the life force. The ti bon ange leaves the body during sleep so that a person dreams, or as I say, "travels."

The belief that the ti bon ange leaves the body during sleep, allowing for dreams or spiritual "travel," corresponds with various mystical and spiritual practices found in different cultures worldwide. The notion of astral projection or entering a trance state is a common theme in spiritual traditions, reflecting a belief in the separation of consciousness from the physical body to explore other realms or dimensions.

It is the ti bon ange that leaves the body during rituals of the spirit possession in Haitian Vodou when a practitioner enters the trance state.

This happens during ceremonies and festivals that honor the lwa. This practice is a fundamental part of Haitian Vodou, and it is something that Vodouisants become very familiar with. During the ritual possession of the spirit, lwa takes control of the participant's body. A person who is possessed by the spirit "floats freely" as long as the spirit stays in the practitioner's body. The person will move, speak, and communicate as the spirit or ancestor and will give messages to the living. Once the spirit departs and the person returns to his senses, the majority of the time, he won't remember or know what happened during the time of possession.

In Haitian Vodou, the act of performing magical acts or rituals, often referred to as *wanga*, can involve invoking the spirits or lwa for assistance, guidance, or intervention. During these magical practices, a Vodouisant may intentionally seek possession by a specific spirit to enhance the effectiveness of the ritual or to receive direct communi-

Fig. 8.1. The author under the spiritual possession of Papa Legba, the lwa of the crossroads. Papa Legba walks with a cane, so when the spirit is invoked into a Vodouisant's body, they use a cane as well.

cation and aid from the spirit world. The process of summoning or inviting a lwa to possess the practitioner's body is a significant and potentially intense experience. It involves careful preparation, including purification rituals, offerings, and a profound understanding of the specific attributes and preferences of the invoked lwa. It requires a high level of expertise in handling spiritual energies. The practitioner must be able to maintain control during the possession, ensuring a safe and respectful interaction with the spirit.

Experienced practitioners such as houngans or mambos are typically the ones who perform such advanced rituals. They have undergone extensive training, often within the framework of an apprenticeship or mentorship, to develop the necessary skills, knowledge, and spiritual maturity to effectively navigate and channel the energies associated with spirit possession. The decision to summon a lwa into one's body during a magical act is not taken lightly.

It's important to note that possession in the context of Vodou is not a negative or frightening experience; rather, it is often considered a form of communication with the spiritual world. During possession, a practitioner may become a vessel for a lwa or spirit, allowing for direct interaction and communication between the human and spiritual realms.

Overall, the practices within Haitian Vodou showcase a complex blend of African, Catholic, and Indigenous beliefs, emphasizing the importance of community, ancestral reverence, and the dynamic interplay between the living and the spirit world.

THE ANCESTORS ARE WITH US

I am sweet and I am sour. I am Vodou.

HAITIAN PROVERB

Good and evil are not God's creations but man's. Therefore, they should not be regarded as absolute in value. A glance at everything that the human mind could imagine reveals nothing that could be considered absolutely "good" or "evil," except for the goodwill and kindness of a person's heart. All the talents we possess—courage, the ability to make decisions, intuition, intelligence, sharpness of mind, ability to judge, the ability to think, and perseverance—are desirable qualities for a person. But they can also be very evil if, and when, the will or character of the person using them is not good.

Haitian Vodou arises from African belief systems, and as such it is an ancestor-based tradition in which the dead play a primary role in the daily lives of believers. The ancestral spirits, "the ancients," continue to live, and they need to be remembered and honored to continue helping their living descendants. It's the very foundation of the Vodou tradition. The central doctrines of Haitian Vodou include the belief in one Supreme Being God (Bondye) who can only be worshipped through secondary deities emanating from him, nature, and deified ancestors; these entities are the lwa, which we have spoken about earlier. Bondye remains on the sidelines as he is "busy" with other things. Vodou practitioners serve the lwa to help people in their daily lives.

Since God is omnipotent but does not interfere, then everything we do is our own choice. We are entirely independent. That's why God gave us the lwa. Ancestors and spirits are sometimes emotional and sometimes devoid of emotions; they have their own characteristics and desires. Essentially, they come together to create the human mind. Not everyone looks at morality in the same way—everyone has their own understanding and makes their own choices.

Vodou is passed down from generation to generation orally, from mouth to ear, from eldest to youngest. There are no scriptures. A mambo or a houngan will never teach you online. You can have the theory for free, but you will never know the practice; that is, the complete "how." It's not possible. Usually, Vodou tradition and its secrets are handed down from one generation to the next inside the place of worship, the peristyle.

What we can share is that ancestor worship is an integral part of the Vodou religion. At the beginning of every Vodou ritual and Vodou wanga (magical or spiritual work), practitioners first invoke and honor their spirits' entire genealogy. Vodou practitioners believe that the visible world intervenes with the spiritual world. Ancestors play an important role—they communicate with their living relatives and guide and protect their loved ones in everyday life.

The emphasis on ancestral guidance and protection in Haitian Vodou highlights the significance of the relationship between the living and the deceased. In this spiritual framework, the concept of an ancestor extends beyond biological lineage to include spiritual ancestors. The relationship with spiritual ancestors is not solely based on blood ties but is also established through spiritual connections, rituals, and practices. The recognition of a spiritual ancestor is considered just as important as acknowledging a biological ancestor, emphasizing the broader and inclusive nature of ancestral connections within the Vodou tradition. These ancestors are often considered guides, protectors, and sources of wisdom for their descendants and the broader community. In Vodou, the relationship with spiritual ancestors is often fostered through rituals, prayers, and ceremonies conducted by practitioners, including houngans and mambos. These rituals may involve offerings, libations, and invocations to honor and communicate with the spirits of the ancestors. The spirits of these ancestors are believed to be accessible and can provide assistance and insights into various aspects of life. This inclusive approach means that the lwa, or spirits, can communicate with individuals regardless of their Haitian ancestry. The spiritual connection allows for a broader understanding of lineage and heritage, transcending biological ties and fostering a sense of community that extends beyond familial boundaries.

Furthermore, the idea that houngans or mambos may choose to teach and initiate someone who is not biologically their child underscores the openness and universality of Vodou practices. The tradition recognizes the potential for individuals from diverse backgrounds to engage with and be initiated into the spiritual teachings of Vodou, emphasizing a shared humanity and interconnectedness that goes beyond cultural or ethnic boundaries.

The mention of ancestors in the national anthem of Haiti further underscores the significance of this connection. The opening line, "For our country and our ancestors, we walk together," reflects a deep sense of unity and continuity. It highlights the idea that the journey of the Haitian people is intertwined with the legacy and guidance of those who came before them. This cultural perspective aligns with the broader African and Afro-Caribbean traditions, where ancestors are considered integral members of the community, actively participating in the daily lives of their descendants. The notion that ancestors "live, breathe, and take action daily" signifies a dynamic and ongoing relationship, where the spiritual realm is seen as intimately connected with the earthly existence of the living.

In Haiti, people believe that the worst thing that can happen to a person is being born into this world without family ties. You become a tree without roots. Whatever happens on your path, you can go astray very quickly. Our roots define who we are and where we come from, but as soon as we no longer know about their existence, anything can harm us because we have no one standing behind us.

Vodou recognizes a theology that can explain the nature of death and man's soul and further defines the spirit world's geography, including the afterlife. The entire spiritual world is called Ginen, which is synonymous with Africa and comes from a reference to the region of Africa called the Gulf of Guinea (present-day Togo, Benin, and Nigeria), from which many enslaved people were taken to the New World and Haiti in particular.

For Vodouisants, Ginen no longer necessarily refers to the geographical mother continent of Africa but a mythical island said to lie beneath the waters below the Earth—where both the dead and the lwa live. Ginen is called "the original home of all things in the universe" and "the place where dawn begins." Ginen is an idealized primordial paradise, an Africa untouched by human corruption, guarded by the group of lwa called the Gede (the spirits of the dead, and the spirit of the first dead human ancestor). It is from Ginen that deceased ancestors and lwa return when they are called to communicate with the living, and it is "here" that these same spiritual and biological ancestors greet the human soul after death.

I always say that if the branches of a tree are rotten, the root is already dead. Ancestors are the beginning of the existence of every person. We stand on their shoulders. Their blood flows in our veins, and their spirits surround us with bonds of the same blood. And for these reasons alone, we should respect our ancestors and invite them to "participate" in our daily lives. Those who came before us possess knowledge about our souls, us, and the world as a whole. We are just earthly beings, mortals who see only things that are in front of our eyes, but spirits who have existed in two different worlds for centuries can see much farther. When you honor your ancestors, it's a two-way street. You give what you receive. The crop you have planted is the fruit you will harvest. Respect yourself and respect them, and you will succeed.

In the Haitian Vodou tradition, we say that "we stand tall because we stand on the shoulders of our ancestors" because the foundation they build under us (whether good or bad, it doesn't matter) is still part of who you are today. You may have inherited materialistic values, moral values, cultural values, skills, a religion, or a belief, to mention a few. Who your ancestors were, what they did, what they achieved or did not, their mistakes, the lessons they had to learn, their hard work, their minds, hearts, and actions are all within you. You, as an individual, would not be who you are today without the foundation that was already built.

The Ancestor Altar

Vodou is our love and gratitude to our ancestors and the spirits. You need to understand how to honor and respect these entities because it is only thanks to their contribution that our freedom has become possible today. In Haiti, almost everyone has an ancestor table or ancestor altar in their homes. An ancestor altar is a very personal and special space that is specifically designed to help you communicate with your ancestors. Ancestor altars are usually very simple; they can be a table with a white fabric covering the top. At the center of the table there is usually an oil lamp in a white bowl and a glass of water, which is meant to provide spiritual warmth and refreshment to the ancestors.

There are only a couple of fundamental rules that guide what happens in this space. Everything about this table should reflect your family. Later, as you get to know your ancestors better by creating a stronger connection with them, you will learn what they need. When you start to hear them, they will tell you precisely what they would like you to include on their table. The creation of ancestral altars is very simple. Images of deceased loved ones, along with personal items or mementos that belonged to them, serve as a way to connect with and remember the ancestors visually. Please do not put any photos of the living persons on this table. Lit candles symbolize the presence of the spirits, providing illumination and representing the spiritual light of the ancestors.

Burning incense or aromatic resins is a common practice in many spiritual traditions. The smoke is believed to carry prayers and messages to the spirit world. Offerings of food and beverages are made to nourish and please the spirits. These offerings often include the favorite foods and drinks of the deceased during their lifetime.

Flowers, often fresh or in the form of arrangements, symbolize beauty, life, and the transient nature of existence.

A bowl or glass of water is commonly placed on the altar to quench the spiritual thirst of the ancestors. Water is also a symbol of life and purity. A clean and preferably white cloth is often used to cover the altar, signifying purity and respect for the sacred space. Items with special significance to the deceased or symbolic of the spirit world may be included, such as religious symbols, stones, or other meaningful objects.

The arrangement of these elements can vary based on the personal and cultural preferences of each person. The ancestral altar serves as a place for prayers, remembrance, and communication with the spirits of the ancestors. Practitioners may engage in rituals, meditation, or offerings at the altar to maintain a strong spiritual connection with their forebears. The act of tending to the ancestral altar is a way of showing respect, gratitude, and a commitment to honoring the wisdom and guidance of those who came before. Above all, the table should be kept clean, with clean water and lit candles. Care for it just as you would care for the grave of your loved one.

Most Haitians offer daily service to their ancestors by pouring water for the spirits. In addition, on an annual basis, usually in November as part of the Festival of the Gede, they provide offerings to the deceased ancestors. Haitian Vodouisants will usually serve their ancestors at family grave plots in the cemeteries, at particular trees, or at sacred crosses that are part of the temple.

Since ancestors are the basis of all religious practice, it is very important that when someone from another culture starts to practice Haitian Vodou, she first needs to call or address her ancestors. If she doesn't first establish this connection with her family, it will lead to problems for her in the future; the person will encounter many obstacles in learning the tradition as well as many bad omens during her life course.

9
Witchcraft and Healing in Haitian Vodou

The tallest tree sees far, but the seed that travels sees even further.

HAITIAN PROVERB

As with many other branches of Afro-Caribbean religious traditions, Vodou doesn't distinguish between the roles of priest and doctor. It is expected that a mambo or houngan will cure diseases, both mental and physical. Haitian Vodou ranges from healing with homeopathic remedies, to preparing potions prepared for various diseases, to witchcraft and curses.

It is believed that there are two types of disease: Natural and non-natural. Vodou practitioners must know how to treat both types of disease. In the direct intervention, a spiritual illness is treated by the lwa, spirits summoned *mèt tèt* or "into a patient's head" (as the Haitian saying goes) by possession, either by the houngan or mambo performing the treatment or by another practitioner. They summon the spirit of a sick person or other lwa who can eliminate the root cause. Some treatments occur almost instantaneously; some take longer.

Then, after the spiritual problem is solved, the person is treated with special remedies for weakness and exhaustion. Natural diseases or injuries are treated with herbal teas, roots, special baths, and other treatments.

In Vodou, we conduct witchcraft—or spiritual work, as I prefer to say—on people. It is best to get something that belongs to that person for the houngan or mambo to manipulate this person best. You must at least have a full name, photos, hair, pairs of nails, and dirty clothes; all of the mentioned are appropriate when working magic.

The logic and structure of magic represent wanga, the practical part of Haitian Vodou. It follows the laws of association whereby an object that is directly associated with the person—for instance, the DNA present in a strand of hair—is directly linked with the person. These things continue to have magical power at a distance: magical power that exists between a person (his soul) in any part of him, such as human remains or earth from a grave, endowed with the power of the deceased, personal items, and so on. A Haitian Vodou practitioner who has taken possession of someone's hair, nails, or other parts of the body or personal belongings can influence this person with his will, at any distance, for absolutely any purpose. Although the objects themselves can be trivial and common, the faith of the practitioner who works with them gives them their true "power." The spiritual presence that governs the magical ritual when it is performed is more important than the magical principles of imitation and contact.

In traditional African religions, as is the case with a lot of folk magic around the world, it is believed that amulets are either endowed with an inner spirit (a spirit summoned into an amulet), or allow the user to contact the spirit directly, like a channel, and direct it in the right direction. This is usually where the bearer of the amulet is most needed at that moment. Gods, prophets, demons, saints, or the dead (depending on the faith of each individual and religious system) can be summoned with the help of a spell. In African American folk Hoodoo practices, the religious concept of the spirit dwelling in the amulet is sometimes lost. The user may believe the amulet itself is performing the desired action. The principles of imitative and portable magic and the invocation of the spirit behind magical work is to achieve the practitioner's goal through the choice of ingredients, such as magic itself and associated ritual actions.

Constructing a wanga is one of the most commonly requested magical works from the houngan or mambo. There are many different wangas and many different ways to "cook" them. Most of the wangas are the houngans' or mambos' personal secrets, and a few are "traditional," that is, they are known among all the Vodouisants in that specific line. Uninitiated Vodouisants also practice magic. Houngans or mambos djakout, bokors, kwakwa men, medsyen fey—these are just some of the uninitiated Vodouisants known for their successful magic. The terms *djakout*, *bokor*, and *kwakwa men* are less common in general descriptions of Haitian Vodou. However, it might be used to refer to someone who is skilled or knowledgeable in certain aspects of Vodou practices. Most of the time, they specialize in the tradition's darker or more malevolent aspects. They are often associated with sorcery, curses, and the use of supernatural forces for personal gain.

Medsyen fey translates to "leaf doctor" or "herbalist." This individual specializes in the knowledge and use of herbs and plants for medicinal or magical purposes within the context of Haitian Vodou. They may work with natural remedies and spiritual practices related to herbalism. It's important to note that the roles and specializations within Haitian Vodou can vary, and different communities or lineages may use slightly different terminology.

But initiates differ from noninitiates; the initiates have a close relationship with the lwa, which gives them great opportunities and significant help to solve their problems and those of their clients. The initiation/dedication ceremony enhances and clarifies the ability to create wanga, puts you in direct contact with the lwa, and lets you in on the secrets associated with properly working with them.

Houngans and mambos have an arsenal full of magic when they approach someone's problem. Sometimes spells require the client to do some work on their own, sometimes all the work will be performed by the houngan or mambo. Much more often, it will be lwa in the houngan or mambo's head who will cook the wanga and create the ritual itself.

Many different charms can be created to solve people's problems. Houngans and mambos must have a tremendous amount of knowledge to practice magic because the number of different problems they face throughout their life and work with clients is endless. Some people want to get rid of their enemies calmly; others do not. Some are seeking new love; others need to get an old lover back, find a job, call on luck, get rid of bad luck or a curse, divorce their partner, be successful in business, cure sickness, to name just a few.

It is not unusual or inappropriate to use magic against enemies in Haitian Vodou. In Vodou, we attack those who attack us; but of course, we try not to get into situations in which we are attacked and can be harmed. Sometimes, the houngans and mambos are able to disperse their enemies calmly. Sometimes the situation vanishes. In other cases, enemies will be forced to retreat.

Houngans and mambos also work with *pwen*, meaning a living force or a creature that exists outside of time and space. Since pwen is considered alive, it must be cared for with respect on a regular basis. An example of this can be seen in processing ritual initiation objects or the Vodou tools that practitioners receive during initiation. The *asson* or sacred rattle of the houngan or mambo must be kept clean in a sacred place and also ceremonially "fed" on the altar at least once a year. Another example is ceremonial beads, *kolye*, which represent a specific spirit that must also be fed once every year, two years, or five years, depending on the rules of a particular Vodou lineage. Pwen has unique attributes. The most famous of these are associations with specific objects such as roots, leaves, flowers, foods, drinks, and unique rhythms.

Pwen exhibits a multidirectional movement that is also reciprocal and balanced. The Vodou act of creating pwen reflects this type of movement. When someone prepares pwen (makes someone a talisman for good luck, for example), the practitioner first winds a thread or fabric on a designated object in a specific direction at a controlled speed. The practitioner then repeats the exact movement of the same object but in the opposite direction. This alternating action continues until the practitioner feels that pwen is complete.

The concept of pwen in Haitian Vodou is very significant and plays a crucial role in the practices of houngans and mambos. It is considered a dynamic and potent source of energy that practitioners can harness for various spiritual and magical purposes. It can be associated with a particular lwa or a specific aspect of spiritual power. It represents a concentrated force that practitioners cultivate, maintain, and utilize in their rituals and magical workings.

In Haitian Vodou pwen does imply a spiritual or magical orientation and intention. A pwen is considered a point of spiritual power or a living force that practitioners intentionally work with for magical and ritualistic purposes. This can be a ceremony, a lwa, a sacred object, a spell, a song, a dance, or a special ritual or service to the ancestors (all dead family members), for example continuing every Monday for three weeks in a row. Essentially, this is what focuses and gains tremendous energy.

The traditional public Vodou ceremony is pwen, manifested through a group of practitioners and the use of specific spaces, objects, regalia, actions, songs, dances, or gestures that "call" spiritual entities to "do the work." There are also other types of pwen; these are not available to the public but are conducted and prepared in secret. It is also important that pwen in Haitian Vodou adapt to the needs of their practitioners. While Haitian Vodou maintains its general structure and rules, practices have evolved based on social, economic, and political status.

There is also a nonritual use of the term *pwen* in Haitian culture. In particular, the personal power of the uninitiated can be a kind of pwen. For example, if a Haitian gets hit by a car but nothing happens to her, not even a single scratch, Haitians often say "Se pwen cap travay," which means that the person's luck saved her from harm. This broader interpretation aligns with the understanding that spiritual concepts, even those rooted in rituals and formal practices, can also be woven into everyday life and language. It highlights the cultural and spiritual perspectives that shape how individuals perceive and explain various aspects of their experiences, including instances of luck, protection, or survival.

The kanzo ceremony is the biggest pwen in Haitian Vodou. It goes on for almost two weeks; people pray, sing, cook, dance, nurture, grow and prepare herbs, craft objects, play instruments—all to accumulate energy for new initiates. We will discuss the power of initiations in more detail in the next part of this book.

PART 2

Transitions, Initiations, and Burial Traditions

10
An Initiation as a Rite of Passage

A person's rite of passage to a new stage of development is called initiation. Initiation serves as an individual's ceremonial journey to a new developmental stage. These rites come in various forms, such as shamanic, military, professional, and coming-of-age ceremonies. Regardless of the specific type, all initiation rituals share the commonality of guiding individuals from one status to another. In the context of traditional practices, particularly those ushering individuals into adulthood, the primary aim is to shift them from the world of childish irresponsibility and naivety to a reality that demands personal responsibility and willpower. Complete personhood, as seen across various cultures, involves not only one's natural and biological self but also the acquisition of a higher cultural and religious dimension. This transformative process occurs during initiation ceremonies, which persist globally, shaped by diverse customs and beliefs.

In many cultures, a child is taken away from his parents and sent to take tests (real or symbolic) at a certain age. Usually, initiations occur in sacred places far from away settlements, such as in the forest, prairie, caves, fields, and so on. This knowledge is necessary for a person to become an adult. It is believed that it can be given to him by the spirits of his deceased ancestors. A person needs to be transferred symbolically to the realm of the ancestors, to another world, the space of the dead. Therefore, symbolically, the actual space where the initiation takes place needs to resemble the space of another world.

The concept of spirits was always ambivalent in early civilizations, and the dead could bring both good and evil to the living. Therefore, the dead were feared and revered as a source of various kinds of knowledge: predictions, advice, and experience. In particular, it was believed that the knowledge necessary for a person to become an adult could only be given to her by her deceased ancestors. To obtain that knowledge, she had to go to the Kingdom of the Dead—that is, to temporarily "die."

The journey to the afterlife was never an easy task. At first, a person had to "die" successfully so his ancestors accepted him as one of their own. He would subsequently safely return to this world without losing his humanity. These experiences could be thought of as symbolic, or they could be thought of as an actual exit from and return to this world; some cultures today still believe the latter. Amulets and special rituals were supposed to guarantee a person's safe passage to and from the other world. A person was dressed in special ritual clothes, and special magical attributes were used to make the intersection of worlds clearer. It was customary for those undergoing initiation to be buried (symbolically) in graves in the ground or covered with branches. After some time in this place, the person would meet with a being from another world.

A real entity could appear to a person during a shamanic initiation, a spirit that would later become his assistant. During a coming-of-age initiation, a shaman entered a special state of trance, and a spirit possessed his body. This practice is also common in Haitian Vodou.

One of the initiations we can talk about as a rite of passage is a wedding. In many traditional cultures, the wedding ritual was a real mystery, during which the bride and groom, being in an altered state of consciousness (which was achieved with the help of complex shamanic techniques: special songs, ritual actions, ritual clothes, fasting, and so on) and playing out the sacrament of dying and the rebirth and connection of opposite principles, became entirely different people—adults and family members.

In a traditional Slavic wedding, many of the songs the bride sang in the first part of the wedding were related to death. She was preparing to go "beyond three forests, three mountains, and three rivers," that is, to another world. In some cases, she even sang about the shroud she wanted to receive as a gift. The word "bride" (*nevesta*) itself comes from "not knowing" (*ne vedat*) and means "unknown" or "impersonal"—like all the dead.

One may ask: Why do we need such challenges at all? After all, you can become an adult and a married person without any of these fancy rituals, can't you? Of course, physical and biological maturation occurs by itself, and no special ceremonies are needed to make it happen. But with a psychological transition to a new state, it's not so simple. Indeed, a person often continues to behave like a child even after getting married, and her parents continue to perceive her in the same capacity. And, of course, this usually has unpleasant consequences, including the collapse of a marriage. Perhaps the lack of a rite of passage for coming-of-age in contemporary culture is one reason why society is becoming increasing infantilized. Many people who have matured physically remain children psychologically. Of course, the rite of passage itself does not guarantee maturation either. Still, it can clearly demonstrate to a person and the people around her that she has moved to a new stage of psychological and social development.

Another important rule in interactions with the "ordinary sacred" was the principle of a special way of interacting with the world of the dead. The concept of the ordinary sacred is a way of acknowledging that the sacred is not always found in grand rituals or extraordinary experiences but is also present in simple, everyday activities and inter-actions. It highlights the idea that there is a sacred dimension to the ordinary aspects of life, and recognizing this can lead to a deeper con-nection with the spiritual or mystical. It suggests that even in ordinary, day-to-day life, there is a sacred aspect that must be approached with a certain level of reverence and distinction, especially when dealing with the spiritual realm or the world of the deceased.

The other world must be treated differently and not how a person is accustomed to behaving in his day-to-day life. This has major psy-chological and magical significance; after all, if you keep the door to another world constantly open, it can impact the living world in ways that no one would enjoy. For example, followers of Slavic traditions believed that a person must communicate with the deceased in the form of a chant that sounded like wailing; if not, then the deceased would not understand them. The wailing took the form of a recitation reminiscent of crying, with a clear, rhythmic structure: a non-rhymed verse that began with traditional words but spiraled into an impro-visation. Traditionally, wailing was performed exclusively by women. The wail was often accompanied by tears, swaying from side to side, a wringing of hands, and other actions that made the situation more dramatic.

Psychologically and ritualistically, wailing is a technique that leads to a change in a person's state of consciousness, allowing her to enter a trance. With the help of wailing, two things are achieved: First, in such a state, it is easier to contact the other world to obtain the neces-sary information. Second, the act of wailing provides "protection from foolishness." After all, the wailing makes it quite difficult to acciden-tally perform a rite of passage and, thus, unknowingly open the door to another world.

Wailing was a universally recognized form of communicating with representatives of the other world. People believed it necessary to wail at funerals, at memorials to the deceased, and when they wanted to turn to the dead for help. However, traditionally, a wail was to be performed before noon, and it was strictly forbidden in the dark because undesirable spirits could hear the wail and respond to it. It was even impossible to mourn a person if his death occurred at night as it was imperative to wait until dawn.

It's believed that otherworldly creatures themselves engage in acts of wailing. For example, some people believe that mermaids wail this way when asking for clothing gifts. And, odd as it may seem to you in the contemporary era, wailing was traditionally used during a wedding; namely, in the first, "sad" part (we will discuss the wedding rituals in more detail in chapter 12). This element of a folk wedding was present in the Russian tradition and those of almost all Eurasian communities. When the traditional wedding ceremony began to decline (in approximately the second half of the nineteenth century), it was this custom that suffered the most. At first, the wailing was significantly reduced and lost its original format. Ultimately, it completely disappeared. However, to this day, people have preserved traditional Russian wedding lamentation songs, and they are fascinating to listen to. The wedding lamentation is one of those parts of the wedding ritual that makes it an initiation ritual and a mystery, allowing the bride and groom to take a symbolic (and psychological) journey into another world and return as new people.

Attention to such transitional moments in human destiny is something that we should learn from traditional culture. After all, especially during these transitional stages, people need to be aware of their reality and not confuse, for example, the role of a child with that of an adult or the role of the dead and living. The latter happens all the time—a person dies, but his relatives still cannot come to terms with the death and continue to treat him as if he were alive. Psychologically, this reaction is very understandable, but from the point of view of the rules of energy exchange, this is a big mistake. It violates the established order of the flow of energy in the family system, as we have discussed earlier in this book.

TRANSITIONAL RITES
AND UNDERSTANDING DEATH

It is not surprising that modern people have forgotten how to interact with the dead. After all, the transition of the living to the dead is a natural process. This is how the world works, the cycle of nature; this is who we are. And if you cannot truly realize that death is real and part of your existence, you will not understand that life is real. You will probably witness the deaths of your older relatives before you die yourself. However, you may not recognize that you constantly interact with the energies of death in your everyday life. Take, for example, food: by eating, you take away the energy of a living entity, even if it is "inanimate," like fruit and vegetables.

To avoid disrupting the harmony of the system, it is necessary to maintain a balance between the living and the dead, recognize the importance of both states, and follow the rules of their interactions. People can properly let go of a deceased being so her spirit can continue to exist safely in other forms, and the energy remaining from her will not bring harm, but benefit.

Transition rites are special rituals that societies use to help their members at key moments in their lives. These life transitions follow recognizable patterns of behavior in all cultures, for example, when babies are given names, when young people enter adulthood or get married, or when people pass from the world of the living to the world of the dead. For a new "me" to appear, the old "me" must die, symbolically or literally, through the ritual. Each end is the beginning of something new.

Let's take a look at funeral rites as a specific example. Funeral rites represent a rite of passage that can be observed in the vast majority of human societies. They mark an individual's transition from the status of "person" to the status of "ancestor." Numerous changes in identity are associated with burial sites, including the status of the deceased, the relatives left behind, and members of the wider community. The time spent preparing the dead for burial or cremation is a transitional phase as well. At this very moment, the dead are neither what they were nor what they will become.

These transitional moments are often associated with uncertainty. People pay tribute to the dead, celebrate their former identity with them, express their grief, and, through doing so, confirm their continued relationship with the deceased.

Cultural principles usually determine the preparation and final disposition of the body and prescribe a period of mourning for the close relatives of the deceased. These are unique to each society. Rituals of death, like many other human behaviors, are an expression of the culture, attitudes, values, and ideals passed down from parents and grandparents. Each person learns these values as a member of the society and family to which they belong.

The ritual of death begins when a person stops breathing or is otherwise recognized as dead. The body can be washed, anointed, shaved, combed, dyed, or scented. It can be left naked or clothed, covered with a shroud, and sometimes adorned with jewelry. The body's mouth, nose, and rectum may be blocked, possibly to prevent evil spirits from entering it. In the modern-day era, the purpose of securing a body's orifices is to prevent the leakage of bodily fluids. Some cultures place coins or weights on the eyelids to keep them closed so the corpse does not "look" at the living or to ensure a person can "pay" his way to the other world.

When a death is announced, family, friends, and neighbors all gather together. People express their grief by crying, screaming, singing dirges, and so on. At the death vigil that precedes a burial (or another form of final disposition), mourners "sit with the corpse." In some cultures, the goal of this practice may be to ensure someone is present in case the dead stir and come back to life or to protect the soul of the deceased from malevolent spirits and, thereby, defend the deceased's soul against a spiritual attack. Alternatively, the purpose may be to give support as a companion to the poor soul recently separated from its bodily home.

Inhumation, or burial, is probably the most common way to deal with the remains of the deceased—although the position of the body in the ground varies by country and tradition. The body might be buried lying on its side or back, seated, or bent over. Often, it is buried with "grave goods" such as jewelry, tools, or weapons. In some traditions, the body is buried temporarily, exhumed after some time has passed, and then reburied in a second ritual. For example, cemeteries in Greece are so overcrowded that bodies are often only kept in the ground for three, seven, or twenty years. The families then have to exhume the body. The bones can be kept in a building known as an ossuary if the family can afford it, or they are buried at a different cemetery.

All dedication rites follow a standard pattern. The rite of separation is followed by the rite of transition and then the rite of reunion. Separation, transition, and reunion are a part of each life cycle ceremony, although each is emphasized differently depending on the tradition and occasion. Separation rites are important upon a person's death, during the transition into the afterlife, pregnancy, betrothal, coming-of-age, and marriage. Separation means giving up a previous social status to transition to a new social position. To be born is to pass from the world of the unborn to the society of the living. To die means to leave the world of the living and enter the home of the ancestors.

The transition from one status to another is gradual. A person enters a transitional or enlightened period, a sacred and dangerous time during which normal, ordinary activities come to a halt. The person is suspended between two worlds, between the past and the future, between her previous status and a new one.

In ancient Egypt, death was considered the beginning of the afterlife. The cult of the dead was an essential part of Egyptian culture. It was believed that corporeality was unchanged in the afterlife, so the Egyptians became very skilled in the art of embalming and mummification and in the construction of pyramids used as tombs for the pharaohs. In the Christian tradition, death is the cessation of sin introduced into the world by free beings, fallen angels, and man. This is not the destruction of life but the cleansing of its sinful nature, the liberation of the soul from the captivity of sinful flesh so it can pass into perfect eternal life. In Hinduism, death is believed to be a transition from a lower level to a higher one, a gradual improvement of the spirit, which must eventually reach the Absolute.

In many cultures around the world, people link death with birth. The exit of one person from the family system requires him to be replaced by someone else. For example, in Chinese culture, after a person dies, his grandson or granddaughter must either marry or have a child. In Jewish culture, there is a custom to name a newborn child by the name of the closest deceased relative. In almost all cultures, there is a belief that contact with death transfers a person into a sacred dimension. Only by touching death (in reality or symbolically) does a person learn the value of his life, become genuinely human, and comprehend the greatness of the universe and his place in it. Only through knowledge of death can we reach the true depth of understanding, including the understanding of life itself. Death is terrible, but we lose the ability to see reality in all its diversity and richness by turning away from it or closing our eyes when faced with it.

When people are alive and among other living beings, they rarely recognize the enormity of life as a gift and how much an ethereal spirit longs to receive a physical body and reincarnate on Earth. And as often happens with gifts that are not appreciated, people cannot take advantage of the opportunities that life gives them every day and every minute, often only arriving at that understanding when they are on the verge of their death.

On the topic of funeral and memorial rituals and the range of ideas that they express (death, life, immortality, the soul, good fortune, ancestors), we touch upon the very core of traditional Slavic culture. All researchers of Slavic antiquities agree that death and the deceased ("grandfathers," "parents") belong to a unique, pivotal place in the Slavic faith. This was true also for the archaic pre-Christian segment, which is usually referred to as "folk Christianity" or "Christian-pagan syncretism" or dual faith. The tradition of honoring the dead is the most intense moment in the religious life of the Slavs and, in general, was integrated into church life without difficulty to become one of the distinguishing features of the Orthodox Slavic tradition. In the field of ethnology, funeral rituals are the most necessary and richest source of describing and interpreting the other traditional rituals of the people and calendar cycles. The code of conduct for funerals demonstrates the connection between weddings and funerals, and this is especially significant.

The obscured symbolism of other rituals may also become clearer when researchers discover information about funerals and memorials (this is especially true for Slavic Christmastide and the rituals of the winter solstice).

Funeral rituals clarify (often quite unexpectedly) the most ancient motifs of Slavic folklore. A researcher of Slavic lullabies will undoubtedly note their close connection with the metaphors of death and burial. The oldest genres of oral folk poetry help clarify some information about burial rituals, making them a verbal parallel.

The material of traditional burial rituals is essential not only for the reconstruction of some fundamental ideas of Slavic Paganism, but also for general theoretical, typological definitions of the ancient religious system of the Slavs, which scholars usually and, in my opinion, erroneously, try to reconstruct according to the model of classical polytheism of the Greek or Germanic type. The systematically presented information about burial and memorial rites can become essential to the arguments about issues such as Prince Vladimir's artificially codified Pagan pantheon and methods of reconstructing the functions of his gods (Volos, Perun, etc.) or the genesis of Slavic folk demonology, including the Domovoy, mermaids, and Leshy.* We will explore Slavic burial rituals in more detail in the rest of the book.

---

*The Domovoy is a house spirit or god of a given kin; he is usually represented as an old man but could manifest in the form of animals. Mermaids are water spirits, see the box on pages 95 to 96. Leshy are guardian spirits of the forest often depicted as masculine with horns, but could assume any shape; like most creatures, they could be either harmful or helpful to humans depending on the circumstance.

11
Haitian Vodou Initiations

Vodou cosmology focuses on developing a cohesive community group in which people support each other. Individuals are initiated into this group via special ceremonies through which the individual regresses through life stages leading to the death of the old self and the birth of a new self. As part of the ritual, the initiates are subjected to days of seclusion in the *djevo* (initiation chamber), during which they regress through childhood, infancy and, ultimately, death. At each stage of the process, they are treated in a manner befitting these life stages. Eventually, the initiates experience rituals that enable them to relinquish fear, selfishness, and pain to be ultimately born again not as individuals, but as a collective consciousness. Having been initiated into Vodou, the individual enters a new state of maturity through which he is at one with all living beings and the four primary forces of nature: earth, water, fire, and air.

The initiated leave the seclusion chamber with their heads covered and remain as such for forty days following the initiation. The process of initiation represents a moral lesson in and of itself: it serves to challenge the bounds of knowledge and power, celebrate truth and faith, and challenge the forces of life and death via an experience in brotherhood and humility. During the ceremonies, the initiates share their moral dilemmas and life conflicts. During these ceremonies, the role

Fig. 11.1. A salute during a Vodou ceremony led by the author. The author is making an offering with a bottle wrapped in the color of the lwa being honored; sprinkling or pouring alcohol at specific times symbolizes reverence and connection with the spiritual realm.

of the song leader (called *hougenikon*, often a mambo or houngan) is to choreograph the process through which Vodou overcomes these moral dilemmas and enables the initiates to understand their choices. This role involves delicately balancing the choice and rhythm of the music, the spirits' arrival, and the possession rituals.

In Haitian Vodou, there are three different levels of initiation. The concept of mèt tèt represents a central aspect of the individual's spiritual being. Mèt tèt is usually placed into the initiate during his first initiation into Vodou, but it can be placed also during his *lave tèt* (literally "washing the head") ceremony. The first initiation is often a significant and transformative experience in many spiritual traditions, and it marks the beginning of the individual's deeper involvement and connection with the religious or spiritual practices of Vodou.

Fig. 11.2. Saluting a lwa with ritual items: a sword,
a burning candle, and offerings

Hounsi (sometimes called *hounsi kanzo* or *hounsi senp*) are members
of the family (congregation) of Haitian Vodou. They are responsible for
assisting in ceremonies with saluting the spirits, organizing materials,
preparation and setup, cleanup before and after ceremonies, and much
more. Saluting the spirits is a vital part of any Vodou ceremony or ritual
to acknowledge the lwa and show them respect. Saluting is accompanied by specific gestures, words, and offerings. Hounsi represent the
vast majority of a Vodou society and are intrinsic in the function and
flow. This level is considered the basic level of initiation.

Mambo su pwen or *houngan su pwen* (sometimes written as *si pwen*
or *sou pwen*) are priests and priestesses with the same responsibilities as
hounsi. Su pwen initiates hold the asson (ritual rattle), but it is considered "borrowed" until they are ready to be initiated at the next level. Su
pwen can perform divination and spiritual work for their clients.

Mambo asogwe or *houngan asogwe* are the highest level of initiations available. Some folks describe asogwe as the high priest of Haitian Vodou, but I tend not to use that term because it overlooks the fact that the most knowledgeable person in the temple might be a hounsi who has been serving the spirits for fifty years. Instead, an asogwe priest carries the most responsibility. An asogwe can initiate others; or to be more exact, he can bring other people to the lwa Papa Loko to receive the asson. Asogwe has access to the full range of tools for spiritual work, and the "license" to speak with any spirit on behalf of a client or themselves. Asogwe is expected to know all aspects of the ceremony and spiritual work, so it is an ongoing learning process that lasts a lifetime.

Haitian Vodou requires strict adherence to African *reglemann*, meaning the rules or law of worshipping the spirits. This knowledge is taught, as a rule, by an elder during initiation and for several years after, because it is a whole religious system that simply cannot be learned during the short period of the initiation rite itself.

12

The Slavic Wedding as a Rite of Passage

According to the Eastern Slavic tradition, a bride gets married in the same dress in which she will be buried. In this chapter I will discuss wedding traditions after Christianization of Rus to show how the lines between Paganism and Christianity blur in this regard. We are accustomed to imagining a Russian folk wedding as several days of unrestrained and tireless fun, where guests drink a lot of alcohol, eat a lot of food, dance to the point of exhaustion, and sing until they're hoarse. However, during the Middle Ages, the Russian ceremony was a sad affair (not the whole wedding from the initial matchmaking to the wedding feast, but the ceremony itself). In Russia, a wedding day was a funeral rite for the bride and was officially considered the bride's funeral; as such, she wore a mourning dress.

Our ancestors believed that a bride "died" as a member of her father's family and was "born" into her husband's family. This was marked by a week of lamentations and wailing right before the wedding. (As we discussed earlier, wailing is the method used to communicate with the world of the deceased.) The bride said good-bye to her parents, her single female friends, and her life as an unmarried woman; young, single girls were specially trained back then to lament and sing tearfully. The bride mourned herself as a deceased person. In the Novgorod region (Russia), brides still sing about the shroud they want to receive as a gift.

During the weddings of the Middle Ages, the bride, crying, often turned to the cuckoo bird with a request to convey a message to her parents, because the cuckoo was considered a bird that flew freely between two worlds. The cuckoo holds great meaning and importance to Eastern Slavs; it is one of the most mysterious and mythologized birds, the main figure of several omens, beliefs, and ritual actions. The cuckoo holds special significance in Eastern Slavic folklore, and its behavior and characteristics have contributed to the creation of various myths, omens, and beliefs. Here are some aspects that make the cuckoo a mysterious and mythologized bird in Eastern Slavic traditions:

Nesting Behavior. The fact that the cuckoo does not build its own nest but instead lays its eggs in the nests of other birds is a unique and notable behavior. This behavior has led to symbolic interpretations, with the cuckoo sometimes representing cunning or slyness. But it also has a negative interpretation. The host birds unknowingly raise the cuckoo's chicks alongside their own, often at the expense of their own offspring. The symbolic associations extend to notions of unfaithfulness or neglectful motherhood. The cuckoo's behavior can be seen as a metaphor for taking advantage of the efforts of others, representing cunning and opportunism.

Repetitive Voice. The monotonous and repetitive cries of the cuckoo, particularly during the breeding season, have captured the attention of people. In some beliefs, the call of the cuckoo is considered both mystical and prophetic. It is often associated with the arrival of spring and is sometimes seen as a foreteller of events or a bringer of change. It is also considered a mournful and repetitive call that has led to associations with death and mourning. In certain cultures, the call of the cuckoo is considered a lament or a wail for the dead. This dual nature of the cuckoo's symbolism reflects the complexity of cultural interpretations.

Symbolism. The cuckoo's behavior may symbolize different things in Eastern Slavic folklore, such as unpredictability, transformation, or the cyclical nature of life. The idea of the cuckoo laying its eggs in the nests of other birds might be interpreted as a metaphor for unexpected events or influences entering one's life.

A significant number of cuckoo-related beliefs concern love, marriage, and fertility. In addition to having prophetic significance, the cuckoo also has a magical effect, with tradition asserting that those who first hear the cuckoo will benefit from health, happiness, or wealth. Cuckooing and the first appearance of the cuckoo are credited with the ability to heal diseases. In some legends, the cuckoo is a grieving widow turned into a bird; a wife waiting and calling for her dead husband; or a sister mourning her brother's death. In folk ballads, it is a daughter driven out by her parents who, yearning for her home, turns into a cuckoo and flies home. In Russia, there was a belief that tears dripped from a cuckoo's eyes and onto a tree branch when it cuckooed. The word *kukovat* (to cuckoo) held the meaning to "cry, grieve, lament, complain."

In folk wisdom, the cuckoo personifies unbearable heartache for departed loved ones and acts as an intermediary between the worlds of the living and the dead. In some areas, it is customary to sing along with a cuckoo. Women who have lost their loved ones go deep into the forest and, upon hearing a cuckoo, begin to lament and cry about the pain they've accumulated. They say the cuckoo itself flies up to such a woman and "consoles" her. She then asks the cuckoo about her loved ones living in the other world and, through the bird, transmits requests and orders to the lost souls seeking their help and guidance.

There is also a belief that a bird can predict bad things: Its cry is said to be a bad omen. The cry of a cuckoo near houses is a sign of crop failure that coming season. If the cuckoo is positioned on the roof of a house, it is taken as a sign of death, disease, or fire. An alternative belief is that if a cuckoo cries directly in front of your eyes in the early stages of spring, you will cry all year; if it cries right behind you, you may get sick and even die. When a cuckoo cries at sunset, it is a sign of death and misfortune. Using a cuckoo's cry to foretell your death is a commonly known method of fortune telling. Young women use cuckoos to ascertain how many years they have left before they will get married.

In folk custom, the cuckoo was also seen as a heavenly messenger that announced the onset of summer and the beginning of thunderstorms and rains. In ancient times, people used its voice to judge the future harvest: If a cuckoo cried out at sunrise on a "green tree," the year would be a fruitful one; if it cuckooed at night on a "bare tree," there would be hunger and pestilence. Hearing a nightingale before a cuckoo in spring meant a happy summer, and hearing a cuckoo before a nightingale meant an unhappy one.

A twig from a tree on which the cuckoo sang its song has magical properties. It was worn as an amulet to protect against misfortune. Hunters carried it in their pockets in the hope it would bring hunting success. Women would make a circle with a cuckoo feather along the inner edge of a jug before pouring milk into it. They believed that this "charm" would help form an especially thick layer of sour cream in the jug.

In love magic, the root of the orchis plant was often used. This plant was colloquially known as "cuckoo tears," because people believed that the specks on the leaves of the orchis are traces of bitter tears that the cuckoo cries from being lonely. Newlyweds were given a decoction made from this root so they would live in love and harmony. Given the importance attached to cuckoo symbolism, it is unsurprising that it was associated with the bride and her symbolical death.

Returning to the bride, on the eve of her wedding, a bride was sent to take a bath in a specially prepared bathhouse. This was not for hygiene's sake; rather, it represented cleansing the body as if before a funeral. Our ancestors considered the bath to represent a sacred act by which anyone could communicate with the world of the dead. Originally, the

Russian-Eastern Slavic bathhouse was a small room or building designed for wet or dry heat sessions, heated with a wood stove. The steam and high heat make the bathers perspire. The bathhouse for the Slavs served as a place where the two main forces of nature—water and fire—met. Baths were often associated with overcoming evil, cleansing from filth and all negativity. It was later that they came to be considered a symbol of hospitality. To welcome guests, the owners would offer to "heat the bathhouse."

Before the wedding, dowry and wedding clothes were usually prepared, which also had a sacred meaning. The white dress was directly associated with the other world; according to legends, such clothes were also worn by the other world's inhabitants—mermaids, ghosts, and angels. As the bride was considered an otherworldly being, it was dangerous to look her in the eye; as such, she covered her face with a veil. It was also undesirable to touch her bare skin. Therefore, elegant embroidered gloves were an obligatory part of wedding attire, or the groom would have to hold the bride's hand through long, low-hanging tassels, sleeves, or a towel.

In Russian tradition, it was customary for the bride to sew her wedding dress, or at least part of the wedding dress—usually the undergarment. After the wedding, the bride could sometimes wear this undergarment on special occasions as a talisman; she also kept the veil and used it as a talisman. For example, she would use it to cover her child if he was fussy or ill.

The traditional head covering, which later became the modern veil, was originally intended to hide the bride's gaze, which was once considered to have the same ill-fated consequences as a witch's gaze. In Ryazan (a city in western Russia) brides are still called "mermaids." Nowadays, this is a metaphor, but back then, it wasn't. Mermaids were considered the "lost dead," who died before their time. They would drift between the worlds of the living and dead—and bring evil to the living—until they reached the originally intended age of their death and died for good. Brides were the same.

An important event during the prewedding period was what we know today as a bachelorette party—the last time the bride met with her close female friends—their ritual farewell. This was also when the ceremony of "untying the braid" took place. In traditional culture, hair was one of the most important magical symbols. Girls would not cut their hair throughout childhood—it was considered their life power and wisdom. As such, it is not surprising that special manipulations with hair were an integral part of a wedding ritual.

After the bride's parents gave their blessing, the wedding procession would leave for the church. The bride rode with her matchmaker and, in some cases, lay on her lap, pretending to be dead. She would carry a broom in her hands—a talisman against evil spirits—that would enable her to return to the world of the living. In the Kostroma and Rostov provinces (western Russia), the wedding procession usually stopped by the cemetery on the way so the ancestral spirits would not be offended that what once belonged to them was being taken away.

After the marriage ceremony, the bride changed her white dress for a bright one (usually red) and was considered a married woman. She no longer lamented, the wedding ceased to be sad, the time for cheerful

Fig. 12.1. Wedding procession on their way to the church
(Painting by Alexander Alekseevich Buchkuri, 1913)

songs came, and the wedding feast began. The ceremonies that took place at this time were designed to indicate a new relationship; the bride would call her father-in-law "father" for the first time, and mother-in-law "mother," and so on.

Much time has passed, wedding ceremonies have been forgotten, and many symbols have changed. Now the bride doesn't hold a broom as an amulet, but a beautiful bouquet that complements the image of a newlywed. The veil has replaced the head covering, and its purpose is purely aesthetic. Wedding parties no longer go to the cemetery, though some couples lay flowers in front of an eternal flame in Russia and Ukraine.*

The idea of a bride as a *laminar* (from the Latin *limen*, "threshold") between the world of the living and the world of the dead has its roots in the era of preclass societies and is found in many cultures. Here, we are talking about the rudiments of rites of passage (initiation), which allow a person to change the status of her existence, such as birth, coming of age, marriage, and death (the number of stages varies from culture to culture). All these ceremonies had one thing in common: they were all necessary for successful contact with the world of the dead.

Omens and Superstitious Tips of Old Believers for the Wedding Day

- If the bride is given roses, she should carefully cut off all the thorns with scissors, ensuring she does not prick herself.
- A bride must wear a wreath with a veil on her head. There should not be any flowers inserted into the hair, and she should not wear a hat or a tiara.
- The bride should put on her dress first, pushing her head up through the collar.

---

*The eternal flame is a continuously burning fire that symbolizes the memory of fallen heroes and freedom fighters. By Russian law, it's an element of every military memorial structure.

- A friend who has the same name as the bride cannot help her get dressed.
- The dress should have an even number of buttons, if any.
- If the bride's hem rips during the wedding, she cannot hem the dress herself.
- Young couples should be seated at the table on a shaggy fur coat or sheepskin coat with the fur facing outward so they will be wealthy.
- The spoon that the groom uses to eat must be put away until the fortieth day after the wedding. On the fortieth day, the husband can use it to eat again, and the couple will have a happy and long life together.
- On the wedding day, it is good to plant a tree for the bride and groom to help them put down "roots" together.
- When the young couple has wreaths on their heads during the wedding in a church, they should not look into each other's eyes, or there will be betrayal in their future. They should not look at their candles, either. They should only look at the priest.
- Couples should leave through the doors they first entered through during the wedding. Otherwise, there will be a disaster in their future life together.
- Matchmaking: Dates including the numbers 3, 5, 7, and 9 are good days.
- No matchmaking on Wednesdays or Fridays.
- The wedding ring should not fit over a glove.
- If the bride wears a hat on her wedding day, it means the couple will divorce.
- To ensure her son-in-law is a good partner to her daughter, the bride's mother should put a pin in her bra near her right breast on her way to the wedding, and pin it on her bra near her left breast on her way back. When she arrives home from the church, the mother should put this pin on her daughter's skirt. The pin should not be removed until after the skirt has been washed once.

- When putting wreaths on your children, make sure there are not three people of the same gender behind the groom and bride when walking into church, or the children will get very sick.
- If the couple uses their wedding tablecloth on the anniversary table on their wedding anniversary for three years in a row, they will live to a ripe old age.
- If the groom or bride drops something during the wedding, no one should pick it up (flowers, gloves, etc.).
- You shouldn't hold a wreath over the heads of the bride and groom in a church when they get married. The wreaths must be placed on their heads.
- A wedding dress, veil, and shoes cannot be rented or sold to anyone.
- You should not give wedding photos to everyone. It is very easy to put a curse on them. As a newborn baby, a new bride is vulnerable and unprotected since she just "came to life" again.

THE BROOM IN SLAVIC FOLKLORE

In Slavic folklore the broom is an important symbol. In general, the broom represents money and the destruction of grime, of both the physical and nonphysical variety.

The wedding broom has its own specific place in the Slavic belief system. Traditionally, the wedding broom is a bunch of birch branches decorated with ribbons that was made by the bridesmaids. The broom stands in the red corner of the bride's home for the entire prewedding period. On the day of the wedding, the bride hands out ribbons from the broom to her friends. Because they don't yet have their own wedding brooms, they use the ribbons to decorate a Christmas tree, a burdock bush, and so on. It was believed that a wedding broom symbolized the loss of girlish beauty after marriage.

Some common beliefs related to brooms in general are as follows:

- You cannot use an old, worn-out broom, or insufficient money will come into your home; you will always be in need.
- Sweeping the floor in the evening means sweeping money out of the house—all your wealth will be lost. Sweep only in the morning and only take the garbage out after the sun goes down. Otherwise, you will take all you have and throw out all your riches; you will always be in financial trouble.
- You cannot sweep for three days after close relatives have visited your home. Otherwise, they will no longer visit you at your house.
- If people who aren't kind to you are coming to visit you all the time, you need to immediately sweep the floor once they leave. It will guarantee they won't return to your home.
- Keeping an old broom in the house will cause illness and lead to financial losses.
- Place a new broom by the front door with its brushes facing up to invite money and good luck into the house.
- After a departed person has been taken out of a house, the floor must be swept, and the broom that was used must be thrown into the trash.
- A broom should be thrown into a strong wind or burned, but it's better to put it in a bag and put it into a trash can while saying:

> You have served me well.
> You swept away my troubles,
>   and your time has come to an end.
> Thank you for everything!

In the old days, people believed that when someone moved house, Domovoy visited the new home on a broomstick. The house owner would go to the middle of the kitchen, put a broom on the floor, and say: "My dear master Domovoy, sit down and come with me." He would then take the broom and drag it along the ground to the new house. Nowadays, you can carefully move it with you in a vehicle.

Domovoy could also be invited in a boot or a sandal made of bast. Bast is a fiber obtained from the bark of trees, such as the linden tree; strips of this fiber were woven and shaped into a shoe traditionally worn by poorer people in Northern Europe. This boot or shoe containing the Domovoy would then be carefully carried to the new house and placed in the northwestern corner of the home. The homeowners would then position a saucer of milk and bread in front of it. If the milk in the saucer disappeared during the night and crumbs were scattered on the floor, it indicated that the Domovoy had successfully moved with them and was satisfied with the new home. The broom was then placed in its traditional place on the threshold, and the shoes could be hanged in the house.

If there were no changes to the saucer of milk and bread, they treated the Domovoy with sweet candies, milk, baked goodies, and so on. He would forgive the owners for changing homes and would settle

Fig. 12.2. Sandals made of bast
(Photo by Maxim Shanin, cc by-sa 4.0)

into the new house. The homeowners had to perform a ritual to please Domovoy for seven nights after moving into a new home, leaving goodies for him each evening. On the eighth day, they had to thank him, respectfully and lovingly addressing him with a promise not to disturb him anymore.

Domovoy's attitude could be determined by the behavior of children and pets, who see what many adults are unable to see. If they were healthy, cheerful, calm, and happy, Domovoy was taking care of the family. If they became shy or aggressive for no apparent reason, were cranky, or started to get sick, the family needed to improve its relationship with the Domovoy.

The Domovoy are very similar to the Scottish household spirits called brownies or broonies, who are said to come out at night to perform various chores, but only if they are treated with respect. Brownies protect their master's well-being with dedication. Still, they're also very touchy and vindictive, just like Slavic Domovoy. If they don't get a bowl of milk, cookies, or beer at the right time, these spirits begin to harass pets and then people. Children won't want to clean up their toys; they'll be naughty, become hyperactive, lie to their parents, and get into all kinds of mischief. There will be problems in the house, like plumbing and electrical issues, arguments, heavy atmosphere, and so on. Furthermore, the homeowners won't be able to drive him out no matter what they do; they'll have to sell the house.

THE THRESHOLD IN SLAVIC FOLKLORE AND ASSOCIATED OMENS

When a young woman gets married, she must wash the threshold in her parent's home with soap and a scrub brush to erase the traces of her energy, so she won't get divorced and run back to her parent's house. The next time she returns to her parent's house, she will be a guest.

Some other common beliefs related to the threshold are as follows:

- You must not step on the threshold, as Domovoy love to sit and relax on it and might be accidentally kicked and hurt.
- Sitting or standing on the threshold is also prohibited. "Whoever sits on a threshold will miss out on happiness." A threshold has never been a porch designed for gatherings. You will never see your fate from the threshold.
- If you stand on the threshold with the doors open, money will escape your house.
- You must not hold a conversation on the threshold. You might develop an illness, as the energy of the border between the worlds will taint your energy.
- You should only step over the threshold with your right foot when you leave the house. Otherwise, you will encounter many obstacles that day; whatever you do, you will find only "closed doors."
- You should greet any guest before the threshold and allow him into the house ahead of you. This enables you to close the "protective circle" of your home and remain the master of your space.
- It's forbidden to greet someone or say good-bye from across the threshold of your home. The energy of health should remain in the house. The energy of a farewell should remain beyond the threshold, separate from the home space.

The underlying belief system regarding the threshold is simple: Anything, especially any object, held over the threshold (the border) carries a different quality of energy of external and internal space; one "gives away" and another "owns what's given." These are the energies of different houses that belong to different people to be forced out of the lives of both the giver and the taker. If you give something to someone, you must do so inside the house to ensure information about the gift or loan stays contained. Space will inscribe everything in the house's energy of cause and effect, creating a returning flow of energy of love and kindness. It will show you gratitude for your sincere gift or help.

Our ancestors endowed doors with special magical meanings: doors to heaven, doors to hell, doors to the universe, doors to the world, and so on. All peoples have developed their protective system of door talismans and amulets that protect a dwelling from the intrusion of "base" energy influences. The ancient Greeks placed an image of Hecate, the goddess of magic, witchcraft, the night, moon, ghosts, and necromancy, and the most important figure in the history of magic and witchcraft, on doors. The Jews nail a box with selected texts from the Hebrew scriptures to the doorjamb to protect the home and frighten away evil. In China, the images of two spirits who served as the house's patrons were placed on doors to protect the home. In the Gospels, Christ is defined as "the door to the Kingdom of God." But the most basic and universally important function that a door fulfils is as the gateway through which the energy vibrations of people and objects enter and leave a house. Doors are a portal between the inner and outer worlds. Naturally, a door should be surrounded by a powerful positive energy field and stand as a barrier to negative manifestations. All bad things should remain outside the door of your house. Therefore, our ancestors protected the integrity of their earthly matrix with the help of various symbols and amulets with protective qualities.

13
Bridges and Crossroads

We all encounter bridges and crossroads in the course of our lives, in a metaphorical sense as well as a physical one. Perhaps bridges and crossroads guide us to carefully and productively use the tools found at every step to reveal our potential and create our reality. The magic of bridges themselves within witchcraft practice is not well known, because they are customarily viewed only in the context of the specific magical working to be performed, where they are used as a complementary tool.

Nevertheless, bridges are widely and frequently used by practitioners all over the world, because they are one of the leading "tools" in magic. They cover a wide range of meanings—accomplishment, implementation, achievement of balance, to name a few. Ultimately, the meaning will be different for everyone. The magic of bridges can sometimes have absolutely no rules of execution. It can be spontaneous but no less powerful. Bridges represent transition zones that obey laws unknown to us. It is here we meet with the lost. Furthermore, on the path that unites two conditional "shores," we can release what is no longer useful for us.

The bridge itself is a striking symbol of connection between two points separated in space or time. There is a clear division in this context: We talk about the bridge as a physical object or consider it an allegory. The bridge is a link connecting two points separated by something, but its symbolism is broad. It would be enough to say that, in ancient times, bridges were considered the creation of the devil. The human mind itself could not think of such an "amusement." Perhaps partly due to such representations in many fairy tales, the hero of the tale meets with the devil, and this meeting typically takes place on the bridge. It is a well-known fact that folklore reflects the realities of the time of its creation. Therefore, the devil and witches on stone bridges can often be found in the "old Grandma's tales" we all used to hear before bed. Well, at least in my family.

The meaning of a bridge as a transition between worlds of different properties is directly associated with change. The transition from Point A to Point B, as a change of location, from one state to another, from bad to good, from light to darkness. A bridge built over water is symbolically any action aimed at achieving something or getting rid of something. The essence is a transition from one state (for example, lack of something) to another, emergence, acquisition.

Again, the magic of bridges is essentially the magic of transformation. Another example of the magic of bridges is when you may, at a specific time, completely unplanned, coincidentally pass on the bridge exactly when a nearby clock strikes the hour. You may think it is a coincidence. But after analyzing the events that preceded the chime, as well as your mood and thoughts at that very moment, you will most likely identify your inner readiness for the fundamental life changes that lie ahead.

A bridge, especially one that crosses a river, is an extremely powerful place. There is a popular expression "from the bridge to the water," which means an extreme degree of despair, a state from which there is no turning back, death. Many rituals specifically necessitate the use of water that has been taken from under a bridge because this water has long been considered special and to possess very specific properties. Other rituals involve throwing something from the bridge into the passing river. The origins of the symbolism of the bridge as a way of transitioning from one state to another should be sought in mythology.

In almost all world traditions, you can find references to bridges connecting the world of life with the world of spirits.

In Haitian Vodou, the role of bridge between the heavens and the Earth is fulfilled by the *poto mitan*. The poto mitan is the pole found in the center of Haitian Vodou temples; it is a representation of the connection between this world and the world of the spirits and ancestors. The poto mitan forms the central point around which Vodouisants serve the lwa and conduct celebrations and ceremonies. It is both the center of the ritual dances and the path taken by the lwa to come to the human world. It links the heavens with the depths of the Earth—the real world with the spiritual world. It serves as a bridge from one world to another, a transition and passage.

The poto mitan is usually decorated in in lively colors and ceremonial designs (*vèvè*). A vèvè is a geometric design associated with each of the lwa, and it acts as a spiritual communication line to that lwa. The practice of making vèvè is said to be based on an African tradition in the Dahomey (modern-day Benin) region. During Vodou ceremonies, vèvè for specific lwa are drawn on the floor of the temple in cornstarch and Vodouisants dance over them during the course of the night.

Fig. 13.1. Saluting the lwa by pouring offerings onto a vèvè

Fig. 13.2. The author and others performing a salute to the lwa Danbala; the author holds the asson in her right hand and a plate of offerings (flour and eggs) in her left.

The vèvè can also be created as a permanent piece of art to communicate with or honor the lwa. The poto mitan has vèvè for two major lwa: Danbala and his wife Ayda Wedo. Danbala is said to be the Sky Father and the originator of all life; he is represented as a great white snake. Ayda Wedo is known as the Rainbow Snake and lives in the sky with her husband; she is the lwa of fertility, rainbows, wind, water, fire, and snakes. Both these lwa were traditionally worshipped in Dahomey. On the poto mitan, Danbala and Ayda Wedo are represented in the form of two snakes with their heads situated at the two ends of the post.

The division of the worlds into the independent realities of Heaven, Earth, and the Underworld is found throughout world cultures. The Italian magic tradition called Stregheria required the appearance of some connecting bridges as ways through which communication was carried out between the forces of higher and earthly beings. The most obvious symbol of connection we often see refers more often to the lunar deity than to the sun. Night is the time of magic (*streg*) when practitioners can read the messages of the stars and recognize the signs of fate in positions of the astronomical bodies.

The mythology of the origin of Stregherian deities goes back to the goddess Diana, the creator of all things, the founder of witchcraft, and the mistress of witches. In the world's divine pantheons, Diana—the goddess of life, darkness, and magic—is often compared with Hecate. Many parallels between these deities can be noted in the myths that tell their stories.

The meaning of the word *dia* (from the Greek διά) is "separation, division, movement through." One of the myths about Diana describes how she sent her daughter Aradia (whose father was Lucifer, "carrier of light") to Earth to teach people magic. Some researchers, including keepers of authentic knowledge about the Stregherian tradition, tend to believe that Diana, taking care of the preservation of world harmony, sent her daughter to Earth to monitor the observance of the universal balance of light and darkness. Dia separates and draws a clear dividing line, border, and frontier between perfect light and absolute darkness.

Hecate is also considered the goddess of the frontiers, and she constantly keeps the property of the divine "scales" balanced between light and darkness. Only the observance of this balance preserves life on Earth and, since the first days of the emergence of life on it, recognizes the magic of life itself and, naturally, death. Like the wise Aradia, the goddess Hecate teaches humanity witchcraft.

All gods in all traditions have accompanying animals, birds, or other representatives of the animal world who are their helpers and guides. They carry out a special mission as the executors of the highest will. With the help of animal spirits, the gods find a way to get in touch with weaker creatures, people, who cannot perceive the true divine form and endure their strength. Aradia's guide is an owl. Interestingly, in Latin the word for owl is *strix*, and its etymology leads to the ancient Greek word στριγξ, which means "screamer."

The influence of the ancient beliefs of the Etruscans (ancestors of modern Italians) on many religious and mystical movements is obvious, and many elements of *la vecchia religione* ("the old religion") noticeably overlap with Christian myths. The latter, in turn, are based on Jewish mythology in many of their aspects. Thus, it becomes impossible not to recall the "demon of the night," Lilith, who is often presented as a half-woman, half-bird—a naked maiden with the wings and talons of an owl. The demon Lilith was called the Owl.

It is noteworthy that living beings taking part in the creation of worlds usually do not need special bridges to carry out their actions. Birds, which often become conductors of divine will, move through the air and across the sky as the bridge. In the Nordic tradition, these are usually ravens, like the legendary Huginn and Muninn, the ravens of the God Odin. Huginn, whose name translates from Old Icelandic as "thinking," is responsible for the thought process as an aspect of the mind, and Muninn, which translates as "remembering," is responsible for memory. Odin sends the ravens to fly around the world so they return and bring him truthful news. In other traditions, various insects can be divine guides—for example, flies, the ruler of which is Beelzebub (Baal-Zebub), who co-rules with Lucifer.

Slavic mythology commonly features fish and other animals. For example, Pushkin's "The Tale of the Fisherman and the Fish" is a classic example of interpretations of authentic folklore motives. A goldfish served as a grantor of wishes and a messenger from the Underworld. In another tale, "Ruslan and Lyudmila," Pushkin described a wolf guide. We also observe the wolf motif in the Russian folk tale "Prince Ivan and the Gray Wolf." The gray wolf serves as a guide in the form of a horse on which Ivan rides to Elena the Beautiful. The mythological significance is, again, noted as obvious parallels between the mythologies of different cultures.

A guide horse carrying a hero away to other worlds is a typical element of shamanic mythology. The horse acts as a guide to the

Underworld, the world of the dead. A tambourine is also referred to as a horse because it helps the shaman reach a trance state that allows him to go beyond his consciousness and move between different worlds.

There are no random things in the world of magic. The closest and seemingly fantastic intersection and fusion of mythologies, in fact, can be explained by quite simple phenomena. If you carefully read the texts of folk poems and fairy tales, you will notice special nuances that clearly came from shamanism as the fundamental principles of ancient Paganism.

PRINCIPLES OF MAGIC WORK ON BRIDGES

The bridge can be stretched over anything and connect any points with each other. For example, a board thrown between two elevated parts of land, such as a bush or a stone gorge, functions in practical terms in the same way as any other bridge—it serves as a means of passage. If the structure acts as a bridge through a gorge, abyss, or ravine, it is called a viaduct, from the Latin words *via* ("way") and *duco* ("led"). The term itself hides a special symbolism because any path is taken by someone for something, and you can travel the path in different ways. However, the esoteric—or perhaps it would be more correct to say magical—meaning of the bridge over the land will be fundamentally different from a bridge over a river or lake. The combination of the elements and bridges of various types with their own history of origin give rise to a whole direction of witchcraft as a method of influencing people and processes. Before proceeding with the implementation of the practical part of any magic work, you should study the individual characteristics of the future parts of your ritual.

The Earth element allows you to materialize intentions associated with self-related meanings. Money magic, status transformation, and stability all work on the development of processes lying in the plane of material and physical resources and are carried out with the help of the element of the Earth. Also, negative magical influences, designed to destroy or "bury" something literally and figuratively, are often carried out with direct participation.

Bridges stretching over bodies of water carry different meanings. A bridge built over water signifies any action aimed at achieving something. First of all, as already mentioned, the bridge is a symbol in itself, unifying or transforming, like a transition. Second, water, an independent magical element known in all world traditions, sets the character of the actions carried out with its help. One of the main magical properties of water is its ability to memorize information that is at its disposal for some time (I will address this property of water in detail in chapter 14). All further actions associated with this information will be transformed by the will, intention, and actions of the person conducting the ritual.

Air conventionally collects and transmits nonconcentrated, disconnected bits of information. The air element affects the mood, the moral state of the individual but does not form the action, only setting the direction and, in some cases, prompting the goal. To a certain extent, the properties of air are similar to the tarot card the Star. The card often features a central figure, usually a woman, kneeling or standing by the edge of a pond or river. She is often depicted as nude, representing vulnerability and openness. In her hands, the central figure holds two jugs. From one jug, she pours water onto the land, and from the other, she pours water into the pond or river. This dual action symbolizes the flow of spiritual energy and the nourishment of both the earth and the soul. Both the card and the properties of air involve elements of inspiration, guidance, and setting a direction. Just as the air element sets a direction and prompts goals, the Star card may encourage individuals to take steps toward their objectives. It emphasizes the act of getting up and walking, implying a journey or progression toward a goal. In this metaphorical connection, the air element and the Star card align in their influence on thought processes, inspiration, and setting a course of action. Both encourage movement and progression, suggesting that achieving specific results requires not only intellectual clarity but also a willingness to embark on a journey toward one's goals.

The Star symbol is most closely related to the elements of air and fire and makes you wonder if bridges over fires are possible. Try to move over a fire from Point A to Point B without burning your feet or setting yourself on fire. The task is not easy and requires a high concentration of willpower and desire for implementation and courage; however, most importantly, understanding what this movement, this transition, and this "bridge" is for. The goal can hardly serve as a stimulus in this case. The goal is the future. It is unknown and exists only in theory until it is achieved as the outcome of a long-term plan of action. The past can serve as a great incentive for the dangerous and difficult passage over the symbolic bridge over a fire.

The past "burns out." "Burning bridges" to the past cuts off the option of returning, which means that one of the possible ways of solving any issue disappears. It becomes impossible to go back.

CROSSROADS

In terms of magic, any crossroads is a place of power. Crossing roads create instability of energy through which other worlds can appear. It is considered easy to contact the devil, demons, ghosts, and the gods when paths converge. The crossroads in black magic are perceived as a point at which the past and the future, the world of the dead and the world of the living, meet. It is here at the intersection that energy is absorbed and you can relinquish negativity, cure diseases, and eradicate curses.

Magic practitioners go to the crossroads with a problem and conduct a dialogue with those who can help. The summoned entities absorb the message sent to them and contribute to the implementation of the plan. Usually, the practitioner takes the ransom to the intersection, paying for the services rendered. Of course, spirits or demons are physically incapable of eating meat or sweets, drinking vodka, or picking up coins. But they absorb the energy of a payment and this leads to a mutual settlement.

In many cultures, a crossroads is a door that symbolizes the transition from the old to the new. The crossroads are a symbol of choice—the choice between life and death and a sign of the transition from one space to another. As such, the intersection has an ambivalent meaning. In some cultures, crossroads were considered sacred; the Greeks and Romans considered intersections to be under the protection of Hermes and Mercury, the patrons of travelers. At the crossroads, Hercules chose virtue over pleasure and Oedipus killed his father. The Greeks made sacrifices to the three-headed Hecate, the patroness of sorcerers and crossroads and the goddess of spirits and witchcraft associated with the Kingdom of the Dead. Hecate appeared in places where roads merged on clear nights, accompanied by spirits and howling phantom dogs. The Greeks left food for her at the crossroads. They also erected her three-faced statue, sacrificed dogs, and placed the bodies of the hanged there. They would pray to ask for help if someone was seized by madness since it was believed that the spirits of dead people sent this disease.

The Romans prayed to the *lares* (female spirits) of the crossroads, and statues of Hermes the Psychopomp, the driver of the spirits, were displayed there. In medieval Germany, trials often took place at the crossroads. In India, the god Bhairava, as one of the manifestations of the great god Shiva, was called to guard the crossroads on the outskirts of the village. Stone columns, phalluses, and statues exalted the vigilant Bhairava as the guardian of borders.

In Christianity, the crossroads, the shape of which is reminiscent of a cross, became a place at which to honor Christ. In Europe, crossroads were once seen as meeting places for witches and evil spirits. Christians installed crosses, chapels, and statues of the Virgin Mary at the crossroads. In African traditions, crossroads are often places of ritual performance where doors are open between two worlds. In Africa, each ethnic tradition has its own version of the god of the crossroads: Legba, Ellegua, Elegbara, Eshu, Nbumba Nzila, and Pomba Gira are just some of the African names (in several languages) for a spirit that opens the doors to the other world, guards the crossroads, and teaches wisdom.

In Slavic mythology, crossroads were considered the favorite "residence" of the devil and a place where you could see witches, mermaids, the devil himself, and demons. For example, in Transcarpathia (the Carpathian Mountain region between Ukraine and Romania), when pasturing cattle, sorcerers cast spells to protect the animals and buried salt with a piece of Easter bread under the path the herd used. The Slavs also commonly told fortunes at the crossroads.

During a mass epidemic that affected cattle in the Russian provinces, witches drew a cross at the crossroads with a plow and buried specially prepared remedies in the ground. This act symbolized that the entrance to the village through the intersection was closed for sickness and ill-wishers.

The dead souls of the unclean were believed to dwell at the crossroads. Victims of suicides, accidents, John Doe, and murderers were buried here, and nearby crosses and chapels were erected "for protection." On days of remembrance, grain was scattered for birds (souls) at the crossroads.

In many areas of the world, the spirits of the dead are believed to appear near the crossroads on the evening of October 31. This once Pagan and then Christian holiday known by many names (Veles's Night, Samhain, All Hallows' Eve, the eve of All Saints' Day) falls on the day when the line dividing the world of the living and the world of the dead is the thinnest. This thin veil means that the opportunities to engage with the ancestors abound, and often crossroads are part of these beliefs. For example, the people of Wales believe that spirits come to the intersections at night, and people's ancestors process back to the homes of their earthly ancestors; if a person stands at the crossroads and rests her chin on a forked stick, she can see the spirits as they walk.

Another Welsh belief was that if a person went to the crossroads and listened to the "wind blowing over the feet of the dead" (the east wind), he would hear the sighs from the houses in which a person would die in the coming year. Among the highlanders of Scotland, it was believed that if a person sat at midnight on a three-legged chair at the intersection where three roads merged, he would hear the names of those who were doomed to die soon. German folklore held that to find out this information, one must go to the crossroads between eleven o'clock and midnight on the eve of All Saints' Day or on Christmas night.

Road crossings were also given special importance in funeral rites. In one ancient Welsh custom, the deceased was laid on the ground at every intersection between the home to the cemetery, and prayers were read over him, perhaps as a protection from spirits who meant him harm. In Hesse (central Germany) it was believed that the ghost of the deceased would not return to the house if his dishes were broken at the intersection. In Finland, those in the funeral procession gathered soil from the crossroads they passed and scattered it across the fields as a means to protect themselves from witchcraft.

Many ethnic groups bury people who have committed suicide at crossroads. However, there are no reasonable explanations for this ritual. Perhaps this custom is attributed to the fact that the cross formed by the roads is associated with the consecrated ground of Christian cemeteries, where victims of suicide were not allowed to be buried. Or maybe it was designed to enable people to leverage the supernatural properties of intersections to prevent the ghosts of those who had committed suicide from returning to the living.

In many folk traditions, there is a belief that crossing lines of paths provided people with protection from ghosts which, according to legends, appear near intersections. For example, once widespread in Germany, one superstition was that spirits and ghosts could not cross intersections. Thus, they were a place of salvation for a person being haunted by a ghost or some demonic being. As soon as a person who was chased by the ghost reached the crossroads, the pursuer disappeared, usually uttering a completely inhuman cry. The Irish believed that crossroads were virtually immune to the magic of the fairies and that mortals abducted by these creatures could regain their freedom in such places.

Fateful encounters take place at the crossroads. If a family experienced the death of multiple children, people believed the best way to remedy the situation was for the father to go to a crossroads and invite the first person he met to become his child's godparent.

Many magical rituals start or end with a trip to an intersection, at which a specific rite is performed. For example, evoking and inviting a certain entity, leaving a ransom, throwing something away, burying or burning something. The manipulations carried out at the intersection vary significantly, but most often, diseases and damage are left in this place.

But why exactly the crossroads? What is it about these places? Why not, for example, an ordinary road or a roadside? A crossroads is truly a sacred place, especially X-shaped crossings. From the dawn of time, it was believed that human destinies and worlds intersected at crossroads. Every place had its own master—be it a house, lake, or forest. According to ancient Slavic beliefs, the god Veles, the patron saint of crafts and all living things, was found at a crossroads. Veles was a strong and wise ruler who guarded the border between Nav (the afterlife) and Yav (the real world, reality).

Our ancestors knew that the crossroads represented a place at which you could both find troubles and relinquish yourself of them. It was universally recognized that no good would come from picking anything up at an intersection. People knew that the more expensive item you found, the greater the sadness you would acquire if you took it. People would never eat at an intersection, and no one would count their money there. It was believed that not observing these rules could lead either to the attachment ("cohabitation") of evil entities or to an eternal lack of money. Older people taught that one should not cross the very center of an intersection because this would change life for the worse. However, if they found themselves in the exact center of the crossroads, knowledgeable people could cast a spell that, on the contrary, helped them acquire happiness and wealth. People also believed that they must not spit or yawn while at the intersection of the roads as it could have negative consequences.

TYPES OF INTERSECTIONS

It is worth knowing that not all road crossings are the same. Let's take a look at what types of crossroads exist in general and whether they are all suitable for the magic practices.

T-junction. This type of intersection is unsuitable for magical work. It is a not a true crossroads, and its energy is not conducive to magic.

Fig. 13.3. A T-junction
(Photo by C. O'Flanagan cc by-sa 2.0)

An intersection consisting of three roads. It is important to understand that all three roads come out at the same angle, from one point. In such places, you can cast magic, but success will depend on many factors: on personal strength, on the place itself, and so on.

An intersection where three roads intersect in one place. It resembles the Cyrillic letter Ж. The roads do not start at one point, as already described above, but they intersect. This option is also called "Devil's Crossroads." In this place various rituals are held, including communication with the devil, demons, the deceased, and representatives of the other world.

Fig. 13.4. An intersection of three roads
starting from one point
(Photo by Pavlo Klymenko)

Fig. 13.5. Three roads intersect in one point

Intersections where five or more roads intersect. It is not so easy to find those, but they are worth it, because these are extremely strong places in terms of energy.

Fig. 13.6. An intersection of five roads

Y-shaped intersection. They are not uncommon. Interacting with a given location can have different consequences. In this case, everything will depend on the place itself, as well as on the energy of the one who performs the ritual.

Fig. 13.7. A Y-intersection

An intersection of two roads, the so-called cross. This option is perfect for any magical practice. It is an elegant example of all of the power of the intersection in a spiritual sense. It is in places like this that magic happens. Ideally, the intersection should not be formed by two paved (with asphalt or gravel), but by two intersecting dirt roads. In ritual practices performed on the crossroads, ransom is very often used. It is customary to present the crossroads with money (especially coins), vodka, tobacco, and fresh meat (especially liver and blood in case you can't perform a sacrifice). However, sometimes the ransom may be different, it all depends on the ritual. If in the ritual it is indicated that the coins must be given away as a ransom, then you should know that they must always be thrown over the left shoulder.

Fig. 13.8. The four-way intersection: the cross
(Photo by Vasile Cotovanu, cc by 2.0)

A very powerful variation of this crossroads is a place where four roads converge to form an intersection; that is, two sets of parallel roads cross each other, making a hashtag shape.

Any practice at an intersection is a mystery. Having done the job, you need to go back in silence, without looking back. This rule must be observed especially strictly if you brought a sacrifice to the crossroads.

In the rituals of black magic, the crossroads becomes the place of the most correct completion; it is at the crossroads that the remains of ritual candles, photographs of enemies, ashes, extra sewing needles, and so on are left as your offerings to the Powers. At the crossroads, you can bury a magical artifact—for example, a witch's bottle—if it is impossible to throw it into the intended recipient's house. Verbal magic is very effective at the crossroads, when you cast spells upwind or against the wind—the wind brings it straight to your target.

Initiations also take place at the crossroads, and these could be applied not only to sorcerers. If you look at what is happening from the point of view of shamanism, the Spirit coming at the crossroads has nothing to do with the Christian Satan or the devil. While some may say that you "sold your soul" by performing rituals like this to gain some skill, none of the Spirits will claim your immortal soul. You can pay for being rewarded with a special talent by offering food, a silver coin, or simply by being present at the intersection—in good faith and fearlessly, with full confidence—for a certain number of days or nights. Then the spirit of the crossroads, "the black man," will teach you what you want for free. The spirit of the crossroads is a teacher who has ready-to-use recipes for specific, practical, useful skills. He will sharpen your skills, give you mental guidance, and provide spiritual support. "The black man" at the crossroads will not steal your soul and plunge you into fiery hell; he will not push you to ruin and force you to make a deal with him. He only hears your call, and then he teaches you by his example and gives you a piece of his strength.

The strongest days in terms of rituals are considered to be the days of the full moon and the days of the new moon.

Don'ts of the Crossroads

- Don't pick up anything at the intersection—you will find trouble. This rule is considered fundamental. We can say that this is not even a custom but a rule that must be strictly observed. There are many rituals in magic when all sorts of items (clothes, food, money, and jewelry) are left at the crossroads to get rid of problems and diseases, poverty, and failures. And the more expensive the item you pick up at the intersection, the more troubles you will invite. Everything from which someone else was freed, you will take upon yourself, only in a larger volume. Therefore, whatever you see at the intersection, never pick it up, even if you really need it.

• Don't eat at the crossroads. The crossroads is a very energetically powerful area, and this energy is far from positive. The crossroads are often used for negative magic. Every person who is at least a little familiar with the peculiarities of esoteric science knows that when we eat, we absorb not only physical food but also its energy. That is, during a meal, both our physical body and the astral (spirit) are nourished. Lower entities can attach to the astral body of our food and then live in you and destroy your life. It is extremely difficult to get rid of such "settlers."

• Don't count money at the crossroads—It will "leave" you. Very often, a person who is in a hurry for a bus, as an example, tries to prepare money on the go. Monetary energy doesn't like intersections; crossroads tend to draw it into themselves because money is often thrown at the intersection to buy off something. Therefore, you should not open your wallet, receive or give money, or count money at the crossroads.

• Don't go through the center of an intersection. If you do, your life will change for the worse. Crossroads are a unique place. In its center, the forces of the four cardinal directions converge. Suppose you stand in the center of the intersection, spelling specific chants for good luck; in that case, you can attract happiness, good luck, and prosperity from all sides. But if you stand in the same place without conscious thought, you can, on the contrary, disperse your happiness, luck, and prosperity in all four directions.

Significance of the Distance between Your Home and the Crossroads

1. The first crossroads, that is the crossroads closest to your home, involves the "carrying" of the relevant items (money) to solve mainly family and household relations. This magic should be done during daylight hours.

2. The second is for rituals of a romantic orientation (love spells for attachment or its dissolution)—from sunset to the beginning of a new day.

3. The third will help you positively resolve financial (commercial) issues; this should be done in the morning.

4. The fourth crossroads will assist in the return of any debt owed to you. This type of work is best performed at the beginning of a new day.

5. The fifth crossroads is best for work to punish your offender (enemy, ill-wisher). You many perform this work at any time of the day.

6. The sixth crossroads is where you seek to attract good luck to your side. You should perform this work directly at sunrise.

Of course, the summary presented above does not cover all beliefs and superstitions—there are many more rules and secrets of interaction with intersections. Furthermore, people who practice magic have their own experiences, discoveries, and magic tools that work for them specifically. The best thing is to learn until you feel comfortable, and to discover the methods and practices that resonate most with you.

In the realm of magic and mysticism, the path is often as important as the destination, and each individual's journey is unique. So, continue your exploration with curiosity, reverence, and a willingness to adapt and evolve on your magical journey.

14
Magical Properties of Water

According to folk belief, water is one of the first elements of the universe, a source of life, a means of magical purification. Slavs worshipped water long before the adoption of Christianity. The worship of sacred springs and wells was associated with the cult of Mokosh and later with the cult of Paraskeva Friday. Mokosh is the Slavic Mother Goddess, protector of women in childbirth and traditionally women's work like spinning and weaving. She is the only female goddess that Prince Vladimir included among the gods he placed in his pantheon. In the folk tradition of Orthodox Slavs, Paraskeva Friday is the Pagan personification of Friday as the day of the week, the equivalent of the Christian holiday Good Friday. She is the patroness of the water

Fig. 14.1. The crucifix in water

element. Paraskeva Friday, like Mokosh, is associated with women's destinies and the Earth's fertility. In contrast, the church's consecration of water was aimed at its purification.

According to popular folk belief in many Christian countries around the world, when a holy cross is immersed in water, all the devil's power is expelled and, therefore, the water becomes immaculately pure and holy. In the Christian religion, water is often blessed via a special rite that is performed on the Epiphany; the water consecrated on this day is considered to have healing properties that offer protection against diseases and evil spirits. It is usually stored and used for medicinal purposes. This sacred water is also believed to possess miraculous and magical powers.

We can't imagine our life without water; we wouldn't exist. Water is the source of life and a symbol of life change; it is the foundation of creation. We all came out of the water. Water is the first element that we encounter and in which we live for nine long months in the womb. Therefore, everyone can establish contact with water, as well as with the Earth.

The element of water is associated with purification and renewal. While the element of fire embodies sexual desire, water is associated with pure, spiritual love. Just as consciousness does, water constantly flows and changes, emotions cannot stay in one state for a long time but replace each other. Water is considered a female element. Her qualities speak for themselves: feminine, receptive, supportive, subconscious, creative, and changing.

The magical color of the water is blue and turquoise, and the season is autumn, when the rains irrigate the land. The direction that corresponds to water is west. As such, all rituals associated with water are performed in that direction. Water magic is often associated with mirrors. Water rituals usually involve throwing an object into the water, allowing it to flow, or whispering into the water itself.

Water is considered the best cleanser. The main magical rituals that are performed with the element of water are purification, cleansing, and renewal. Water is capable of transmitting information and "remembering" words and thoughts. You should already know about the importance and significance of the rituals of ablution in magical activities. If you have experienced a severe shock, spiritual attack, or other trouble, water is the first and fastest remedy, and it is always at hand.

Imagine that all the negative energy, just like mud, goes down from you into the water. To enhance the cleansing effect, you can dissolve sea salt in the bath—it also helps to remove and absorb negative energy. It is important to remember that water reads information, so we must perform all rituals in a calm, balanced state when working with the water element.

The water element controls emotions and feelings and everything related to intuition. Therefore, the water element is most often used for love spells, divination, and obtaining wealth. In addition, numerous legends about "dead" and "living" water that could either kill or cure a person and even enable someone to rise from the dead, led to healers often using water to cure patients. Other aspects of the water element that are frequently described are tearfulness, indecision, hesitation, idleness, deceit, excessive emotionality, changeable mood, secrecy, and persuasion. Like all spirits, water spirits are very fond of offerings. If you are performing a ceremony over a natural source—be it a river, pond, or lake—dip a wreath of flowers, some blooms, coins, jewelry, gold, or precious stones into the water.

The ocean is a true mystery. We have been to the moon, and yet no one has ever explored the deepest areas of the ocean. The Earth is formed of 70 percent water, and countless spirits live within it. People usually mistake the peaceful feeling they get when they are by the water for its weakness. Water can kill and destroy; just like during a storm or hurricane, that peaceful feeling is dangerous. Water has drowned many. I have heard many stories in Haiti of children being taken by water spirits. Missing for days and found alive days later. Mermaids are water spirits. The Sea herself is a mystery.

In Haiti, people believe that there is a spirit in the Caribbean Sea. She prevents men from seeing any other women's faces than their partners. They see other women but they don't find them sexually appealing. Many of the tales of mermaids that are shared in Haiti tell of this. A large amount of Haitian Vodou practice involves the sea and water spirits. There is a lot of wanga (spells and magical work) performed at sea to worship these water spirits. In Haiti, we take our Vodou magic lamps, magically charged oils, powders, and many other ingredients that are very specific to each situation to the sea to celebrate and worship.

STANDING WATER AND SYMBOLIC MOVEMENT: MORE PROPERTIES OF BRIDGE MAGIC

The feeling of the continual presence in the life of "ghosts of the past," which an individual is unable to let go of over time, represents subconscious communication. In your psyche, you have "storerooms," which we refer to as memory. Often people become immersed in storerooms that overflow into the past, and these people become guided by the intended interaction with this past more than by the surrounding reality. Because these storerooms overflow and rot, and it is important to clean them. The metaphorical content of these storerooms can be a significant source of love or hate. However, it is often the case that a person is not ready to give it all up, to surrender her "wealth," and subsequently the struggle happens not *with* these ghosts of the past, but, on the contrary, *for* them—for their right to live and continue to be present in your life.

It is better, of course, not to allow your personal storeroom to be overcrowded. However, if this does occur and you find yourself unable to forget your past forever, you can seek to remove it from yourself and symbolically bury it. It is in such psychologically difficult situations, when refusal of something is not possible, that it will be useful to carry out a symbolic "burial" of this heavy load.

Water is a memorizing element that collects the properties of all other elements. As such, it is an ideal storeroom, a cache for the past, that can neither be used nor erased without a trace from life. Think of the motionless waters you may sometimes see in areas of ponds and lakes. These are filled with water that does not flow. Standing lake water can be entered twice. You can talk to it and transfer information to it through words. It will remember and answer at any time, picking up the dialogue, providing you are ready to hear. Submersion in a pond filled with still waters that once "remembered" a certain event is similar to putting on a thematic outfit, an invisible masquerade costume that allows you to forfeit physical laws and combine the times of the past, present, and likely future.

A bridge over water is a connecting transition from one state to another. Being on it allows you to symbolically return to the past and reexperience the emotional states you may need. The reservoirs, across which the bridges are laid, set the character and mood of the actions, and the properties of the structure serve as a vehicle for carrying the intentions of the person performing the ritual all the way to the goal. In this sense, you should always consider the history and origin of the body of water or land through which this bridge was built. Thus, a bridge connecting the passage from the past to the present can be constructed across a river or lake. In this case, in magical transformation, the functions of the bridge become even wider.

The practice of deliverance, which is carried out on bridges on certain days, is an example of the relationship between witchcraft and the magic of intention. In this context, the term *deliverance* pertains to a specific ritual or practice associated with witchcraft or magical traditions. Deliverance involves invoking spiritual forces or setting intentions to achieve a desired outcome, often within the framework of magical or ritualistic practices. Bridges and certain days hold significance in the performance of these deliverance rituals, highlighting the connection between witchcraft and the intentional use of magic.

Such actions are traditionally performed on a seasonal holiday, marking one of the transitional periods. For example, on the solstice days, or eclipse or moon phases. The New Year's holiday in particular is the most favorable time for transforming your life and freeing yourself from any interfering factors, both personal characteristics and external circumstances. As noted earlier, entry into something new is best achieved by converting old spent energy into new resources, literally crossing the symbolic boundary—the bridge—with them. (This is true even if the new energy is only conditional as an *egregore*, which is a nonphysical entity created and fueled by the power of multiple humans' thoughts, a concept we will discuss more later.)

Let's shift our focus for a moment from the bridges over bodies of water and talk, for example, about bridges over railway tracks. What is a railway, and what is the associative feature of trains? Trains and roads allow movement: departure or arrival, transportation of specific cargo, unified mobile movement as a single train. The analogy is simple: The carriages of a passenger train are interconnected and move in the same direction. As they do so, they leave your troubles or hopes behind on the rails, symbolically "attaching" them to the tracks. Works that are most often performed on those types of bridges aim to allow you to "move forward" from a standing situation or position in life—or to dispatch and send away. Movement represents transformation and change. To make this change, it is necessary to give a symbolic "push" to deeds for further development.

These types of works should be carried out at the energy level. Take the symbolism of the flow as a fundamental principle. Formation of the thought that consists of visualization of the intention, created by the mind, and directed by the will toward the goal is a flow that can carry away the obstacle or permit an evolution, transforming all the elements included in it. Such actions could be romantically titled "Saying Farewell to the Train." However, one should not take such a lyrical approach lightly. Escorting trains, being on the bridge over the railway, is no different from other magical works of a similar kind because their essence is the same. It is the release of intention, based on the strong symbolism of the "guide–mediator," the bridge.

What falls, shatters, an elementary law of physics that we should also consider in practical witchcraft actions. In anger, a person sometimes destroys objects that come to hand, and such an emotional outlet has no beneficial effect. Why? After all, it would seem that a strong emotional reaction should set energy into action. However, the opposite effect occurs. The material equivalent of "anger" takes on a solely physical function. Accordingly, the only outcome is nothing but a broken object. Emotions should be carefully and proportionally controlled. The intention is to mindfully move the object toward the goal by reflecting on reality and changing the aspects that need to be changed.

When performing a ritual action, a person aims to setting into motion some kind of intention, making events change according to his will. Thus, giving the meaning to the "thing" (object, condition, thought, etc.) that should be gotten rid of, the person who performs the ritual endows it with the properties of "living force." For example, you come to a bridge with a firm intention to remove a condition present in your life that interferes with your well-being: perhaps a situation in which you feel stuck in the middle and can't move forward. This situation could involve some unpleasant state of mind, an event, or even a real person. You throw an object that is symbolic of this—be it a figurine, a written note, or a picture—over the edge of the bridge. The element that we address in such works is air. Say the words of your spell out loud. Everything you are doing now is transforming reality, so you should remember the connection between all elements. If you reflect on this while performing rituals, you create a road that is paved with the symbolic elements that unite something and build bridges from the starting point to the future.

One common ritual is for newlyweds to hang locks on bridges as a symbol of their union. This is a controversial action from a magical point of view due to the practices that take place on bridges that are associated with the end of any processes, getting rid of something, and magic practices of prolonged action. If you choose to engage in such a custom, after locking the padlock, throw the key into the water. If the work is carried out on a bridge over a reservoir, paying off the river for what was done thus secures your intention.

It will not be excessive to return to the topic of superstitious fears that many practitioners have in connection with the elements of the craft. Any actions, especially those related to certain special attributes and ingredients, may at an unforeseen moment be subject to natural correction by nature and sometimes other people. The lock from the bridge can be pulled off, a candle accidentally (or deliberately) extinguished by the wind or a person. Your actions, chants, and spells can be heard by prying ears; however, this does not mean that higher powers reject you, or that your ritual will not work or will not happen. Nothing will happen if the person who performs the ritual in the process loses faith in herself and her work.

15

Christianity Is the Most Powerful Form of Occult

With this I come to a conclusion and pronounce my judgment. I condemn Christianity; I bring against the Christian church the most terrible of all the accusations that an accuser has ever had in his mouth. It is, to me, the greatest of all imaginable corruptions; it seeks to work the ultimate corruption, the worst possible corruption. The Christian church has left nothing untouched by its depravity; it has turned every value into worthlessness, and every truth into a lie, and every integrity into baseness of soul.

FRIEDRICH NIETZCHE, *DER ANTICHRIST* (1895)

I am walking my path in my way. I never had an urge or need to worship any deities at all. They are as fallible as any human. I still recognize the love I feel for many of them since they have been good to me. I am a free thinker. Details fascinate me. I worship knowledge and my freedom. Gods have stood by me, but so have demons. I am not beneath any god or demon; I am a descendant of the gods. And you are too. Humanity has been cut off from spirit, having been taught by most major religions that people have to give up their spirit to another's rule. This is the lie that has torn this world apart. Self-knowledge is the only way to evolve above the masses. This means letting go of the belief that another holds the truth when you turn a blind eye to your own self-truth.

Generally speaking, Christianity is not significantly different from other religions and traditional beliefs. However, there is one major difference that is often camouflaged with euphemisms. According to Christian Creationism, this hidden source exists above the Universe (Nature) and is personified in Jehovah, God of Judaism. The force of Christianity is destructive because this belief entails that the flow of the worshippers' energy goes into oblivion. Since ancient times, humans received water, food, clothes, and moral and spiritual pleasures from Mother Nature and the universe. Accordingly, all rituals were rituals of appreciation that harmonized the flow of force from the world to the people and, through the ritual, from the people to the world in the form of their spiritual strength, the strength of love and appreciation. Rituals were a means of achieving harmony and being attentive to the place and locality at which humans interacted with one another and lived. For this reason, an enormous amount of the Pagan rituals and holidays are dedicated to natural occurrences, cosmic events, and, less frequently, local spirits. Essentially, rituals of unity connect humans with the acting forces and flows and enable them to enter a state of appreciation.

With the arrival of monotheism, people were initially forced to attend mass rituals where their energy was practically taken away by force, and the flows of energy were directed toward some hypothetical god positioned outside the universe. This force subsequently went nowhere because the god the Christians worship is beyond the universe itself. Accordingly, the energy given to this god did not reach any of the objects of the universe, not a single element, being, or spirit.

I am not arguing that devout Christians are strongly detached from the world, while the Pagans and people of nature radiate integrity and strength. However, Christianity established an energy flow by which man drew energy from the Earth, Heaven, elements, animals, and plants without giving any energy in return. The connection between people and higher powers became severed. Left without attention and love, these forces, as befits any creature, reacted to the betrayal by leaving. They did not go anywhere; they simply closed themselves, turned away from people, and became invisible. That is how the degradation of everything commenced. Therefore, Christianity became a cleverly disguised form of energy vampirism. And where the energy of the "zombified," enslaved peoples is directed, nobody knows.

People believe that the church forbids magic. And, indeed, if we turn to three modern religions—Christianity, Islam, and Judaism—they do, indeed, continue to preach against fortune-telling and all kinds of magic rituals. Many people also mistakenly believe that one needs to move away from the church and the Christian faith to practice magic. But they don't understand that Christianity, Islam, Judaism, and magic are all one big egregore, since all these religions worship supreme beings; all are very well-organized religions.

One of the names by which God goes is YHVH (Yahweh), the Christian Lord. All this is one and the same God, which means one egregore. It's interesting that, initially, there was only YHWH—the Tetragrammaton. YHWH is considered by many scholars to be unpronounceable; its exact pronunciation has been lost over time. The name is associated with the God of Israel and is considered sacred in Judaism. Later, by transitioning this to a readable entity, Yahweh, a great mental trap was created: God became a personality! But, after all, the originally hidden logos was never defiled by speech and name.

And then Yahweh was often replaced and placed next to the concept of Adonai; in Hebrew, it simply means "my Lord." Moreover, so people could refer to their mentor, to the one at a higher level in the community: "My Lord! Master! Teacher!" There is nothing strange here, but when an equals sign was inserted between the words "God (Yahweh)" and "the Lord," this notorious synonymous chain appeared in Orthodox theology: God=Jesus=Christ=Lord. This represented a significant deviation from the initial form god took as an unpronounceable tetragram. Jesus is the name of the prophet. Christ is the Messiah, the "anointed one" in Greek. The Lord is my Lord (Adonai). Thus, the prophet became God, and God himself acquired the traits of a punishing and cruel personality.

All three religions, Christianity, Islam, and Judaism, recognize the Old Testament as a holy book. All three religions recognize Jesus, although in Islam and Judaism he is not the son of God; in combination, we have a powerful egregore. Magic also recognizes and speaks of the same God as religion. For example, *The Greater Key of Solomon*, one of the most ancient grimoires,* is attributed to the same wise Solomon as the Bible. In the Quran, this wise king is called Suleiman. As such, all three religions have one source of one true knowledge—Gnosis. Gnosis is knowledge based on personal experience or perception. In a religious context, gnosis is the mystical or esoteric knowledge based on an individual's direct participation with the divine, rather than the divine as interpreted through another.

Christianity is tidily united with the esotericism of other faiths to establish a universal religion. It is the most powerful form of occult, as this is the only form of practice that consists of every single tradition and religion around the world. From Egypt to Indigenous groups from Celts to India, traditions are brought into one religion called Christianity. Christianity, first and foremost, is a worshipping of the Sun. This subject needs further discussion and to be examined in much, much greater detail but not in this book.

Esoteric refers to information that is designed and understood by a small group of specially initiated people and is restricted to them alone. Esoteric Christianity, as I call it, can only be understood or practiced

---

*A grimoire is a book of spells or textbook of magic. They often include instructions for making magical objects and invoking supernatural entities. In many cases, the books themselves are thought to have magical properties.

Fig. 15.1. Hieromonks in Russia, 1888

by correctly initiated into secret knowledge. Only a small minority of people can reach the enlightenment needed to break the arcane teachings to really know the Gods and their mysteries. Christianity operates from the premise that only a small group of people has access to the internal functioning of the faith.

Esoteric Christianity uses the selected versions of the Gospels for some of its teachings, drawing from Apocrypha and several apocalyptic texts. The scriptures speak of the church, composed of Jews and Gentiles, as a "mystery."

Church rituals are, in essence, occult rituals. Strongly simplified and codified, but even in them, a small piece of true knowledge remains. So why is the church against magic? Simply because the church decided to establish a monopoly in the occult. But let's see here, baptism is a magical ceremonial ritual of purification with water. As described earlier, water is the most powerful carrier of information and energy and a very potent tool for purification (spiritual cleansing). Prayer represents a spell and is often performed by chanting or singing in a very specific rhyme and rhythm that resembles those used in any occult practice. Fire is a symbol of the spirit; when you light a candle, you invoke the spirit—and not one ritual passes without candles. So, we are dealing with the sacred elements of water, fire, air, and earth in a simple ritual of Christian baptism. At the end of this ritual, a strand of hair is often cut from the baptized person in a special way, in the form of a cross. This completes the occult rite. Human hair is also an excellent carrier of a person's vital energy; hence, hair is a common feature of almost all occult practices around the globe.

As the example above demonstrates, the sacraments of the church are very much like those used in ceremonial occult rituals. The church is engaged in the highest magic—theurgy—a return to God. The occult has a comparable direction or branch; it focuses on the intention of action invoking the presence of one or more deities, intending to achieve enosis (uniting with the Divine), and perfecting oneself.

The difference is that the rituals of the church are recognized and approved, while magical rituals are deemed to be apocryphal. The church doesn't like competition. Religion is a pure magical (occult) teaching. Church and occult (magical) rituals go back to one unknown source; therefore, they do not conflict. Magic does not contradict religion in any way; a good Christian can practice magic freely and without fear. Many saints, apostles, and Jesus himself did so. For example, Saint Spyridon of Trimifuntsky temporarily resurrected his dead daughter, which represented necromancy. Pope Honorius III was a magician and even wrote a magic grimoire with instructions for summoning demons. Thus, magic cannot contradict religion. And the only reason why the

Fig. 15.2. Orthodox hieromonk

modern church does not approve of magic is because it sees it as a threat and competitor.

Demons are the same fallen angels and their helpers (demonology). And priests are priests. On the other hand, magic is knowledge that isn't presented through the lens of organized religion. It's hidden and not accessible to the majority. We can see only crumbs of true knowledge mixed with a bunch of wishful thinkers and invented rituals.

The first fisherman to be called by Jesus was Andrew, and he was subsequently named "Andrew the First-Called." However, where is the Gospel of Andrew in the Bible? Nowhere, because it was banned. Chapter 5 of the Gospel of Andrew began:

> And Andrey ask Jesus his disciple: Rabbi! What nations can bring the good news of the Kingdom of Heaven? And Jesus answered him: Go to the nations of the east, to the nations of the west, and to the nations of the south, where the children of the house of Israel dwell. Do not go to the Gentiles of the North, for they are sinless and do not know the vices and sins of the house of Israel (lines 1–3)

Fig. 15.3. Hieromonks and Orthodox priest in Russia, 1889

This book never made it into the Bible, which is limited to four Gospels: Matthew, Mark, Luke, and John. The Bible didn't include all the Gospels, only those Emperor Constantine and his assistants selected to fulfill their objectives. The rest of the Gospels were simply rejected since their interpretation was far from what Constantin and his assistants needed and they were not deemed to be beneficial to the cause. Even the four Gospels that did make it into the Bible were heavily edited according to the goals underpinning the establishment of Christianity as the main religion.

Since the year 364, when the New Testament was approved, and the first edition of the Bible was circulated, its content has been edited countless times. Translational inaccuracies have also played a role. After all, the Old Testament was primarily written in Hebrew, an insignificant part was written in the Aramaic language, and the New Testament was written in Greek. So, the first printed book, published in 1455, was already substantially different, even from the one that was edited in 364. Following all the adjustments made after

1455, we have a very different Bible today than the one that was first introduced.

There are dozens of Gospels that did not make it into the official canon. In 1946, an entire library of works by Christian Gnostics was discovered in southern Egypt. Researchers found the Gospels of Thomas, Philip, Mary Magdalene, Truth, the Apocrypha of John, and Judas, among other literature. But even the apocryphal writings were divided into "permissible" and "renounced/rejected." The renounced, of course, were always doomed for destruction.

It is worth mentioning that the first official list of renounced books was compiled in the Eastern Roman Empire in the fifth century CE. Naturally, after such "blasphemy," the descendants got only the titles and quotations provided in the works by Christian writers of the second through fourth centuries, who argued against these books. For example, there is a lot of information about the Apocrypha, but science supposedly knows nothing about the Gospel of Andrew. Instead, the *Decretum Gelasianum*, also known as the Gelasian Decree or the Gelasian Sacramentary, is an ancient ecclesiastical document that dates to the sixth century, attributed to Pope Gelasius I. This document contains lists of books that were considered either canonical or noncanonical (apocryphal) by the early Christian Church. The Gospel of Andrew, often referred to as the Acts of Andrew, is a second-century Christian apocryphal text detailing the activities and miracles of the apostle Andrew. The *Decretum Gelasianum* categorizes it under the heading "Apocrypha," which suggests that the text was not universally accepted as sacred nor considered part of the authoritative canon by the compilers of the document, and it implies that the Acts of Andrew was viewed with some level of skepticism.

Some of the rejected books were valuable because they reflected the true teachings of Jesus in their original, authentic form, which made people truly free from all their fears. These teachings helped people understand that the body is perishable, the soul is immortal. But had people studied these texts, they would not have become hostages and slaves to the illusion of the material world. They would realize how short life is and the temporary nature of the conditions in which their current body is. They would know that this life, no matter how long it may seem, is just one moment in which their soul dwells. They would understand that any earthly power, politicians, or religious structures, can only control our bodies, not the soul, for the soul belongs only to the true creator(s).

The notion that people could have such freedom frightened those in power. Therefore, they began collecting, editing, and screening the written sources about the teachings of Jesus that were available at that time. After selecting the information that they needed to create a new religion, the undesirable information and knowledge was destroyed. As a result, many of the written sources that shared the true words of Jesus were omitted from the collections of the "new ideology for the masses." Yet, despite all the deliberate omissions, tricks, and selfish ambitions of people in power and religious leadership during different periods, these written sources existed and did not cease to exist.

THE ORTHODOX RITE OF BAPTISM

The Orthodox rite of baptism has immense occult power. In the Orthodox perspective, baptism means to be born for spiritual life. People at their physical births are born only into their mortal lives; to become a Christian is to have a chance to "enter the kingdom of heaven" for eternal life. According to the Orthodox Church, every person is born a sinner, "foul," and guilty before the justice of God, and the only chance for salvation and eternal life is baptism.

The idea of being "born again" is not unique to Christianity. Indeed, as we have discussed before, initiations often serve the purpose of "dying" from one life role into another (i.e., the wedding as a funeral for a bride). Hinduism and a variety of esoteric orders, ancient mysteries, and secret societies all practice some form of it. In Hinduism, someone who passes the initiation rite is referred to as being "twice-born" and receives the right to study the Vedas and become a full participant in the rituals.

Initiations also have the meaning of welcoming an individual into a certain closed community, and then connecting that individual to an egregore for that community. The significant difference is that these rites are always performed on conscious adults or adolescents, never on infants, and they take into account the law of free choice and free will. Your destiny is your choice, and you should decide for yourself what path you wish to follow. Even Jesus Christ made his own choice in the matter; he was baptized at the age of thirty-three. But today, in Orthodox baptism, the initiation involves an infant, who can neither agree to nor prevent the ritual.

In the early stages, the rite of baptism had no biblical basis. Adolf von Harnack (1851–1930), a historian and theologian who called on Christians to question the authenticity of the doctrines of the early church, wrote in his book *The History of Dogma*: "It cannot be directly proven that Jesus instituted baptism since the words cited by Matthew (28:19) are not utterances of God." Matthew 28:19 is the Bible verse that calls on Christians to make disciples of the other nations and baptize them in the name of the Trinity, but Harnack states that the "speaker" is not God in this case. He points out that baptism is administered in the name of the Father, Son, and Holy Spirit, which was not the case in any of the earlier manuscripts. Harnack states that "this trinitarian formula is extraneous to the mouth of Jesus and did not have the authority in the apostolic age that it should have had if it had come from Jesus himself." The verse Matthew 28:19 is often cited as a biblical basis for the Christian practice of baptism. In the King James Version (KJV), it reads: "Go ye therefore, and teach all nations, baptizing them in the name of the Father, and of the Son, and of the Holy Ghost." This passage is commonly known as the Great Commission, where Jesus instructs his disciples to baptize in the name of the Trinity. Harnack's criticism centers around the question of whether this specific trinitarian formula, as found in Matthew 28:19, was originally spoken by Jesus. He argues that the attribution of this formula to Jesus is not conclusively supported by the text and suggests that it may have been a later addition to the Gospel.

Another point is the impermanence of the sacrament of baptism in general Christian theology. Baptism, as it is now understood, means that the Holy Spirit, the third member of the Trinity, enters a person and removes his sins. If one accepts this, it is not clear how later in that same person's life, Satan drives the Holy Spirit out of him and, by temptation, leads him into sin. It turns out that the ritual has no "divine" power. Or does the performance itself please Yahweh? Then what is the point of the ritual? This raises the question: Can the devil tempt a person who is filled and protected by the Holy Spirit? Have you ever thought about that? So, it is quite clear that baptism is not based on the teachings of Jesus at all.

It is my view that the church's main task is to instill a sense of guilt in man, make him pray and repent, and keep him in fear. During the baptism rite, the priest reads, "The servant of God is baptized in the name of the Father and of the Son and of the Holy Spirit" as a "sheep slain," and he joins the "flock" of Christ's sheep and becomes ideologically governed. The infant is immersed in the baptismal font. As we have discussed, the element of water is excellent at holding memories and preserving information. Imagine what information church water carries.

This is compounded by the energy bondage placed upon the person during the rite of baptism. The church believes that baptism seals all of the body's natural energy channels and separates her from the forces and energy of the Earth. They call this "renouncing one's own sinful nature." But Pagans believe that there is nothing separate from Nature, and so this renouncement is a complete rejection of the life-giving mother who birthed us, raised us, and nourishes us.

During the rite of baptism, priests often seal hair in wax, glue it to the back of a patronal icon, or throw it into the baptismal font. Small strands of hair are cut crosswise at the back of the head, at the forehead, and on the right and left sides of the head. While ritual text and chants are read, the hair is rolled up in a piece of wax and thrown into the baptismal font. In magic, a token of this nature is known as a puppet or doll and is used to curse an individual or impose a certain outcome. With the help of this ritual, a man becomes completely attached to the Christian egregore.

This tradition of cutting hair during the mystery of baptism has persisted since Roman times when slaves had part of their hair cut off to demonstrate loyalty and devotion to their master. In general, the cutting of hair has long been a symbol of sacrifice and obedience, and it is likely it evolved on the basis that ancient civilizations believed that hair contained an individual's main strength, the concentration of powerful energy. It is likely you have heard of the Old Testament hero Samson, whose long hair was the source of his incredible power. It is for this reason that hair is cut in many rites, such as the initiation of monks.

Parents and witnesses, called "godparents," must be present when the baptism is performed. All four must be guarantors of the child's future Christian upbringing. During the rite, the baptized person undergoes the symbolic procedure of death and new birth into the Christian faith with a new name. In this way, it is believed he repeats the earthly path of Christ, dying and resurrecting, cleansed of sins. It is no secret that the name carries a certain program for a person, imposing a particular imprint on his whole life.

What names does the Russian Orthodox Church assign to Russian people during baptism? These are mostly the names of biblical heroes and canonized saints. More than one critical book has been written on the moral qualities of the participants in biblical history. On a personal note, if an Orthodox believer thoughtfully read and analyzed the "holy" scriptures (the Bible), she would become not just an atheist but an ardent opponent of the cult. In my opinion, virtually none of the characters are worthy representatives of humanity.

Who does the church canonize? Most of the people who are canonized by the church are great martyrs and hermits or people who died tragic deaths because they preached or pursued Christianity. Ask yourself a question: Would normal parents want to identify their child's future in any way with such fates? I'm sure they wouldn't.

Thus, during the baptismal ceremony, the human soul passes through a symbolic death. Then, through a special set of actions, the essence of the child is erased from the program that was laid down by the name given to him originally by his parents, and a new one is given, corresponding to the one assigned by the representative of the church. In this case, it is extremely unlikely that the child will be given a Slavic name during baptism. The majority of names permitted by the Russian Orthodox Church are biblical; therefore, they are Hebrew or Greek in origin.

Churching

The pre-baptismal rite of churching is an imitation of the Old Testament tradition that prescribed that male children should be presented to God in the temple forty days after their birth. Most Orthodox priests recommend that children be churched once they are around forty days old. During this time, it was also common for the mother of the child to be churched as well—a further hallmark of Old Testament tradition that represented the mothers' reentry into the church after participating with God in the birth of their child and their confinement. After being churched, the mother could once again participate in Communion and receive the Body and Blood of Christ. During the churching initiation, the priest read a prayer:

Lord, now lettest thou thy servant depart in peace, according to thy word; For my eyes have seen your salvation, which you have prepared in the sight of all nations: a light for revelation to the Gentiles, and the glory of your people Israel. (Luke 2:29–32)

Everything is clear; no comment is needed. The word "Israel" is not substituted for anything. It has been firm and holy for centuries. Only Muslims don't use it; they have their own interpretations. Not for the glory of the child's parents' kin, but for the glory of the tribal society, which has nothing to do with the Russians and other nations.

Chrismation

In the Orthodox Church, chrism (holy oil) plays a part in many liturgical services and sacraments. The first sacrament that uses chrism, the sacrament of chrismation, is the second of the three sacraments of initiation (baptism, chrismation, and divine Eucharist), which are all performed on the infant in a short period of time. The order and administration of these sacraments can vary among Christian denominations. In the Western Christian tradition, particularly in Roman Catholicism, confirmation is often a separate sacrament that comes after baptism, usually during adolescence. However, in many Eastern Orthodox and some Eastern Catholic traditions, chrismation (or its equivalent) is typically administered immediately following baptism, emphasizing the unity of these initiation rites.

During the anointment in the rite of chrismation, one receives what is called "the seal of the Holy Spirit." These seals are placed crosswise on the forehead, eyes, nostrils, mouth, ears, chest, hands, and feet. There is a connection to the chakras (energy centers) in the body: the second, third, and fourth chakras—which are responsible for the person's integrity of will, clairvoyance, creativity, and senses—are closed.

For the Orthodox, chrismation canonically must be administered in conjunction with these rites, except in the case of true necessity. Chrism was also used to consecrate church buildings by anointing the walls and the altar table. In addition, chrismation was used to anoint the dead and to prepare the body for sacrificial service.

Holy Communion

During the rite of Holy Communion, a person is given bread and red wine—the body and blood of Christ. The person doesn't have to drink and eat it. The important thing is that she consciously sets herself up to eat the living man. In Haitian Vodou magic, this form of ritual is used to destroy enemies: eating the flesh (symbolic consumption of the meat) of your defeated enemy and drinking his blood (symbolic consumption of wine) to make his essence your slave forever. The rite of Communion uses the principle of identification. Identification means the transfer of astral-mental properties from one essence to another. That is, by identifying himself with Christ, a person takes the properties of a dead person upon himself, thereby joining the world of the dead while he is still alive.

The Pentagon Star and the Sign of the Cross

Another major occult connection between rituals of the church and Paganism involves the process of crossing oneself. The Christian "sign of the cross" is not of the cross but the pentagon star. As you see in figure 15.4 the path that your hand, forearm, and elbow make when crossing yourself actually forms a five-pointed star. The right hand starts from a point above the bridge of the nose, then makes a vertical line downward (approximately to the solar plexus), then it goes to the right shoulder and then the left shoulder (or the left and then the right for Catholics). The points on this star correspond to chakras in the body: *ajna* (forehead or "third eye") and *manipura* (solar plexus). If you were to connect all the lines, you get a pentagon star without the lower-left leg. From the point of view of magic, having both sides be symmetrical is not crucial because all processes are mirrored: the left

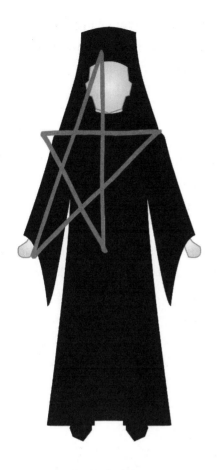

Fig. 15.4. The five-pointed star is created when one makes the sign of the cross (base image by Tom Lemmons, cc by 4.0, star added)

side of the body reflects what is happening in the right. So, whenever you baptize and "cross yourself," you put the pentagon star on yourself.

The five-pointed star, as we know, is a good sign; it's a sign of protection against negative influences. It is said that if the star is pointed up, it signifies evolution or enlightenment; if the star is pointed down, it is the devil's star.

The tradition of placing the pentagon star on oneself as a protective sign can be traced back to the Egyptian pharaohs. People in all sacred drawings and bas-reliefs are depicted with their arms crossed on their chests. The mummies of the pharaohs exhibited the same hand position; depending on which hand was on top, the magical purpose of the gesture changed.

When you cross yourself, know that you are making a pentagon star and that you are taking back your strength—it is your intention and will behind it. Despite all of the efforts the Orthodox Church makes to impose certain beliefs on you, both overtly and in the occult meanings behind the rites, you have a choice. With knowledge, you bring the magic of yourself and your ancestors back into your actions.

16

Spell Text as a Legacy of the Prophetic, Enchanted Word

Spells belong to the sphere of verbal magic, and magic played an important role in the life of ancient people, including our ancestors. The magical power of these spells means that the text (spoken, written, or nonverbal action) can act as an amulet, driving away evil forces and attracting good ones. Performing the spell, and seeing it performed, affects the consciousness and body of a person, who subsequently creates and manipulates the energies at her discretion and will. Verbal magic is the prophetic, enchanted word.

The spell texts that we have now are often described as "the wreckage" of ancient Pagan prayers. They couldn't reach our times "fresh"—or completely intact. Like other folklore genres, spells have undergone significant changes due to the destructive influence of time and the adoption of Christianity, which has consistently influenced the development of popular beliefs. From the point of view of modern times, many aspects of the spells appear mysterious or inexplicable. Closer examination shows that this "strangeness" was a legacy of the distant past where the Pagan worldview of the Slavs were closely intertwined, and Christian prayers influenced the content, structure, and language of the spells.

The oldest sacred texts emerged at the early stage of culture in the form of incantations and myths. These later evolved into prayers, hymns, chants to the gods, and other types of texts. They exhibited a mythological worldview; what we now call a magical type of thinking. The uniqueness of such thinking is clearly manifested in sacred texts, and contains clear marks of the language and culture in which it originated, even though it has changed over time.

The strength of verbal magic, in all of its forms, is due to the meaning that the spells have accumulated over the ages in the life of the people. If other genres of folklore (fairy tales, riddles, songs, etc.) were a means of entertainment, spells were not used for fun. The enchanted word contains a tremendous force that shouldn't be invoked unless absolutely necessary; otherwise, you will incite misfortune. In the context of a spell, which is treated as a sacred text, the use of speech goes beyond the mere expression of information and emotions. Instead, it is considered a unique form of inviting or motivating a desired outcome through the magical function of words. The message conveyed is that the use of enchanted words carries a significant responsibility and should be approached with respect and care.

In essence, the difference between magical speech and regular speech is that the speech audience is not a conversational partner in a spell text but some "higher" force. In regular speech, communication typically occurs between individuals, addressing immediate concerns, sharing information, or expressing emotions within the human realm. However, in magical speech, the words are often considered to have a transformative power when directed toward the divine, spirits, or other supernatural entities. The intent is to influence or invoke a specific outcome, and the speech is seen as a means of connecting with forces beyond the mundane world. This distinction underscores the ceremonial and ritualistic nature of magical speech, where words are chosen and spoken with the belief that they hold a unique influence on the mystical aspects of reality.

SPELLS: THE PRIMARY TOOL
OF MAGIC FOR HEALERS

In comparison with other folklore genres, spells are the subject of the secret actions of healers, witches. People turn to them when it is necessary to seek the help of ancient magical rituals. The healers, in turn, depend on the power of the prophetic word as the primary tool of magic. To ensure these sacred texts would be remembered (as we will discuss later, the power decreases if the spell is not spoken correctly), witches began to write spells down, often in notebooks. These recordings have become a true treasure for science and research. The spells researchers find in such notebooks carry information about psychological and social aspects of our ancestors' lives. The structure of the spell texts clarify the connection between the magical worldview and the influence of religion. The sacred word is always the main and most natural instrument of tradition. The practical and magical purpose of a "living" spell text is important, and the spell is alive as long as it is believed. Over time, it becomes a part of a cultural legacy.

Each spell contains a deep communicative meaning: the creator of a spell (the healer) feels involved in the supernatural world and unearthly forces. She must, with the help of prophetic words (and actions), inspire others and, in a miraculous way, help people to overcome their problems and bring good into their lives. It is no coincidence that spells were created by people who know how to heal and get rid of mental and physical suffering, believing that the main power of such treatment lies in powerful whispers and special potions, primarily prepared using different herbs and roots.

It is interesting to note the core of the meaning of the popular names of sorcerers (sorcerer or sorceress, warlock or witch, whisperer, healer, etc.) in many Slavic languages contains the *zna* component, which means "know" and "knowledge" (the equivalent of the Sanskrit *ved*). For instance, in Ukrainian and some other Slavic languages, a *znakharka* (знахарка) is someone possessing knowledge in the realm of healing and magical practices. The term *znakhar* (знахарь) for a male healer is another example from some Slavic languages, representing someone with knowledge or skill in certain magical or mystical practices. The idea conveyed is that individuals associated with terms like *sorcerer, witch, healer,* or *whisperer* are linked to possessing supernatural knowledge. A healer, for instance, is viewed as someone with magical knowledge used for benevolent purposes, while a whisperer is seen as a practitioner of divination or spellcasting.

Much like the other initiations we have discussed in this book, note that the ability for verbal magic (slander, whisper, etc.) is not initially given to a person, but that it appears and develops under certain conditions: After preliminary magic, obtaining secret knowledge, reaching a certain age, and other important events. The ability to perform verbal magic is typically passed from the elders to the younger members of the group who vow to comply with certain conditions and perform special rituals. It is believed that one who possesses knowledge (texts and rituals) cannot die without transferring it to another.

Healers are usually viewed as mediators between humans and supernatural forces whose help and cooperation are necessary for the outcome of the treatment to be successful. Observations of the spell texts show that the one who creates the spell (the healer) is not orthodox in his faith: by conjuring, the Christian returns to Paganism, or at least to dual faith when he turns to different, including so-called incompatible, higher forces.

A large number of canonical Christian prayers were included in the Psalms and Trebniki. Trebniki, which translates as "something that is needed, required," in Russian are a special type of day-to-day manual that describes situations and plans of liturgical actions for particular occasions. They were used in many rituals involving so-called private worship, such as baptisms, weddings, funeral services, confession, the blessing of oil and water, and various prayer services (consecration of a house, a new building, etc.). These books are widely utilized in the Orthodox Church because they were most often used (and continue to be used) in divine services. The Psalms were read in full every week. Prayers, as a rule, were memorized word for word. The believer retained faith in the magic, enchanting holy words.

Thus, the magical and aesthetic perception of the word in prayer seems to merge: Not only *what* is said is of interest but *how* it is said. Turning to the Lord God in prayers seems to be a magical act, and the plea to God to allow, help, bless is widely used throughout the world to this day.

STRUCTURE OF THE SPELL

Spell texts are not all the same in content and structure, but they do have certain characteristics that define them. Spells contain three main parts: (1) the appeal, where the higher power that the healer is calling on in evoked in very specific, ritual language, (2) the core, which is where information is given and misfortunes are named and expelled, and (3) the closing, which is a magical formula to lock in the power of the spell.

Appeal

In some ways the appeal section of the spell is the most important and complex part. In the appeal, the healer calls upon the specific higher power to cure that specific problem, using specific language for that higher power to recognize. This complexity is partially due to the fact that the spell texts have a dual origin. On the one hand, they contain elements of Christian texts (both canonical and apocryphal); on the other, aspects of folklore. This is an organic synthesis of elements of different origins.

The appeal has a certain position in the spell and certain linguistic qualities. In most cases, it is found in the first sentence of the text. For example: "To the Heavenly King"; "Lord God, bless . . ."; "Holy Mother, help." The spells are saturated with appeals to Pagan higher powers and Christian intercessors. This demonstrates the belief in the magical properties of the name, which is consistently evident in all folklore texts. Even in later folklore texts (such as stories, legends, oral stories, etc.), the narrative always evolves the name as the primary tool of verbal magic.

Sounding out a ritual name in prayer evokes the presence of the higher power who was called by the name. This is not just the case in Slavic prayers: various prayers and hymns in Sanskrit, ancient Greek and Latin, Old Slavonic, and Arabic also name their gods in a specific manner to fulfill the ritual (magical) function. The texts of prayers and hymns are based on a religious idea that appeals to God in prayers and hymns do not achieve their goal if their texts do not include God's name(s).

In spells, often there is an appeal to Christian intercessors, including names for God and the Trinity, the Virgin Mary, saints, miracle works, and angels. These include: To the Lord God Almighty, Jesus Christ, the Blessed Virgin Mary (Theotokos), the Most Holy Trinity, Saint Barbara the Great Martyr, the great Nicholas, George the Victorious, Vlasiy, and more.

Chants frequently refer specifically to the Virgin Mary (in all of her names). Attributes such as "Most Holy," "Most Pure," emphasize her purity and holiness in the eyes of all believers. She was especially revered among the Slavs. Prayers were offered to her as often as to the Lord God himself. The Most-Pure Mother of God is considered the patroness of all women, especially women in labor (note that the name Mother of God is related to the word "birth"), children, and girls. Her cult in the folk tradition comes close and merges with the cult of Mother Earth, Mokosh, which we have discussed. In the numerous available materials, spells to protect against all diseases, evil eye, damage, and fear, and to facilitate childbirth, peace of mind, abundance, and animal charms are associated with the name of the Holy Virgin.

Spell texts frequently contain appeals (contrary to the prohibitions of official Christianity) to the "small higher" forces, which reflect the belief in what has been preserved since Pagan times. These appeals may be issued to natural elements and cosmic bodies, such as the mother-water; holy water; the moon (moon you are a moon, silver horns, your golden legs); Earth; stars (clear stars); the sun; the wind (that is free); diseases (burn you, [name of the disease or misfortune]); and objects that help create a spell (salt, ash, coal).

Appeals to Christian intercessors, of course, are borrowed from prayers (canonical and apocryphal), which had a significant impact on the spells' wording. Apocryphal prayers are essentially spells that feature apocryphal prayer characters (Adam and Eve, Abraham, Christ, apostles, archangels, saints) and seek to drive out unclean spirits and fight diseases, misfortunes, evil eye, and so on. Some of them were contained in the prayer books of the fifteenth and seventeenth centuries. Apocrypha such as the teachings of the apostles (the Acts of Andrew, for example), Bible-based legends, and apocryphal torments (Fedor Tiron, Irina, etc.), all have a significant influence on the texts of spells.

In the mythological consciousness, the name of the higher power and/or especially important ritual verbal formulas become a fetish; that is, they become worshipped themselves as an icon or relic. As a result, the success of the prayer becomes directly dependent on the authenticity of the sacred text. It is extremely dangerous for the believer to distort the prayer text and, thus, create a perilous loss of its power. When the magical motives and sacred meanings of spells are forgotten, ritual actions and verbal forms become a rote, meaningless custom.

It is important to note that a very distinguishing feature of spells in Slavic languages is the use of the variety creative diminutives (more frequent and varied than English "nicknames") to express both affection and familiarity with the spell "helpers." This is one feature that keeps the spell's magic alive.

Core

Prayer texts are structured to enthrall a person. All components of the prayer text are characterized by skillful rhythmic construction, expression, and figurative use of words. They enchant with the rhythm and sound, and the unconventional, yet also highly accurate, choice of words and metaphors that are capable of discovering the mysterious connections between the concepts and the bottomless depth of meanings.

The spells are often characterized by descriptive forms of the imperative (command) with the meaning "let it be so." The tone of this section of the spell can vary. It can be a positive request: "Come and dwell in us and cleanse us from all filthiness and misfortune"; "Help, save, have mercy"; "Wash away ailments." Or it can be slander (insults, curses): "Turn into a dark whirlwind and drown yourself in the sea"; "From the relics of the veins of the dead"; "Angels, take this pain, carry it over the mountains, over the valleys, over the dense forest." The healer directly appeals to the "higher" and "small" forces and asks for their help.

Quite often, the expression of will in spells is expressed by the infinitive: "You won't be here, you won't walk on this ground, you won't break your bones, you won't spin your head, and you won't kill the servant of God [name]." It is, generally speaking, a typical feature of Slavic language: "Let you fail!" "So that you choke!" "Let him not see the daylight!" and so on. They express a negative wish, a spell, and contribute to the implementation of the intentions of the witch. These prophetic words also affect the listener, who is convinced that there are grounds for fulfilling the will of the spell caster.

Closing

In the East Slavic spell tradition, the ending of the spell is called a closing, setting, key, lock. The lock, the key in the magical language of the spell, always has the symbolic meaning of the instrument of closing the disease, the bearer of danger, or bringing protection. Closing the lock serves as a symbol of securing the desired result, as expressed in the will.

There are always phrases like: "Amen"; "My word is strong"; "In those words, the lock is the sea"; "So be it."

These closings have different origins; the Hebrew biblical "Amen!" (meaning "true," "so it is," "so be it!") can be found most often. The same is true of liturgical texts; speakers verbally confirm the truth of what was said (or written). This formula passed into the sphere of folklife and folklore and is often used in spells to this day. Moreover, in Russian folk speech, "Amen" has become a noun that not only denotes the end of a prayer, but also the end of the affair: "Amen, amen, break up the evil spirits," "Amen saves a man," "Amen does great things." There is even a verb in Russian dialects, "to amen," which has the following meanings: "complete, finish, fix or strengthen"; "destroy, cast out the disease"; "protect from evil spirits."

Physical Components

Like a religious rite or prayer, a spell is formed through the combination of verbal components and physical actions: the "tangible" word and "deed." The verbal part conveys a message and expresses the practitioner's will. Actions performed during spells encompass a variety of practices such as pouring, sprinkling, washing, rubbing with water, slandering in water (or possibly slathering), spitting (often over the left shoulder), smearing oil on the affected area with the ring finger, blowing on a wound, licking, waving hands, and so on.

EXAMPLES OF SPELLS

Depending on the scope and object of application, the following types of spells are common.

✳ MEDICAL

There are many medicinal spells of a general and specific nature (from the evil eye, injuries, sore throat, headache, bruises, etc.).

For example, here is a spell from the evil eye:

> Mother-water, the Lord's helper, wash away the grief from the servant of God [name], wash away the ailment from the servant of God [name], wash away the evil slander from the servant of God [name]. Give her mother water, good health, not for the coming year, but forever. Amen. Amen. Amen.

Pour water into a glass and add salt. Give it the sick person to drink, wash the sick person's face, pour the remaining saltwater into the heel of the door, and close the door.

✳ THERAPEUTIC SPELLS

Therapeutic spells are for children and women in labor (to facilitate childbirth, ensure the baby is not cursed, prevent insomnia and nightmares).

> Mother, evening dawn, Midnight Irina, Morning Catherine, Midday Maria, Mother Maria. The dawns are engaged, and the servant of God [name] is crying out. And you, cockerel, take a cry and give the servant of God [name] Peace."

Read three times and spit on the floor over your left shoulder.

✳ SPELLS TO AVERT ALCOHOLISM
AND PROTECT AGAINST BITES

This class of spells includes behaviors like alcoholism, promotes aversion to wine, and protects against a snake or dog bite.

This is a spell to protect against alcoholism. Whisper to the water:

> You, heaven, hear, you see what I want to do over the body of God's servant [name]. You are clear stars, descend into the wedding cup. And in my bowl is water from a cold mountain spring. You are a handsome moon, come into my cage, and my cage is a bottom-

less one. Sunshine, you are free, come to my yard, and there are neither people nor animals in my yard. Stars, take away the servant of God [name] from wine. Moon, turn away the servant of God [name] from wine. Precious Sun, pacify the servant of God [name]. My word is strong."

Read over the water three times, but read the "Our Father" three times before that.

✳ Housekeeping and Economic Spells

These spells are designed to ensure the well-being of the house, the health of livestock, the harvest, and protection from pests. This is a spell for the well-being of the house:

Peace, salvation to this house and those living in it. Settle, Lord, in this house the spirit of holiness, meekness, and humility, drive out from it all the power of the devil and the enemy, visible and invisible. The purest life-giving cross of the Lord, by the power of our Lord Jesus Christ, crucified on you, strengthen me against all enemies visible and invisible, observance and temptation of flesh and spirit. Amen.

Spray all corners of the room with enchanted water and pour the remaining water under the threshold.

Medical Spells and the Evil Eye

Let's focus now on the medical spells that are presented in various forms, from the evil eye to hernia, the so-called universal spells from all diseases. From the Slavic point of view, disease is a form of "sorcery slander."

Spells usually invoke the following actions to overcome the disease:

1. Driving away (knocking out) the disease: "As fire knocks out of the damask, so that it would knock out all the ailments and damage from the servant of God [name]."

2. Removing the disease: "You are a moon, you are a moon with silver horns and golden legs. Take away my toothache, take the pain above the clouds."

3. Coaxing, insults (abuse, curses, threats): "Come out from the bones, from the relics, from the veins."

Tools of the spell treatment are very diverse. They include garlic (to protect against the evil eye), water, salt (to protect against the evil eye, against all diseases). A knife is used as a traditional amulet against evil spirits. Healers often use it to protect an unbaptized baby, woman, groom, bride, livestock, and so on.

The most common spells target the evil eye or curse. To protect against the evil eye, the healer whispers to the water, which is used to wash up or drink. The spell is told over the patient for three dawns, in more difficult cases, twelve dawns. The spell is cast on the water, which no one has tasted (untouched freshwater usually from the well). A ritual tool, as mentioned above, is then added to the water according to the needs of the spell.

Dark Forces in Spells

According to folk beliefs, dark ("unclean") forces and energies, evil spirits, are hostile to man and send him various diseases and troubles, such as harming crops and livestock. Initially, they denoted some supernatural power, forest, water, dark, and so on. Their habitats are unclean places: wastelands, wilds, bogs, swamps, caves, pits, all types of reservoirs (especially whirlpools), unclean trees (dry willow, alder, aspen).

Aspen, in the folk tradition, is an unclean tree cursed by God. In the Apocrypha, it is said that aspen, with the trembling of its leaves, betrayed the Mother of God who was hiding from pursuers under its branches. As a cursed tree, aspen was widely used for magical purposes and spells against various diseases. In contrast, the image of a birch tree is often used against damage caused by the evil eye. (We have discussed how the birch tree plays a role in many Slavic festivals and beliefs, including making the wedding broom out of birch branches and placing a pillow of birch leaves under the deceased's head.) A person could "transmit" their disease to the birch tree; it was considered an effective technique of magic.

Listing unclean places in the spell creates part of the magical atmosphere, the realm of forces unseen. The healer demonstrates her competence by knowing exactly where to banish evil spirits so that the disease will retreat. Just as higher powers must be specifically named for them to heed the spell caster's call, so must all the habitats of evil spirits be named—or else they will remain outside the field of action of the spell.

Additionally, the mysterious, otherworldly atmosphere of a spell is created by describing the time. It is believed that the spell will work if it is pronounced at a certain time and in a certain place. Therefore, healers will chant a spell text at a certain time of the day. In most of the spell texts, the time is called as follows: morning dawn, evening dawn, midnight, day; the sun at sunset, a month at sunset, the sun at sunset, at night, at vespers. The atmosphere of witchcraft is intensified by incomprehensible words, outdated grammatical forms, and an appeal to higher otherworldly forces.

RELATIONSHIP BETWEEN FOLK PRAYER AND SPELL

Folk prayers occupy an intermediate position between spells and canonical prayers, but they gravitate toward spells and incantations in form and function. Many research papers have widely discussed the difficulties of distinguishing between the chants and prayers that appear in Slavic folklore. The question of the origin of spells from ancient Pagan prayers deserves special attention. Representatives of the "mythological school" of folklore wrote about the evolution of chants from this very perspective. In the late nineteenth century and early twentieth century, folklorists discussed how spells and Christian prayers related to each other. In later classifications, "spell-prayers" were often singled out as a special group of sacred texts of "enchantment." As a result, two opposing points of view on the texts of spells and folk prayers have emerged:

1. Spells and folk prayers are nothing more than conventional designations; therefore, the same texts can be called both "spells" and "prayers."
2. Spells and prayers are located at opposite poles of a certain continuum of magical texts.

It is worth noting that folk prayers can be traced back to canonical and apocryphal prayers that originated in books. We have already mentioned two such books: The Psalms and the Trebniki. The Psalms are a collection of religious poems and hymns found in the Book of Psalms in the Hebrew Bible and, to a slightly different extent, in the Christian Old Testament. These poetic expressions cover a range of emotions, including praise, lament, and supplication. Many religious traditions, including Christianity and Judaism, use the Psalms as a source for prayers. Trebniki, a type of liturgical book in the Eastern Orthodox Christian tradition, contain various prayers, rites, and services for different occasions, such as daily prayers, sacraments, and special ceremonies. These books are used as guides for personal and communal worship, and they often include prayers for various needs and circumstances.

In form and function, folk prayers are closer to spells and incantations; however, they differ from the latter by always containing an element of request and always lacking the demanding language we saw in some spells. Prayer as a genre of the Slavic folk tradition does not have clear characteristics that distinguish it from a spell, but it differs significantly from conventional prayer as the texts belong to the folk tradition and use elements of Christian culture. Folk prayers usually have a purely practical purpose of application, specific "usefulness" (for example, prayers read before bedtime, on a long journey, etc.), which functionally brings them closer to spells.

DIFFERENCES BETWEEN TRADITIONAL WITCHCRAFT AND ESOTERICA

In our cultural reality, by *esotericism* we mean not abstract "secret knowledge," which is generally true, but a set of concepts collected from different religious traditions and personal experiences that are combined into a single (although it is an awkward choice of the word) system. Esotericism with a Russian "flavor" is usually a compilation of concepts from Christianity, Hinduism, Buddhism, Paganism, postmodern philosophy, and so on—whatever is within the hands' reach. It is not difficult to understand that these concepts are juggled for the sake of their own ideas, blended, and interpreted in different ways— usually in order to fit the purpose for which they are being used. This is because esotericists create their spiritual systems at their discretion. We cannot get one system as the output because each has its own views and opinions on certain fundamental things—each is authentic and unique. There is no single coordinate system that allows everyone to consider their concepts as the most correct.

However, we have a traditional form of magic called ethnic witchcraft. This form of magic is referred to as traditional for a number of reasons: This system does not have an author (i.e., it was not invented by one person, but was formed among the people); it has continuity (i.e., we can say with confidence that it represents more than a separate knowledge, the entire system has its roots, if not in the dense archaic, then in the distant past); and, finally, it is traditional because it took shape in a specific ethnic group and, thus, is not universal.

Ethnic witchcraft is separated from esotericism by the three traits of systematization, continuity, and locality. Perhaps the most important difference is systematization. In traditional ethnic magic, there is

a system by default because practitioners of ethnic magic are insepara-
bly linked with their ethnic groups and cultural characteristics; their
magic is part of the system. Esotericism, which inherited the legacy of
postmodernism, ignores traditionalism (often as simply not interesting
or convenient), and tries to take separate pieces from traditional systems, randomly combining them and getting, as a result, something
new. This may produce successful systems, systems with a specific creator, a founder. Still, the system will be new each time, which is why
esotericists often argue and do not understand each other—they don't
have a common coordinate system, and there is no joint base. Against
this background, traditional forms of magic look much more attractive
because people who carry on tradition do not need to invent anything,
and each of them works within a single grid system.

Continuity, like consistency, is also an essential difference between
esotericism and ethnic witchcraft. This is, probably, the main "trump
card" of the traditionalist. If the system has been preserved in tradition, it works because generations have tested it before us. Esotericists,
of course, cannot take pride in this, as they predominantly composed
their own systems or, in other words, their programs have an author
and, thus, no continuity of concepts.

The locality of ethnic witchcraft is the third significant difference,
although it does not offer any special advantages. The locality itself is
rooted in geography (i.e., any ethnic tradition only exists where its car-
riers live). For an esotericist, this is not at all essential. In esotericism,
all boundaries of identity are erased, and a combination of spiritual
concepts is obtained. From the point of view of a traditionalist, this is
similar to acquiring not the freshest sturgeon but the one in the most
beautiful wrapper.

17
Burial Rites in Old Russia

From the point of view of our ancestors, death resulted in a transition to another world where people continued to exist, invisible to the living. Therefore, death was treated as a natural phenomenon, especially when it came to the elderly.

There is a custom of preparing for death that is very popular in both Russia and Ukraine. People buy clothes, shoes, towels (for the people who will be performing the vigil ceremony) and everything they want to wear or to "take with them" at the moment of their deaths. They keep them in a special place, separately from everything "living."

Long before the advent of Christianity, incantations and spells were pronounced over the sick and dying, accompanied by cleansing rituals. Spiritual figures also drew from the magic of numbers. Shamans, for example, put seven amulets on the patient, walked around his bed seven times, said the spell seven times, and hit the tambourine the same number of times. Magical actions were used to help heal the patient, including sprinkling him with specially prepared water, which gave him its magical power (strength to make a safe passage), and burning sacred plants, which were believed to protect the deceased soul from malevolent spirits on his journey.

All these elements were adopted and preserved in the Christian sacrament but were transformed into the sacrament of giving a blessing (unction). When this ceremony was performed, the priest not only forgave sins but also drove away the spirits that were sent to carry the person away with them into the kingdom of darkness after her death. At the same time, the sacrament was the last parting word of the church before the deceased transitioned to another world.

Beliefs in the magical power of the number seven were also preserved in the sacrament. The priest read seven sacraments and seven passages from the Gospels during the ceremony, said seven prayers, and anointed the patient seven times with blessed oil (chrism). An unction included other rituals, including the process of burning sacred plants, which were later replaced by incense, the smoke from aromatic resin.

Before the sacrament was given, a cross would be placed on the table, and the Gospels would be laid next to it along with seven candles, seven anointing brushes, a dish made of wheat, and vessels with oil and wine.

The prominence of grains in the ritual is explained by the fact that Earth was considered the main source of life-giving power. Among all peoples of the Earth, including the Slavs, ethnographers have recorded the burial of the sick in the ground for healing. This ritual became part of folklore.

The sacrament began with the singing of the special canon, "On the Health and Forgiveness of the Sins of the Sick." Byzantine hymnographers compiled its text in the ninth century based on ancient spell songs. The priest then performed the Great Litany in which he asked the Lord God to heal the sick. After that, a prayer was read. Then the troparion were sung, addressed to Jesus Christ, the Mother of God, and the saint in whose name the patient was baptized. (A troparion is a type of liturgical music in the Eastern Orthodox Church; it can be a short hymn of one stanza or organized in a more complex form as a series of stanzas.)

After saying a prayer, the priest read seven passages from the Gospels. Each time he finished reading a passage, he anointed the patient with oil on the forehead, cheeks, lips, chest, and hands, and then extinguished a candle. At the end of the sacrament, the priest opened the Bible and put the text on the patient's head, saying a prayer of absolution. It is believed that the performance of the sacrament ended a person's earthly path.

Although, according to the canon, seven priests must perform the sacrament, in most cases, only one priest performed it. Only particularly important patients were attended by seven priests. The sacrament was then called an unction or *soborovanie* (from the Old Church Slavonic *sobor*, meaning "cathedral," and *sobranie*, meaning "meeting"). Usually, the unction included accepting a schema—the monk's rite of tonsure, which signified the breaking of all social ties and the return to God.

The burial ceremony began with washing the deceased. Nonrelatives, usually paid strangers, were invited to wash the dead. This individual needed to be of the same gender as the deceased: If a man had died, older men would wash the body; if a woman had died, older women would perform this role. After the deceased was washed, he was dressed and placed in the home's red corner on a bench with his head facing the icons. It was customary that young girls and single boys were buried in a wedding dress or suit.

Local men made the coffins in the village. It was custom for coffins to be made "to order" in rural villages. When the coffin was brought in, the deceased was placed into it. A pillow filled with dry leaves from a birch tree was placed under the deceased person's head. Objects and things they used during their lifetime were also placed inside the coffin, such as glasses, tobacco, a scarf, a shirt (to have something to change into, just in case), dentures, and so on. To protect the deceased against a curse, metal objects or a container with a manganese solution were placed under the coffin, consecrated eggs were placed behind the deceased's ears. Salt (in a bag), nettles, or mint (under the body) also could be placed in the coffin.

As in many other rural areas of Ukraine and Russia, it is still customary to sit with or spend the night with the dead in my village. In

Fig. 17.1. Vigil ritual by elder women

bygone times, older women were the ones who mostly participated in the sitting, many of whom knew church prayers. They weren't explicitly invited; they often just showed up at your door, agreeing in advance among themselves as to who would sit with the deceased. They would spend the whole night, right up until the morning, "when the roosters crowed," reading prayers and singing memorial spiritual verses (rhymes). At midnight, they would cover the deceased's face, and at six o'clock in the morning, they would again uncover it and wash it with holy water. At this point, the vigil ritual was considered complete, and the women would leave.

The deceased was buried the day after her death, or sometimes on the third day if the family waited for relatives to arrive. No later. The body was supposed to be buried in the afternoon, not before. The funeral procession lined up in a particular order: In front, they carried the grave cross, then the lid of the coffin (even today, coffins in Russia and Ukraine have separate covers), and then the coffin itself, which was carried on foot by six men or transported in a hearse.

On the way to the cemetery, the procession would make regular stops at relatives' houses, crossroads, and places where the deceased often visited or worked to allow the final good-byes. When the funeral procession moved onto the road, it was customary to throw spruce branches behind the procession, as it was believed that the deceased came home for the night before the fortieth day after his death, and the branches would show him the way home. Everyone who helped at the funeral—those who washed the deceased and participated in the vigil, made the coffin, and dug the grave—were invited to a hot meal right after the burial was complete.

The next commemoration dates were the ninth and fortieth days. On the ninth day, only close relatives were invited. In the morning, they visited the cemetery before returning home for a memorial dinner. On the fortieth day, they invited relatives and those who had washed the body, performed the vigil rite, and friends of the deceased. It was believed that until the fortieth day, the deceased spent the night in his house. During this period of six weeks, it was customary to put a glass of water on the windowsill with a piece of bread on top. A candle would also be lit every night until the forty days had passed.

CLEAN AND UNCLEAN DEAD

A common concept in literature on Slavic Paganism is the opposition of the "benevolent" or "correct" ("clean") deceased in contrast to the "wrong" and "harmful" ("unclean") dead, the latter of which are dangerous to the living. There is a distinction between "those who died their own death" and those who didn't. To be in the category of ancestors, you must die your own death; that is, your death must occur not earlier than your own time or later—not dying young or outliving your age.

The deceased does not immediately become an ancestor at the time of his biological death. The final transition generally takes place a year after death (however, longer periods are considered common—

for example, seven or nine years). Those who died during the previous year are not perceived to be ancestors until the commemoration of the annual cycle is complete. Only after the completion of the annual memorial circle are they included in the general group of parents and ancestors and commemorated along with everyone else.

The separation of the dead into clean and unclean ancestors is not nearly as categorical as it might seem. It doesn't coincide with splitting them into friends/enemies or good/evil. Thus, those who died not by their own death could become, according to popular beliefs, natural spirits who control the natural elements (wind, rain, hail clouds) and, subsequently, objects of veneration.

The path to something new always lies through the death of the obsolete. The path to life lies through death, the path to light through darkness. To some, the world seems quite simple—day means "unconditional good," and night means "absolute evil." But without night, there will be no day, and without winter, there is no summer. Thus, death is a natural cycle of rotation, a law of nature that cannot be violated by a person, for life and death are two sides of the same coin.

According to Russian custom, if a person was dying a painful death, close direct relatives would drill holes in the ceiling over the deathbed. Later, they would remove one of the ceiling boards. This "released the soul" of the dying person, for earthly affairs didn't allow the soul to leave. To this day, in some rural villages, healers and sorcerers are "liberated" in this fashion. During their lives, they take on a lot of the ailments and concerns of the people they have helped or, on the contrary, cursed. As a result, their soul needs assistance to leave their bodies.

Traditionally, to "let the soul pass," as in the case of childbirth, all doors and windows in the house were opened, the latch from the chimney was removed, any clothes were unbuttoned, and the belt knots were untied. All this was performed so that everything was "open" and the soul could pass. After the person died, she was washed and dressed according to custom and placed on the bench with her feet facing the front door.

It is believed that the unclean dead "walk" until the time of their real death. The souls of these deceased, not receiving the proper transition to another world, become temporary interworldly entities. People who committed suicide, drowned, and women who died during childbirth are among the unclean dead. A particular category of the unclean dead are deceased summoned back by the longing of the living; for example, a deceased husband returns to a grieving widow in the form of a ghost, animal, or bird. Unclean dead are believed to disturb loved ones and those with whom they have unfinished business, take revenge on their murderers, guard treasures, scare animals, and haunt the people they were friends with. In popular Christianity, there is a belief that the unclean dead pass into the power of the unclean force or become demons themselves. The energy that the unclean dead person hasn't used during his life is now transformed into a destructive force that haunts the dead. Based on such ideas, for example, the image of a vampire was formed—a restless dead man who feeds on the fortune of the living.

18

Funeral Rites and Their Connection to the Folk Magic of Old Believers

From time immemorial, humanity has thought about death and what awaits us beyond its borders. Both believers and atheists respect death—after all, it remains unknown to us all. Modern science cannot provide evidence-based versions of what happens to a person after death, so all philosophical treatises, magic rituals, and reasoning are based on assumptions.

Encountering death has always been a sacrament for man. Funeral rituals are considered the oldest rituals. Archaeologists have also found ritual objects in graves that are hundreds of thousands of years old. To this day, even skeptics follow ancient rituals when saying good-bye to their loved ones, even though they may not remember why memorials are celebrated on certain days or why the dead are usually buried with their heads facing west.

The topic of death was given great importance in the age-old tradition of spells and witchcraft. The cemetery was considered one of the main places of power. Every village medicine man had "his" cemetery where he could communicate with the spirits of the dead and ask them for help. The forces of death were called for many different purposes: To heal people, remove damage (curses) from a clan, rid an individual of her addictions, and attract or get rid of someone.

When discussing the funeral rite as a rite of passage, it is necessary to find out how the rite of a person undergoing this transition is represented. What part of his being goes into the world of his grandfathers, and what part should be buried? According to the traditional Slavic worldview, this is concerned with both the mortal and immortal beings that reside within a human. One of the functions of the rite is the final separation of the body and the soul, which begins with the soul's exit from the body (see below about special acts designed to help this exit in the event of a difficult death). In the most ancient forms of the rite, we find actions that can be defined as "killing the body of the deceased," the destruction of the mortal part of a person. In a later rite, this kind of ritual destruction—more precisely, damage to the body (dismembering, etc.)—applies only to the unclean or walking dead.

As the traditional concept of the body is very complex, I will only touch upon the ones that are essential for the rite. The body is the mortal half of a person, and preserving it after death can be harmful and dangerous for the living, but ritual actions and beliefs recognize some parts of the body as immortal, specifically the bones, hair, nails, and teeth. They are considered to be of high value for old faith believers' magical purposes (healing and cursing).

There is a widespread Slavic custom of binding (tying) the hands and feet of the deceased with red ribbons or ropes. The ropes used to tie the arms and legs of the deceased are called dead bonds. Before burial, they are supposed to be cut and removed. Various beliefs are associated with these ropes. Depending on the relatives' wishes, the bonds can be left in the coffin and buried at the deceased's feet, kept by loved ones for use in healing rituals, or taken (stolen) by a witch for use in her practices.

If relatives decide to keep the bonds, they should be kept outside of the living space—such as in a garage or basement. It is believed that the bonds used to tie the deceased's legs help heal various diseases, including cancer. This belief is explained by the solid destructive energy that the ropes absorbed from the dead. Witches love to use those bonds in their practices. Curses and hexes are greatly enhanced by the use of ropes. They can make a person mentally ill, disabled, tongue-tied (mute), bind a person to another against their will, cause bad habits (alcohol, drugs, etc.), and many more.

Some believe that it is essential to remove the ropes before the burial. If the deceased is tied up forever, she will haunt the living in their sleep and may even bring them back to her grave by choking people while they sleep. It was believed that the bonds on their feet would not allow the dead to rise from the coffin, and the soul would remain tied to the mortal body so it would not possess the living. As such, the ropes kept the spirit contained in a place and, before burial, it was important that they were cut to allow the spirit to leave its physical shell. If the bonds were not taken off the dead person's arms and legs for one reason or another, relatives were required to visit another funeral as soon as possible and place scissors in the coffin and "ask" the deceased inside the coffin to pass the item along to her loved one.

The Christian religion disapproves of superstitions. The priests believe that the deceased's soul doesn't care about his dead body, and it now belongs to the Earth. But the tradition of securing the limbs of the dead with a rope appeared much earlier, long before Christianity. The binding of the arms and legs began because, after rigor mortis, the body takes a strange shape that cannot be easily corrected. Putting ropes in place kept the body in the proper position to be set in the coffin and buried properly. Usually, an observer was specially chosen for this at the funeral—an older woman familiar with mystical rites, as witches would often come over to take ropes and other magical necessities. A hair comb, remains of the candles, water that family members used to wash the deceased, cloths, hair, anything that could be used by rural witches in their rites. For instance, to better preserve the body of the deceased, manganese was dissolved in a basin of cold water that was placed under the table or bench. Raw eggs were laid near the deceased's ears and were then thrown into the burial pit during burial. Water, eggs, and a basin of it were considered to be very powerful magical tools.

My grandmother on my father's side was what we call a "bad witch." Her favorite recipe involved using woolen threads to cast deadly curses. She would ask a family member or a person who requested such a service to take the measurements of the person's body for whom the curse was intended while they slept. Then, after performing a particular rite, she would place thread into a coffin under the heels of the deceased, chanting very specific prayers.

After the funeral, witches would collect what was left of the soap for use in magical rites. With its help, it was possible to cast fatal curses or, conversely, cure incurable diseases. The "corpse soap," as I call it, helped manage various conditions—for example, it reduced inflammation, chronic pain, gangrene for a person who had bad skin (fire burns, chickenpox scars, etc.). If a piece of soap had been used to wash a deceased man, it could only be used for men; if the deceased was a woman, the soap could only be used in magic for women. Soap was, and still is, used for other purposes, such as removing hexes, addictions, or performing strong cleansing. It could also be used to make someone very sick, with a deadly outcome. Corpse soap absorbed the energy of the dead. In my village, this soap was often used by women whose husbands were alcoholics who refused to address their addiction. There was also another use for soap: To wash the underwear of men who cheated on their wives.

The corpse soap was also used by one of my grandmothers to "cure" the husbands who beat their wives. As soon as the husband washed his hands with this soap, he became calm and quiet, like standing water. My grandmother also gave this soap to people who were on trial. If they washed themselves with this soap, the court would not see them as guilty. There were (and are) so many uses for corpse soap and water—it's impossible to describe them all here. The water used in the ceremony also held significance. Ponds and lakes near cemeteries were also very powerful sources of tools in magic. However, the water needed to be still; it could not be flowing water, like a river or stream.

Even today, people may encounter dubious requests and actions from others during the burial process in remote villages. Someone may ask you to lie on the bed where the deceased slept. A person saying her good-byes may wish to leave the house behind the coffin, walking backward. Some may tie knots somewhere in the corner while the deceased's body is carried out of the house; someone will try to throw fresh flowers at the feet of the people who follow the coffin or try to place needles inside the deceased's mouth in the form of a cross.

THE MOST COMMON OMENS AT THE TIME OF THE FUNERAL

Our ancestors attached great importance to weather conditions on the day of a funeral. Bad weather could be a sign that the deceased was somehow not clean. A sunny day was a sign that a person was righteous and lived his life with dignity.

It is believed that pregnant women should have nothing to do with organizing a funeral. They would be removed from any preparation tasks associated with burial. If for some reason, a woman still could not avoid this ceremony, then she had to leave the house where the deceased was staying before the body was removed. This was due to the belief that the deceased could take the soul of an unborn child.

Also, much attention was paid to young children at funerals. There was a belief that if a baby eats something or drinks water intended for the deceased, she can get sick. It is also a bad omen for a child to take something belonging to the deceased or, on the other hand, put something into the coffin, like a toy or candy.

One bad omen is a funeral that takes place shortly before the wedding of the deceased's relatives. This omen suggests that the upcoming marriage will not be happy and will not last. Therefore, it's customary to have a long mourning period.

Several omens show that a series of negative events for the relatives of the deceased are just beginning. Most of them are devoted to impending deaths in the family of the deceased:

- To cross the road before the procession of the deceased passes is a sign that the person who crossed may die for the same way that the deceased died.
- If the relatives of the deceased do not put an ax under the coffin, this may be a sign that death will soon return to the family's home. An ax laid under the coffin is a symbol of death being separated from the house of the deceased.
- If, during the burial, relatives forget to untie the hands and feet of the deceased, according to superstition, death can threaten the whole family.
- If the coffin or grave for the deceased is too spacious, it may be a sign that soon someone else will be in the grave.
- If the coffin falls, it may be a sign that, in the next three years, there may be more deaths in the family of the deceased.
- If the deceased falls out of the coffin, death in the circle of people who were at the funeral may happen very soon.
- An incident with the coffin lid is believed to be a sign of the imminent death of someone close to the deceased.
- Cemeteries in Eastern Europe often have low stone edges or borders around the graves that are called *coping*. These low stone structures typically outline the boundaries of individual plots, creating a defined area for each grave; the style and design may vary based on cultural and regional practices. The coping serves both functional and symbolic purposes, providing a clear

demarcation of the burial space while also contributing to the overall aesthetics of the cemetery. The collapse of one side of the coping is an omen of the death of one of the relatives. The collapse of the south side means a man will die, the north—a woman, the west—a child, the east—an older adult.

- A person who stumbles at a funeral, according to superstitions, may soon die.
- A funeral on New Year's Eve is a very bad sign. According to omens, this means that the next year there will be a funeral in the family of the deceased again.
- If for some reason a funeral has to be postponed, it's a bad omen. Tradition says that it's a way for the deceased to tell us that soon there will be another death. The person who has already passed is waiting for someone else to join him.
- There should never be items belonging to living people in the coffin. If this happens, the object's owner may die sooner than was intended or get very sick.
- And, finally, when leaving the coffin with the deceased in a grave, after leaving the cemetery, you must not look back.

These rules are very important to follow for the health of the family members who remain in our world, the world of the living. In addition to the omens regarding funerals and the burial process, there were other special signs that foreshadowed the death of a person: if myriad flies, cockroaches, bedbugs, or mice appeared in the house, a bird knocked into the window, a dog howled at the house, or a cat slept in a red corner, then someone in that house would soon be dead. Knowing these omens helped our ancestors understand what the future could bring, and what they could possibly do to change it.

19

Death and Burial Rites in Haitian Vodou

Like all human traditions and religious practices, Haitian Vodou also has a clear belief system about what happens to the body and soul after transition into the other world. When someone dies, Vodouisants believe the deceased's soul remains next to the corpse for seven to nine days. During this time, the gros bon ange (great guardian angel, the part of the human soul that transcends the individual personality) is vulnerable and can be caught and turned into what the sorcerer calls a "spirit zombie." If the soul is not captured, the priest or priestess performs a ritual called *desounin* to separate the soul from the body and send it to live "underwater" (in the spirit world) in complete safety for a year and a day.

At the moment of death, the gros bon ange leaves the body to begin its journey back to the watery abyss of the primordial world, Ginen, the abode of spirits. However, this journey will only be successful if the gros bon ange is correctly cared for through special funeral rites. Otherwise, it will wander and end up taking revenge on its living descendants for their negligence, persecuting them, and creating chaos in their lives.

Before the physical burial, the mèt tèt ("master of the head," which was installed in the practitioner's head during her initiation into Vodou) needs to be removed. A year and one day after a person's death, the ceremony *retire mo nan dlo,* "to take the dead out of the water," can be performed. The deceased's spirit is invoked through a vessel of water under a white sheet and is ritually placed in a clean clay pot called a *govi* during the sacrifice and special ceremony.

The deceased's voice can be heard from the govi or through another person's mouth, which is briefly possessed for this purpose. The govi is placed reverently in the djevo, the inner room of the sacred Vodou temple. From this new "body" (the ceramic govi), the restored ancestor will continue to interact with the community, giving valuable advice to his living offspring. As it is passed from generation to generation, the restored spirit of the ancestor in the govi is transformed from an ancestor of a certain bloodline into a generalized ancestor of all Vodou temple members. Through this process, the soul can eventually rise and become an independent lwa. This ritual is one of the largest and most important rituals in Haitian Vodou—the ceremony of extracting the deceased's soul.

People are born to die.

Haitian proverb

20

The Transmission of Magical Power at Death

Shamans, witches, and sorcerers can change their reality at will, but it isn't simple. Magical abilities in a family are often the source of problems, especially if they're unknown. First, I should clarify what I mean by magical abilities. Magical abilities don't have to take the form of magic or witchcraft as they're traditionally understood. Rather, magic is the ability to independently create your own destiny, changing your own reality to better suit your needs. This ability is often manifested as strong personal energy, an understanding of the structure of reality, a special sensitivity to the phenomena of the subtle world, and the ability to influence the flow of someone else's energy, will, and characteristic waywardness. The power comes into play when a person is not satisfied with what her destiny offers her and looks for ways to change the situation. A lot depends on how much that person consciously uses her abilities. After all, real magical power has incredible potential, and whoever wields it must be able to handle and understand it.

Often, someone who has magical power but doesn't realize it thinks that he is just lucky or hardworking. He may simply believe that he achieves everything he wants through his own effort. Sometimes, he's right. If a clan's connection is very well established, hard work does make a difference when it comes to achieving important life goals. But in some cases, a person can achieve success because he unconsciously changes the flow of energy around him and transforms reality, bending it to his liking. You must understand that energy does not come from nothing. If a person unconsciously draws energy from somewhere, he is most likely drawing it from his own blood and, as such, that of his ancestors.

Magical abilities are a gift, but also a huge ordeal. Until a person has learned to master this power, their manifestations are often destructive. Often, at first, abilities manifest as temptations and inappropriate behavior, such as the desire to escape to the subtle reality with the help of alcohol or drugs. Since one of the characteristics of a sorcerer is self-sufficiency, sometimes he also breaks away from his family and clan.

In traditional shamanic culture, there is a concept called "shamanic disease," which is a period of physically and, especially, mentally painful experiences that a future shaman experiences in his youth. This is comparable to what happens to an ancestral witch who didn't receive or accept the transmission of power from her family. This illness is a sign that the spirits have chosen him, that his ordinary essence is in a state of "decay" and, in its place, a new identity is being born—the identity of a shaman.

This condition can only be healed by going through shamanic initiation and becoming a shaman. That is, the person himself does not decide to become a shaman—he is forced to become one. Shamanic illnesses most often emerge in shamanic families where the gift hasn't been passed down continuously. In that moment, when the magical power awakens and tries to push a person toward the magical craft, it's important for someone to be nearby who can explain what is happening. It usually doesn't seem like magic at first, and the person himself may not want to become a shaman or witch.

There are rules for the transfer of a magic gift. If the sorcerer doesn't transfer his magical abilities to another person before he dies, he can become a restless spirit. In the best-case scenario, his gift should be transferred to one of his descendants. If that doesn't happen for some reason, the witch will try to contact the closest person to her, which can be a neighbor or someone she knows, and inform them that they must accept their magical power, a gift.

But a spirit's methods of communication are not particularly easy to understand for everyone or pleasant for many people. Most often, people perceive spirits as otherworldly entities that have set out to scare them, or as inexplicable problems and difficulties that affect their health, personal relationships, and other aspects of their lives.

This misunderstanding is especially common these days because, under the influence of historical twists and turns and changes in generally accepted beliefs, even in shamanic clans, at some point, the descendants renounced their magical ancestors, and the continuity is interrupted. But this power cannot disappear just because the living ceased to believe in it. As such, it begins to manifest itself destructively. When this happens, a special rite is necessary to restore the correct flow of the power. For example, in our time, this type of ceremony has become very popular among the Buryats (a Mongolic people, one of the two largest Indigenous groups in Siberia) for whom shamanism is a traditional religion. The ceremony is usually performed when a family or whole clan has various problems, and the clan is known for having shamans in its history. In this case, it is believed that the likely cause of the family's misfortune is the influence of the ancestral spirits seeking vengeance for their descendants' forgetfulness.

Since ancient times, many rituals and ceremonies have been associated with the death of a witch. During their lives, witches perform many rites associated with evil spirits, damage, curses, and so on. Unlike an ordinary person, the one associated with evil spirits dies painfully. In the old days, the house of a dying witch was boarded up, and no one was present at the time of her death. Sometimes people heard wild screams and screams for several days and nights in a row. But, if a witch transferred her gift before death, she died a quick death, without torment. It was believed that the souls of those whom the witch killed came to her just before death, and it was the souls of the innocent who made her suffer torment. Also, the life of a dying witch was supported by the entities that served her. These spirits and demonic beings couldn't be left without their host. Therefore they supported her body, increasing torment and suffering until she could transfer her power (entities including) to another person.

Rural witches do most of their magic with low spirits (low-frequency streams of energy). As a result, the astral body develops so much low energy (for example, those working with the dead) that it creates a concentration of much greater power than the high-frequency energy of the soul. And since the astral body is the connection between the soul and the physical body, when this power weighs down the soul, it can hold this connection for a very long time. As a result, the soul already wants to leave, and the astral keeps it.

In the old days, for the witch's spirit to leave the body faster, men (who had to be sons of a witch or very close male relatives) dismantled the roof of the house, opened a hole above the room in which the witch lay, or raised the ridge on which the roof slope was installed. These actions were based on the belief that a sinful soul cannot find a way out of a confined space. But even in situations where it was not possible to take such actions, you can help a dying person. Windows and doors must be opened throughout the house at the time of the witches' death; entities that were the sorceress's assistants leave through these portals. And with the departure of the evil that served the dying, her torment decreases. It is also necessary to cover all the mirrors in the dying woman's home, so the witch doesn't pass into the looking glass. If she does so, she may harm the people who live in the house after her death.

A witch's torment can also be relieved through the transfer of power with the help of a spindle, which is made of aspen. (As we discussed, aspen is considered a cursed tree, which gives it some particular magical properties.) The spindle must be new. If placed into the hands of the dying woman, she can speak out all her deeds and temporarily transfer her power into the spindle. After the witch completes her "transfer," the spindle must be broken in half and burned in the fire (if the person doesn't want to accept her ability). Only spruce logs can be used to make the fire. After the spindle burns out, the witch calmly and without torment gives up her spirit. Watching death can be a long and scary process. I witnessed the death of my grandmother at the age of twelve. I still remember it as if it happened yesterday.

From Our Ancestors to Our Future

Haitian Vodou and Slavic customs and beliefs are traditions without a written moral code or strict definition. Practitioners have not compiled a complete written history of any of them, and the material we possess today has not always benefited us nor the reputation of either tradition. Writing about Haitian Vodou and Slavic tradition in a way that accurately depicts the culture and its history is not an easy task.

The histories of Haiti and Vodou are inextricably linked. We can observe the same exact link in Slavic tradition. The connection between people, societies, social status, and geographical location, the suppression of people's will, and the formation of a new tradition based on current conditions and circumstances are very similar between the two practices. In Haiti, like in earliest Rus, people never recorded their history in the way Western thinkers believe. Over time, the elders have passed down the practice of Slavic tradition and Haitian Vodou through many generations, nurturing their children through old ways and sharing their knowledge orally through stories, memorized songs, lullabies, proverbs, and legends. Another way to retain tradition is by association with a landmark, such as an altar or remains of a shrine, that will remind us of the past.

By serving the gods in the Slavic tradition and the spirits in Haitian Vodou, a history and morality have been created that cannot be found in books, but only one born and raised by the believers can understand it. This is only possible due to the unique history of both countries.

The aim of this book was to give you a closer look at Haitian Vodou and Slavic folk tradition, not as misunderstood syncretic traditions; rather, as ways of life that reveal how spiritual practice has served as a survival tool. People perceive Haitian Vodou to represent an avenue through which they can experience spiritual healing, secure a better future, and be at peace in this life and the next world. Like Slavic tradition, Haitian Vodou does not involve any notion of a utopian Heaven or Eden. On the contrary, it emphasizes that the afterlife may be no more peaceful than the present life. As such, the most important value in the present is survival—survival of both the self and the wider community.

The sentiments of Slavic and Vodou customs become a way of life for the followers of these worldviews. The traditions are entrenched in both daily existence and history, with the devotees' experiences serving to uphold and permeate the culture. Throughout history, both believers of Slavic old ways and Haitians have been forced to turn to their roots and the associated ancestral power to rise to the challenges of the betrayal, ostracism, and isolation that have accompanied the New Era. However, unlike Slavic Paganism, Haitian Vodou has better endured and overcome the ideological assaults associated with modern capitalism, colonialism, slavery, and oppression.

People often condemn my principles, saying I confuse Slavic witchcraft for Vodou and that what I share and write about is not Slavic tradition at all. Those people's practice and knowledge of Slavic and Haitian traditions are unenlightened. Their practices have nothing to do with real Slavism since they have forgotten about the foundation of the tradition itself: Ancestors! Paganism is built on the clan, the ancestors, and the gods themselves. Worshipping, or more suitably, honoring the gods, includes and is based fundamentally on honoring your lineage, roots, and origin.

A sorcerer's practice, what we call the practical part of the faith, witchcraft, is exclusively a person's personal—intimate, if you wish— path. It is like shoes or clothes that are never meant to be "worn" by another person.

This path is passed to you by your clan, your family through many generations. People who practice and have no idea who they pray to or worship and what stands behind them, or on what all tradition is based, are like empty shells. I often like to compare them to a broken pot. You can glue the broken pieces back together, but the pot will never be the same. Those people have to go back to the beginning and start over. Knowledge is the difference between heirs to a lineage and those who are self-taught. People run from one tradition to another, collecting initiations, trying to find the "strongest" magic, all along ignoring the fact they already have all the power they need within them.

I'm not afraid of the judgment of ignorant people. If they judge me, it is because I'm doing something right in front of them. When the drums beat, I unreservedly dance a certain rhythm, my rhythm. I let the ignorant criticize me. They don't have enough strength or intelligence to connect with the ancestors who live in them. They cannot dance to the beats of drums that resemble their existence in this life, so they run away from themselves. They want me to follow in their footsteps so they can alleviate the jealousy and disappointment they feel in themselves. However, that will never be possible because, although we are all the same, each of us dances to the beat of the drum in our own way in line with life's rhythm and our understanding of life. Others have their ways that are suitable for them and their societies, but no one should worry about someone else. If you are afraid to step out of your comfort zone to explore the unknown and mystical, look inside yourself and discover what is unknown within you. How will you untangle the chaos you live in or find a way to feel at ease with your own life?

In most cases, a correct explanation of things does not always help to destroy the delusions that have penetrated the minds of the masses of this world and greatly paralyzed them; they remain unable to recognize the truth of their reality. No matter how hard you try, as long as the people themselves do not show interest in learning and exploring the secrets of our world, all communication will be useless. In the Haitian Vodou faith and the Slavic tradition, we believe in people's right to freedom of choice and, of course, in their respect for their ancestry, which is their heritage. These principles are the same ones I was brought up with within my own family. It is why Haitian Vodou is the only tradition that gives me a feeling of being home.

Man is, in many ways, a natural being. Like all living things, we do not exist in a vacuum. We are influenced by a variety of things in our lives, the most important of which is our ancestors and the history of our clan. All cultures emphasize the importance of a respectful attitude toward a person's ancestors, and there are certain rituals to show them the respect they are due. Of course, a modern person does not need to mindlessly imitate archaic rituals; in many cases, that would be inappropriate. But the people of the contemporary era do need to know about them and understand their meaning to use the important tools intended to help us strengthen our connection with the spirits of our ancestors.

Many people in the West do not even know who their ancestors are because they are not taught to consider them as important. Many people cannot even call their great-grandfathers by their first names! But in Haitian Vodou culture and the Slavic tradition, knowing your ancestors and communicating with them, whether they be your biological or your spiritual (clan) ancestors, is a very important part of everyday life. Ancestors are always present. We should always remember that we live and breathe thanks to those who came before us. Honor your ancestors, and they will honor you. Watch how you grow strong within yourself. You are suffering only because you are running away from yourself. Demonizing your ancestors is, in reality, demonizing yourself.

I fundamentally disagree with the erroneous doctrines of modern Paganism and Wicca, which do not follow a specific lineage from the ancestors. In the modern world the transmission of magical tradition in many cases has been interrupted, and a mixture of different traditions and religions all blend, sadly often contradicting each other. In this case, someone having great power and little knowledge can cause serious mistakes that harm the person and her loved ones and descendants. If a person feels like she doesn't have the energy she needs to accomplish her goals, it usually means she doesn't know how to use her power and navigate her energy. Without our ancestors, you would not be here, plain and simple. For this reason alone, you must regularly honor them and invite them into your life.

There are people who close their eyes and demand answers without taking any action or making any effort. It is contrary to the way nature works. And there are people who demand answers, taking all the necessary measures to receive what they seek. All that we have received in our life so far is all those things that we have worked very hard to obtain, no matter whether they are good or bad. So, in Haiti we say, "Sa w fè, se li wè," which means "what you do is what you get." Strictly speaking, this is life. Whether you pray to the Spirits of Life or fictional stories of people, pray, but know why and what power is behind it.

Bibliography

Afanasyev, A. N. *Russian Folk Fairy Tales. Complete Edition in One Volume.* [In Russian.] Moscow, Russia: Alpha-Book, 2010.

Afanasyev, A. N. *The Tree of Life.* [In Russian.] Moscow, Russia: Sovremennik, 1982.

Avdeev, Vladimir Borisovich. *Overcoming Christianity: Experience of Adogmatic Preaching.* [In Russian.] Moscow, Russia: Russkaya Pravda, 2006.

Dahl, Vladimir Ivanovich. *On Beliefs, Superstitions, and Prejudices of the Russian People.* [In Russian.] St. Petersburg–Moscow, Russia: M. O. Wolf Typography, 1880.

Desmangles, Leslie G. *Faces of the Gods: Vodou in Roman Catholicism in Haiti.* Chapel Hill: The University of North Carolina Press, 1992.

Ermakov, S. E., and D. A. Gavrilov. *A Time for Gods and a Time for People: The Basics of the Slavic Pagan Calendar.* [In Russian.] Moscow, Russia: Ganga, 2009.

Evstifeeva, N. "Dolls of the Dead." *Tribune,* January 29, 2010.

Globa, Pavel. "Time Is the Connecting Thread: Communicating with Ancestors." [In Russian.] *Mitra* no. 5–6 (2003): 41–65.

Grof, Stanislav, and Joan Halifax. *The Human Encounter with Death.* New York: Plume Publishing, 1978.

Grushko, E. A., and Y. M. Medvedev. *Dictionary of Slavic Mythology.* [In Russian.] Nizhny Novgorod, Russia: Russkij kupec i brat'ya slavyane, 1995.

Harnack, Adolph. *The History of Dogma.* Translated by Neil Buchanan. Boston: Little, Brown, and Company, 1907.

Metraux, Alfred. "The Concept of the Soul in Haitian Vodou." *Southwestern Journal of Anthropology* 2, no. 1 (1946): 84–92.

Nevsky, Dmitry. *Slavic Rituals of the Ancestral Circle: Ancient Ancestral Power.* [In Russian.] Moscow, Russia: Ripol Classic, 2009.

Sáenz-Badillos, Angel. *A History of the Hebrew Language.* Translated by John Elwolde. Oxford, UK: Cambridge University Press, 1996.

Samsonov, D. A. *Korean Etiquette: The Experience of Ethnographic Research.* [In Russian.] St. Petersburg, Russia: Nauka, 2013.

Schneider, Lidia. "Thanatos-centration and Its Manifestations: Generalization of Empirical Research." [In Russian.] *Bulletin of the Moscow Region State University* 3 (2020): 9–17.

Schutzenberg, Anne Ancelin. *The Ancestor Syndrome: Transgenerational Psychotherapy and the Hidden Links in the Family Tree.* Abingdon, UK: Routledge, 1998.

Sedakova O. A. *Poetics of Ritual: Funeral Rituals of the Eastern and Southern Slavs.* [In Russian.] Moscow, Russia: Indrik, 2004.

Sharaya, O. N. *The Value-normative Nature of the Veneration of Ancestors.* [In Russian.] Minsk, Belarus: Tekhnalogiya, 2002.

Soldatov, Alexander. "Overcoming the Fear of Death in Different Religious Traditions." [In Russian.] *Otechestvennye zapiski* 5, no. 56 (2013): 46–59.

Strongman, Roberto. "Transcorporeality in Vodou." *The Journal of Haitian Studies* 14, no. 2 (2008): 4–29.

Sudnitsyn I. I. "Living Tree: In the Year of Russian History about the Descendants of M. V. Lomonosov." [In Russian.] *Prostranstvo i vremya* 4, no. 10 (2012): 119–25.

Tolstaya, S. M., ed. *The World Is Sound and Silence: Semiotics of Sound and Speech in the Traditional Culture of the Slavs.* [In Russian.] Moscow, Russia: Indrik, 1999.

Tsydenov, E. M. "The Cult of Ancestors in Modern Buryat Shamanism." [In Russian.] *Vestnik Buryatskogo gosundarstvennogo universiteta* 8 (2011).

Zelenin, Dmitry. *A Folk Rite "To Warm a Deceased."* [In Russian.] [N.p.]: Kharkov, 1909.

Index

About the Author

Natasha Helvin is an author, occultist, hereditary witch, and priestess in the Haitian Vodou tradition. She is a passionate researcher of tradition and religion and simply a woodland creature who feeds on folklore and magic!

Natasha grew up in the Soviet state in a secluded small village among dense woodland and endless rivers. Every morning, for as long as she can remember, she loved to go out into the backyard of her house, where in front of her lay an infinite field (as it seemed to her at that time) bathed in the golden glow of the morning sun. On the green grass, under the windows, the dew was still glistening; in the distance, on the horizon, in the misty pinkish haze of the morning, huge trees led into a dense, dark forest. She vividly recalls the smell of damp grass and earth that blew from the fields and into her room through the open windows. She loved the sounds of owls and other animals that came out of the forest at night, the silence of a hot summer afternoon, the hypnotic singing of field crickets, the solemn stillness of the snow-covered fields in the winter, and the heart-squeezing melancholic feel of autumn. Natasha spent a lot of her time as a child discovering the underbrush, searching for wild berries, "befriending" ancient trees and forest spirits, and exploring ruins covered in moss and ivy—elements that, unsurprisingly, Natasha blends into her magical work today.

With a deep-rooted connection to the mysterious natural world, Natasha inherited her passion for magic (manipulation of the energies) from her mother and previous generations. She learned the ancient secrets of magic, healing, and the boundless potential of the human spirit from her family. As a child, Natasha saw her grandmother and mother use magic in their everyday lives to help neighbors, friends, and anyone simply seeking help.

Natasha tends to trust in the experience that goes back many thousands of years. Traditionally, man was in harmony with the universe, nature, and his essence; he knew how to draw strength from both the outer and inner worlds. Natasha believes you can bring forth peace by first learning to love and appreciate yourself and your ancestors. She believes that rules are not arbitrary but made by you in accordance with your own belief system and worldview. She adheres to the wisdom of her own voice because she knows the greatest gift in the universe is free will—ultimate and omnipotent—bound only by love and ameliorated by the practice of magic.

BOOKS OF RELATED INTEREST

Slavic Witchcraft
Old World Conjuring Spells and Folklore
by Natasha Helvin

Russian Black Magic
The Beliefs and Practices of Heretics and Blasphemers
by Natasha Helvin

Veneration Rites of Curanderismo
Invoking the Sacred Energy of Our Ancestors
by Erika Buenaflor, M.A., J.D.
Foreword by Luis J. Rodriguez

Familiars in Witchcraft
Supernatural Guardians in the Magical
Traditions of the World
by Maja D'Aoust

The Path of Elemental Witchcraft
A Wyrd Woman's Book of Shadows
by Salicrow

Runes for the Green Witch
An Herbal Grimoire
by Nicolette Miele

Icelandic Magic
Practical Secrets of the Northern Grimoires
by Stephen E. Flowers, Ph.D.

Pagan Magic of the Northern Tradition
Customs, Rites, and Ceremonies
by Nigel Pennick

INNER TRADITIONS • BEAR & COMPANY
P.O. Box 388
Rochester, VT 05767
1-800-246-8648
www.InnerTraditions.com

Or contact your local bookseller